LOVING
SOMEONE
GAY

LOVING SOMEONE GAY

fourth edition

UPDATED AND REVISED

Don Clark, Ph.D.

CELESTIAL ARTS
Berkeley | Toronto

CELESTIAL ARTS PUBLISHING
P.O. Box 7123
Berkeley, CA 94707

Celestial Arts titles are distributed in Australia by Simon and Schuster Australia,
in Canada by Ten Speed Canada, in New Zealand by Southern Publishers Group,
in South Africa by Real Books, in Southeast Asia by Berkeley Books,
and in the United Kingdom and Europe by Airlift Book Company.

Cover and text design by Lisa Buckley Design

Printed in the United States

1 2 3 4 5 6 7 8 9 — 09 08 07 06 05

Library of Congress Cataloging in Publication Data:
available from the publisher.

ISBN 10: 1-58761-236-4
ISBN 13: 978-1-58761-236-7

To Michael A. Graves

[CONTENTS]

[PART ONE]

Being Gay

1

OUR WORLD

BEING A GAY MAN, woman, girl or boy is neither common nor ordinary but, like having blue eyes, blond hair, great artistic talent or being left-handed, it is absolutely natural. Gay people have been present on this planet, in all times, in all places, throughout all of human history. Sometimes gay men and lesbians are more visible and sometimes less so. It depends upon the welcome extended to us and the quality of the observer's vision.

A friend described a long conversation with a man who was assigned the seat next to hers on a flight from Europe to the United States. He had attended an international conference of sixty people held in Amsterdam. Rather than gaining good will for his employer, he had embarrassed himself. He told her, "I left there the last day feeling dumb as a piece of wood."

He had made the mistake of assuming that "most folks aren't gay and if they are you can tell." He had further assumed that "a woman wearing a wedding ring has a husband and a guy wearing one has a wife." On the final day of the meeting a Norwegian woman corrected his assumption when she mentioned her wife.

"Then I found out that the guy from Boston has a husband, the California guy got married in San Francisco and is retiring and moving to Rotterdam with his husband, the gal from Barcelona is engaged and getting married to a woman from Canada and my Amsterdam tour guide and his husband are planning to have kids with a pair of married lesbians who are their friends."

He said he felt ashamed. "I know that I've said that I believe marriage is between a man and a woman whenever it's come up that I live in a state that's outlawed gay marriage. I'm sure I sounded like a little parrot saying just what my senators and my preacher says. Dumb as wood. It's like I just woke up. As if the world doesn't have enough misery without me going out of my way to make trouble for people who just want to get on with their lives like anyone else."

A good cautionary tale. Eyes open, the truth unbalances the *presumed* reality of people who fail to question assumptions that rest on prejudice and the belief systems of those who docilely accept easy answers designed by their leaders to reassure them of their superiority. Anyone who looks will find that gay people are many and varied. Some of us are cowardly, some heroic. Most of us are ordinary individuals, sometimes forced into extraordinary behavior in order to maintain our integrity and dignity. Most of us do not call attention to ourselves—in part because it can be dangerous.

Anyone who is aware of lesbians and gay men in the world will notice that we are most visible in those places where civic leaders and lawmakers show they appreciate individual differences in the population and are sufficiently enlightened to understand that only a government which celebrates diversity can reap the rewards that diverse cultures contribute to a society. In parts of the world where repressive regimes demand conformity, we are less visible. If government or religious officials decree that we do not exist and promise punishments of imprisonment, torture or death to anyone who proves them wrong, we must be assured of discretion and consideration toward our safety before we will reveal ourselves.

Repressive rulers fear us—with good reason. We are not conformists. We break rules in order to express our love. They cannot see us. They do not understand us. They do not appreciate our worth in society. When they threaten us, our protective caring for one another easily can cross whatever boundaries they choose to draw on their maps.

Letters have come to me from such places, thanking me for my work. These letters, sometimes smuggled across borders before being mailed, were written as a response to books that were smuggled across those same borders. These are acts of quiet courage that I have been unable to applaud appropriately because any direct communication might put the correspondent at risk.

Repressive rulers need to reinforce their delusions of grandeur, feed their personal greed and retain privileges that only political power permits. Consciously or not, they know they must stay in business at any cost or they will see both privilege and their artificial sense of worth disappear. Distributing bribes of money, privilege and prestige to loyalists who offer their support in return is helpful, but it is essential to keep the general populace in line. Threats and punishment go a long way toward meeting that objective. Morale must be tended also lest the citizens become ominously restless. Fascist dictators make use of stereotypes and prejudice to vilify any group which might lack unquestioning loyalty and therefore prove a threat.

Propangandists advertise the presumed faults and evils of the groups to be despised, making them responsible for any discomfort currently being endured by the public. Poverty, war, food shortages, new ideas among the young, bad weather or epidemics are routinely blamed on the unfavored people.

Before the collapse of the Soviet Union and its network of client states, the official party line was that gay people did not exist—and any who did appear were shipped away to labor camps or mental hospitals in order to "protect" the public. Yet soon after the Berlin Wall fell, announcing the beginning of the end for Soviet-style communism all over Europe, a Polish edition of *Loving Someone Gay* (Clark, Don. Lesbijki I Geje: *Jak ich kochac*, Przelozyl Jerzy Jaworski; Warszawa, Wydawnictwo Da Capo, 1995) appeared. People there were ready to translate, edit, publish and distribute such a book and others were ready to purchase it and read it because, of course, the gay people had been there all along.

We have been called many names in many languages, most of them are meant to be unflattering or shameful. *Faggot* and *dyke* continue to be favored by bigots in English-speaking parts of the world where words such as *nigger* and *kike* are also used. French-speaking people may use an abbreviation that sounds like *payday* in English and means *pederast*. Spanish speakers sometimes use *mariposa* which means butterfly and might bring up positive associations if one were to think of *all* that a butterfly represents. The sixteenth-century English word *faggot* actually refers to a bundle of sticks used as kindling to fuel the fires that burned people alive at the stake, people killed because they were different. Their "different-ness" was assumed to be a supernatural gift or curse, endowing them with powers that could be used to do great harm. Today, as in centuries past, people who are different frighten people trained to narrow-minded conformity. Panic, hysteria, vandalism, mob violence and murder result from the discomfort of such people.

Gay is the name for us that has taken root in most places around the world. It has origins in the nineteenth century and referred to people who deviated from the straight and narrow, first theatrical people and then prostitutes who were said to be *in the gay life*.

I once had the honor of introducing the gifted writer Christopher Isherwood to an audience. Picking his English-American words as carefully as one might expect, he looked out at the mostly gay assemblage and said he wanted to make it clear that "... while I can not always say truthfully that I am gay, I am certain at all times that I am *queer*."

Politically active gays sometimes prefer to call themselves *queer*, thereby being clear in their language and robbing potential tormentors of a tool. More conservative gays sometimes simply refer to themselves as *homosexuals* which, again, points to the simple facet of their lives that makes narrow-minded people so uncomfortable.

As more and more of us claim our identity publicly and are recognized, mystery and misunderstanding disappear. A gay person is simply a man who is fully attracted to men more often than he is to women, or a woman who is fully attracted to women more often than she is to men. As a gay man I have the ability to experience and express that attraction in all ways, including sexually. It does not mean that I am indiscriminate or uncontrolled in my attractions, nor does it mean that I am never attracted in any way to women. It definitely does not mean that I hate women. It is an ability, not a disability.

Many lesbians and gay men have heterosexual experience. In fact many of us have been, or are, in heterosexual marriages and many of us have children. We are a varied population and can blend into the scenery. More and more, however, we are choosing to take the risks and stand up, or *come out*, so as to make ourselves whole and fully known.

Unfortunately, unquestioned fears and prejudice continue to drive us out of our communities and away from our families. Those of us who survive this exile find role models and mentors among others of our kind. I wonder still what happened to the young American I met while I was a student passing through Paris in 1957. He and I, both caught in a sudden summer downpour, dashed from different directions for cover under the same blue awning. We waited while the thunder and lightning flashed around us with the dozen or so other people sharing the small but relatively dry space. We discovered that neither of us spoke French well but that we both spoke English.

Later, he told me how he had been set adrift by his wealthy family when he told them who he was. He could go to Europe, Africa, Asia, New Zealand or Australia but he was not to return to North America. Checks arrived each month. The cover story at home was that he was attending college in France. As time went on, the story would change to an import business operating from wherever he happened to be living or traveling at the time. The hard fist of ostracism was no less cruel for being clothed in the glove of financial generosity.

Other young people are punished more directly. Boys and girls are sent to unethical psychotherapists who claim that they can "cure" the *malady* of homosexuality. Others are prayed over, exorcised, excommunicated or shunned according to the dictates of the family's religion. Too many of us are hounded into misery and suicide, especially during adolescence. We humans are social animals and do not thrive when we are excluded.

Homophobia is a word that was first used by psychologist George Weinberg in his 1972 book, *Society and the Healthy Homosexual*. It suggests a phobic, irrational fear of people who are gay or primarily homosexual in orientation and, indeed, of anything having to do with homosexuality. Homophobia, like any phobia, can be subtle or blatant in its manifestation. People who are phobic about snakes may be made extremely uncomfortable when they come across a picture of a snake, though the picture clearly can do them no harm. When confronted by a live snake, they are apt to conceptualize the meeting as a "kill or be killed" encounter. They are unable to entertain the possibility that they are of little or no interest to the snake. Such people are covering some other fear or anxiety that is very personal and too unacceptable for them to face.

Homophobia may cover a person's fear of his or her own homoerotic feelings. If those feelings are damned by family, friends and community, the last thing in the world that the individual wants is to admit such feelings into conscious awareness. It is easier to stay away from such awareness with a socially acceptable distraction. Of course, the perfect distraction is to join the crusade to punish overt *queers*. It is not logical and it is not rational. It is an irrational, illogical pathology driven by fear and the awesome power of buried anxiety.

Humans are peculiarly vulnerable to this sort of pathology because of our social nature and the consequent urge to stay in the good graces of our community. Such pathology makes it possible for a consensus to evolve that requires everyone to agree that the naked Emperor is indeed wearing fine garments, that the madness of ethnic cleansing is somehow justifiable, that Hitler's Nazis were simply social reformers, that Jews are responsible for the world's evils and that there was no Holocaust.

Scapegoating is an ancient, simple-minded trick of superstition, sometimes used by manipulative politicians, but also used by others in quick desperation to quell fear, escape guilt and buy favor from whatever supernatural powers there may be. A goat or a person can be sacrificed to appease an imagined angry god. When the as yet undetected and unnamed AIDS virus began its spread among gay men in the early 1980s, the first name given to the disease was *gay cancer*, then GRID, or Gay Related Immune Deficiency. Though the virus had been at work, unpublicized and unnamed, building in strength and number in other populations for uncounted years, many people, including those in positions of great power, quickly and peculiarly assumed that the deadly disorder could only affect gay men and that it might even be God's punishment for their sins. Therefore, gay men could be sacrificed and investigative research into the problem could proceed at a leisurely inexpensive pace.

Blinded by bigotry, world health leaders failed to see, or chose *not* to see, that the disease would not follow the lines of their own social prejudice. It was not until the infection had savagely torn through the lives of thousands of gay men and their loved ones and spread into *all* segments of the general population that governments began to spend more reasonable sums of money on research, treatment and social aid—too little and too late for the countless thousands of people already suffering or dead, however.

If the virus had first made headlines among legislators of a powerful and wealthy nation and been named Legislators' Immune Deficiency, or LID rather than GRID, one imagines that the response would have been swifter and the suffering and loss of life dramatically reduced. Instead, the ever-ready temptation to assign blame and to assuage fear by scapegoating permitted the virus to get a tenacious foothold, and thus a worldwide epidemic was launched.

During the first decade of the AIDS epidemic in the U.S., there were influential people who, motivated by fear, hysteria, hatred, ignorance and prejudice, wanted all gay men to be forced to submit to an HIV test. Those who tested positive for the antibodies to the virus (indicating that they had been exposed to it) would be marked by a tattoo, quarantined and/or segregated in detention centers isolated far from the general population, thereby stripping them of property and civil rights. It did not happen in the United States but it was a seriously considered possibility. A similar isolation plan was instituted in Cuba, however.

Today, rapid advances in the mapping of human genes and the reality of genetic engineering lurk as threats in a world where medical ethics shift with the prevailing political currents and prejudice based on *difference* remains the world's most costly social disease. Gay people will continue to be born and to find one another, no matter how unwelcome. However, the nightmarish prospect of a deliberate attempt to abort gay people in utero is chilling and not entirely far-fetched. It could happen in a world that is so blinded to its need for differences that it flails and claws its way mindlessly toward mediocrity and extinction.

Each new generation chooses its favored ingredients from the rich variety of human differences. These choices fashion new styles of adaptation that will identify theirs as distinctly different from all previous generations. Sometimes, these newly incorporated differences are used to redress old wrongs, and thusly do human beings adapt to change as an evolving species, living on an evolving planet, in an evolving cosmos.

Riding from JFK Airport into Manhattan one day, I discovered that my driver was from Kenya. When I told her that I had gone to college with a young man from Kenya, she nearly drove us off the road when she heard his name. My former college acquaintance had become a very important person in that country. She was homesick for her village and her family, she told me, but glad that she had been able to relocate, first to France and then to the United States. She lived with her lover, a Greek woman, whom she had met in France.

"Our families would not think that we are doing the right thing," she said. "They would think that we are crossing too many lines, plus no children—all of it very bad. But we are blessed. Look how lucky we are to have found one another when we were put on earth in such very different places. I know people like us are everywhere but I had to search to find my own special *one*. Maybe love is not enough to excuse breaking rules, but I think it's got to be okay if you don't hurt anybody with it. I have an uncle who would kill me if he found me, I think. He don't appreciate me. Too bad for him."

Indeed, too bad for him. And too bad for all of the other people in the world who would punish us for our affections because they neither *accept* nor *appreciate* us. Acceptance is a good first step, but appreciation is required ultimately.

I have been a clinical psychologist for half a century, specializing in work with gay people, their families and friends for most of those years. I have seen many people burdened unnecessarily when they try to follow irrational rules, betraying their own nature in an attempt to subdue innocent affections.

It is simply wrong to punish love. No matter how grandiose the intention or how delusional the excuse—whether the motive is to help the individual or to save all of humanity—it is wrong.

As the driver from Kenya said, we are everywhere. We have our place in the world. We are part of the balance that makes human variety work on this planet. Gay people are born every year in every part of the world and it is a better world because we are here. There is a great joy in being gay and it is a great joy to have the freedom of openly loving someone gay. Our value in the human community of this world is gradually being recognized and appreciated as is the injustice wrought by those who have tried to change us, contain us, control us or exterminate us.

2

GROWING UP

I N FEBRUARY 2004 the mayor of San Francisco, California, Gavin Newsom, showed the United States and the world a new picture of gay love. Television, newspapers and magazines flashed pictures around the world of lesbians and gay male couples, some with their children, waiting in long lines to enter City Hall to obtain marriage licenses. The mayor had ordered city officials to issue the licenses without discrimination, disregarding gender. He also made the Hall's beautifully restored rotunda available for wedding ceremonies.

Thousands of gay couples were married before a court ordered a stop. Half a year later the state's Supreme Court declared the licenses invalid. During that precious period gay youngsters saw images of joy that they might claim for themselves one day, images to counteract the photographs and news footage of a gay young man beaten and left to die on a wire fence in a deserted area of Wyoming, a young lesbian raped and beaten to death by a gang, or a boy stabbed at school because he was suspected of being gay.

There are as many different kinds of gay people as there are different kinds of people. The only thing gay people have in common is our awareness that we are attracted in all ways, including sexually, to some people of the same gender. What we do with this awareness varies, as the following tales illustrate, but wherever prejudice against gay people is embraced, a lonely emotional struggle is predictable.

Steve, a young African-American graduate student, grew up in privileged circumstances in the suburbs of Washington, D.C. His parents, both college educated and politically active, had responsible and visible positions in government. "There was no fitting in anywhere—except maybe sort of in the private schools my sister and I went to. My parents never talked about it and they worked hard, but they knew that their jobs were partly window dressing in a city where almost everyone is colored and poor and after the government offices let out, the people who can afford it run to the suburbs. I didn't want to complicate their lives, or mine, by telling them that the reason I had to go to the bathroom so often in public places was so I could look for messages from my home planet scribbled on the walls. I knew who I was but not where I was from or where I was going. Fortunately, I never got caught looking and nobody read my mind. I split for New York and then California for school and just about exploded the first time I stepped into a gay club. I never told my parents or anyone else in the family anything until I met my man in graduate school and took him home for a 'Guess who's coming to dinner' evening. They were nice about it—just treated it like any other kind of national disaster that will be taken care of in time. At least I wasn't pierced or tattooed everywhere or *anywhere*—yes, they asked."

Marie told me that her grandparents had emigrated to Peru from Russia and Finland. "Growing up blonde and tall in Peru was plenty different—more than different enough for me," she said. When she was fourteen, she confessed her secret feelings of attraction to another girl her own age. "She was okay with it. Maybe neither of us fully understood what I was saying. It never got truly sexual, but we did a lot of hand holding and even some risky touching and kissing when no one was around. My pressure gauge was in the danger zone, though. I felt like I was waiting for an ax to fall. When the time came, I managed to persuade my parents to let me go to college in the States and when I had enough miles between me and them, I took a deep breath and came out to them in a letter. That was many years ago and they're still shaking their heads and sorting it out. My mother's mother is sure that I caught *it* from drinking water up north. My folks definitely valued being different in the sense of being superior but not being different like I was different. They're sure I'm going to Hell. I used to think maybe I should just marry some nice guy, tell them I'd seen the light and let them have a happy old age. But I have a problem about lying."

Christian was born into a large peasant family in a small village in the south of France in the early sixties. It is less than a half hour's drive from Avignon and less than a five-hour train ride from Paris today, but to Christian both cities seemed as far away as another country when he was a boy. His family farmed land that lay beyond the village and everyone in the family had assigned tasks and long hours of work. Christian knew that he was attracted to some of the boys and men in the village but tried not to think about it. When he was thirteen years old, a fifteen-year-old cousin, Jean Marc, was apprenticed as a waiter in Avignon. Christian had a reputation as a very hard worker and was sent along with his cousin to work as a dishwasher in the same restaurant and to share room and board with the hope that he too might become an apprentice. Christian had long been attracted to Jean Marc but feared being found out. For the first weeks he clung to his side of the narrow bed in the tiny room they shared and slept poorly each night. Eventually, he fell ill with a fever and a cough and was sent back to his village. When he recovered he was allowed to go to school in nearby Carpentras and there he confided in an understanding teacher, who told him that he had better forget such feelings until he was old enough to leave home. Two years later Jean Marc helped him to secure another job, helping a stonemason, and Christian again moved to Avignon, this time sharing a larger room with Jean Marc and sleeping in a separate bed. After some months there he spoke with a priest, who advised him that his feelings were sinful and must be fought. A year later, at seventeen, he confessed his inner tumult to Jean Marc who listened with care, told him that he had a waiter friend who was gay and working in Lyon, and promised to arrange a meeting so that they could talk. He also assured him that he would say nothing to Christian's family. "That waiter in Lyon and Jean Marc saved my life. I think in another year I would have killed myself from the agony. But Jean Marc seemed to think I was okay and the waiter was a great guy who talked and talked with me and even found me a job in Lyon—far enough from home so that I could begin to be myself."

Alice's parents were souvenir shopkeepers in London who became art dealers in a world where they were friendly with many gay people. When she was fifteen, Alice told them about her feelings for several of her female classmates. Her mother slapped her face and sent her to her room. When her father came home, he told her that they would pay for therapy "to get you straightened out" and that they did not want to hear another word from her on the topic until she was quite ready to introduce them to a suitable young man who interested her. "Twelve years, two nations, and five therapists later, I finally got really angry and started planning to have a life."

Oscar was born in East Los Angeles soon after his parents had managed to cross the border illegally from Mexico. "It seemed like everybody within a mile of where we lived was related one way or another, so there was a lot of sleeping here and there when we were kids because all the parents were scrambling for work and had to park their kids wherever they could. I liked it a lot when other boys fooled around a little, and I noticed all the good-looking guys in the neighborhood, but in school we had to be *bad*—we had to join a gang, be a serious jock, or look tough and busy enough to be left alone. If any guy was suspected of really liking other guys, his life was hell. I saw dancing on TV and wanted to be a dancer, but I knew that was out. I managed to get myself into and through college with the help of a track scholarship. I got married right after school and got a job in a stock-broker's office. A little night grad school, lots of work and, before I knew it, we had a condo in a good neighborhood. I was a father of two boys, got taken on as a broker in a big firm and was able to help out my family. Of course, I had to dress well, go to lunches to charm clients, keep myself in good shape, go to the gym regularly and all that. The locker room drove me crazy. Then I set the record for the youngest heart attack victim in the firm. This gave me some time out to look at myself and my life, and I realized how lonely I had always been and how many tears I never cried. I smiled my way all through school and into jobs and nobody ever knew who I was. I had a lot to untangle and explain to people, but I wasn't ready to be dead."

The gay person, like everyone else, begins his or her life being open and interested in the body, mind and emotions of all other nearby people, regardless of gender, but a prejudiced culture encourages its people to tune out awareness of sensual and erotic interest in people of the same gender. It is not yet known why a certain percentage of the human population refuses or is unable to follow such cultural instruction. The increasingly few social scientists who assume that gay interests are abnormal (and therefore wrong) have looked for causative factors. Their search for causes makes less sense, however, than looking for the reasons why some people *do* manage to follow the cultural dictum and actually tune out their same gender feelings.

If I had not seen it in action so often, I would be surprised at how adept many people are at hiding their prejudices from themselves. A friend told me about a vacation with his sister and his life-partner. He and Paul worked in the same hospital, which is where they met. While on the beach my friend's sister met a man she liked and it was arranged that the four of them would have dinner together. The evening was going well when, in the course of conversation, her date asked, "So, how do you two guys know each other?"

"Paul and my brother work in the same hospital," the sister answered quickly.

The next morning my friend asked her why she had introduced Paul in that way. "It seemed weird," he told her. "Were you embarrassed about us?"

"Heavens, no!" she answered. "You know me better than that. But it's none of his business. He doesn't have to know everything right away."

Or there is the paragraph in an otherwise nice letter, not unlike others, that I have received from someone who had been given one of my books as a gift. "I thank God that there are people like you in our world who are making life better for people like my uncle. He is one of the best men I have ever met in my life. My own two boys worship the ground he walks on to the extent that I have to reassure my wife many times that their loving him so much is not going to make them gay. I know now that it doesn't work this way. Either they are or they're not—and we know they're not."

If the writer was as enlightened as he thought he had become, he would have had no reason to "reassure" himself or his wife. He would have known that it would be quite wonderful for his boys to have exactly the natural orientation they happened to have, gay or not. He would also know that there was no way of knowing what that orientation was, until and unless his sons chose to reveal their innermost feelings of affection and sexuality to him.

Like my friend's sister, there is sometimes a superficial acceptance based on love for a particular individual who is gay, but culturally encouraged prejudice continues to lurk in the corners of the person's mind. When it slips out there is a natural impulse to rationalize and excuse it while pushing it back into the peripheral shadows. And there it remains, causing unfounded judgments about *people like that*. "You're just too sensitive sometimes," my friend's sister told him, relieving herself of responsibility.

There is no doubt that the writer of the letter loves his uncle and had done some difficult growing while learning to accept that his uncle is gay. The lurking anxiety that continues to nag at him is rooted in an unrecognized prejudice and in not knowing what might cause his sons to be gay.

The reasons why some people grow up gay and some non-gay are of little interest unless one presumes it is desirable to alter one condition or the other. As long as we assume that in the future, as in all centuries past, some people will continue to retain their sensuous and erotic interest in people of the same gender, we know that we will always have humans of every age, ethnic background and socio-economic status who are gay. Some would be happy to disclaim such labels as *gay*, *queer*, *homosexual*, *bisexual* or any other label. I use *gay* to designate those of us who have refused the cultural instruction to rid ourselves of sexual interest in people of the same gender. I believe that in any place where prejudice against us continues to be manifest, we need our own separate identity until we are perceived as fully equal and can integrate with *heterosexuals* in a pluralistic society that appreciates diversity in sexual orientation.

Most gay people are aware of their same-gender interest, forbidden or not, early in life—some as far back as they can remember; for others awareness begins around age eight, nine or ten. I remember, for instance, being in Florida at age four and watching an attractive male neighbor go into his outdoor shower stall wearing a bathing suit and carrying a bar of soap. I could see his head, arms, chest and legs as he turned on the shower and started to sing while he lathered himself. I thought he was quite handsome and jolly. I was enchanted by the happy scene and felt a sweet strange feeling in the pit of my stomach. When his bathing suit fell to the floor and was then thrown over the top of the wooden shower stall door and he continued his singing and lathering, I had a terrific urge to join him and help with the soaping. The erotic nature of the feeling is perfectly clear even as I remember it today, many decades later. The scene reminds me of some of today's television commercials designed to sell soap, shampoo and underarm deodorants to men. One must presume that either advertisers believe that women do all of the shopping for men's cosmetics or *they really do understand that most men are quite aware of the erotic attraction of other men.*

We do not know how or why the awareness of sexual attraction to some people of the same gender comes into focus or why it is not abandoned. Perhaps the ostentatious silence or absence of outspoken support for such feelings actually sharpens a self-aware focus. In a prejudiced environment, one easily become emotionally aware that boy-girl interests are a matter of constant comment while boy-boy or girl-girl interests are played down, considered appropriate in very young children only, laughed at or condemned.

It is a tired sight gag that still appears with sickening frequency on television, in films and on the stage. One boy looks at another and says, "Nice pants..." and everyone else in the scene looks at him for a silent second while the audience is reminded to laugh. One tough-acting girl says, "I can fix that for you..." to the second girl who is in tears because of her broken mechanical gadget and everyone else in the scene freezes as one or more of them raise eyebrows and the audience is reminded to laugh.

For some of us there is an awakening in adolescence, perhaps set off by a sexual experience. Looking back, people often report that they can see the interest was there earlier but remained dormant because of a reluctance to acknowledge it or because they simply never thought about such things. There is the vivid adolescent memory of a camping trip during which two boy friends had to double up in one sleeping bag because the other bag got misplaced or dropped while crossing a creek, or of being one of two girls who rolled into one another's arms during a sleep-over while each pretended to be dreaming of the world's most popular male rock star.

Not infrequently, there is a story of an attractive cousin, neighbor, young aunt or uncle who is pursued by the youngster until the moment of passion is achieved. The youngster may disown responsibility on the basis of being a few years younger, but honest recollection often brings back memories of a pursuit and longing for intimate body contact that had determination and a clear sexual component.

More unfortunately, the awakening can also come under less favorable circumstances when the youngster is seduced by someone in a position of greater physical or emotional power. That kind of experience brings with it the terror, trauma and confusion of rape that is guaranteed to contaminate the sexual awakening and consequent emotional-sexual development.

Whatever the age of awareness (and for most it is quite young), a long period of quiet, internal struggle may follow. If so, the person is burdened with a lonely secret. Consciously or not, he or she becomes an alert gatherer of information. One listens for news of others who have the same feelings and too often the available news is bad. Rarely is there a truly respected friend of the family or truly beloved relative who is openly gay. Though gay men and lesbians may appear in films and on TV, there are few, if any, apparent respectable models. The child, adolescent or young adult feels caught, pulled in the direction of the impulses and feelings, yet held back by the fear of becoming an outcast.

She or he may try talking to a trusted friend, but support may be curiously absent. All too often the friend is secretly doing battle with some of the same feelings. A brave person may try talking to a relative, parent, school counselor, teacher, priest, minister or doctor. But there is the risk of a negative reaction or visible retraction of respect and good will. There is also the risk of outright censure and persecution. The gay person may be cautioned to mend his or her ways, repent, get well, seek help, confess, pray for forgiveness or, at the least, remain silent.

In enlightened communities there are telephone counselors and other resources, but where there is prejudice, gay youngsters grow up in a lonely, unfriendly world. Older gay people may want to help but may be understandably reluctant to become involved, even when invited, because of possible legal consequences. There are gay adults who have spent years in prison because they tried to give aid and comfort to a gay child.

It is during these growing-up years that some gay youngsters build an invisible wall between themselves and their parents. It is built as a protection. They have listened carefully and seen no sign that their parents are likely to be supportive if their gay identity is discovered. The more open and sharing they are with parents, the more likely is the discovery. Hence, the transparent wall is erected and parents wonder why their offspring have suddenly become so uncommunicative.

Some gay youngsters immerse themselves in religion; some become model students and perfect children. These same children may have emotional breakdowns, the result of having carried too large an invisible emotional strain. Some commit suicide. Families and friends grieve while having no idea that they themselves may have contributed to the youngster's misery. One hears that Juan or Suzie "had everything to live for—why this?" Family and friends may speculate that someone slipped a drug into the unsuspecting young-ster's food or drink. It does not occur to anyone that the lethal agent may have been the socially approved conspiracy of disapproval that is born of, and sanctified by, pious prejudice.

3

INVISIBILITY, OPPRESSION AND SELF

W HEN I WAS A CHILD, I looked forward each week to the next episode of a radio drama called *The Shadow*. The title character, Lamont Cranston, could render himself invisible in an instant, thereby enabling him to hear and observe others without being seen. The opening line for each episode was, "Who knows what evil lurks in the hearts of men? The Shadow Knows."

He also was honest, good, well-informed and very clever. Since he could hide from his enemies with ease, they could not harm him. He was well positioned to see to it that wrong-doers would be punished and that persons threatened with mistreatment would be protected.

In addition to my keen enjoyment of the adventure and suspense of the drama, I felt a mysterious kinship with the hero. Perhaps it was because, though I was unable to make myself physically invisible, I knew that I needed to hide a vital part of myself. I was beginning to see the evil that lurks in many hearts. Unfortunately, however, I was too young to be able to chastise, correct or punish the people who threatened me and caused me to live in fear.

Instead, I did a curious thing. I tried to convince myself that those people were right and good and that it was I who was evil, bad and guilty of wrong feelings. This peculiar adaptation to a world that is upside down or inside out is a phenomenon observed by the psychotherapist Bruno Bettelheim, among prisoners in concentration camps. He labeled it *identification with the aggressor*. It is an attempt to hold on to rational sanity in a world that has become irrational and insane.

A concentration camp survivor with whom I worked many years ago when I was a clinical psychology intern in a Veterans Administration Hospital, told me, "You see, I was only a kid and I started to feel ashamed of my family. I thought that they must be too ignorant or too stubborn to admit what an inferior lot we were. Why else would the guards have all the power while we were penned up in there and treated like animals? Even though the guards were the immediate cause of our misery, I began to imitate them. I wanted to walk like them and talk like them. I wanted to grow up to be strong, powerful and *right*, like them."

Most gay children do their best to hide the developing erotic orientation that is a vital part of themselves. In a society that subscribes to beliefs that homosexuality is bad, wrong, evil or inferior, there is a better chance of survival if the child is invisible. These are the children who are only partly seen and not ever really heard. They do, however, listen and observe while trying to hide their true feelings, well aware of the evil around them. Some try hard to imitate the guards.

Many gay people do not outgrow their need for invisibility. The longer it is used, the more time one spends trying to imitate the oppressor so as to be thought acceptable, the more time one has to shape the self-concept of an *inferior*. The deeper the roots of that misshapen self-concept, the grater the ultimate harm to self-esteem. The more harm that is done to self-esteem, the more predictably troubled a person will be and the more hampered in establishing a satisfying life.

It is a nasty, tortured cycle. The innocent person is assumed to be inferior by an oppressor and is treated accordingly. Over time, such treatment alters the victim's self-perception until he or she also comes to assume himself or herself to be inferior. Ultimately, such victims will present themselves as inferior people—and the circle of oppression is complete.

A man who, with the help of psychotherapy, emerged from a disabling depression said "From way back in fourth or fifth grade, I always thought of myself as the ugly, skinny, hunched over nerd with bad skin who couldn't think clearly except when I was alone in my room with the computer. Most of my family's business and social friends were too well-behaved to say anything really bad about gay people. It was more in what they didn't say—the condescension, as well as the smirks and smiles when someone was mentioned who was gay. I sure as hell wasn't going to show who I was. It took a long time for me to be able to look in a mirror, go to the gym, learn to smile, and then ask for that first promotion and know that it was overdue. Now, I've cleared the fourth promotion and I like myself well enough to think that some guy might really love me. I figured I'd never be *best*—not good enough for the people I grew up with, but not now. Hey, I like being gay. I like the guy I see in the mirror. What I want now is to be a more compassionate person than most of those people were. They weren't *best*, they were just *normal*—you know, *average*."

There are people in every walk of life, in every part of the world, who experience oppression every day. They may be held in disfavor because of the color of their skin, the religion they practice, the village or town in which they were born, the language they speak, their political beliefs, their height, their weight or their sexual orientation. The bad news is that this worldwide epidemic of oppressive social insanity persists today much as it did when the earliest human tribes made war on one another because of greed, envy or fear. The good news is that some people, everywhere in the world, are now aware of this insanity.

This is important. We are reminded of the problem of systematic oppression because it is newsworthy. It is flashed into our awareness via conversation, radio, newspapers, magazines, television, the Internet—and as it often comes from a different part of the world, the long-distance perspective tends to make it look as weirdly insane as it really is—and sometimes this fresh perspective facilitates social change.

Unfortunately, some forms of oppression are so commonplace that they hardly seem newsworthy. Forty years ago, few people noticed how women were manipulated to stay in *their place* in the home or in lower prestige jobs. Only now, as women enter positions of power previously reserved exclusively for men, are we becoming more aware of how oppressively excluded they have been.

Too few people today are aware that there are gay men and lesbians being held in prisons, detention centers, relocation centers and mental hospitals around the world because their sexual orientation is primarily homosexual. They are considered to be *criminal* or *emotionally disturbed* because they insist on going public with their full identity, including their gay thoughts, ideas and feelings.

It is not unusual for public officials, family members and professional colleagues to warn against public pronouncements of such nonconformist feelings. Prohibition of such displays of affection as two men walking down the street holding hands or two women kissing with true tenderness, or talking and writing about such humble events, is quite common. Overt expressions of affection between people of the same gender are *not done* in many parts of the world. They are considered an offense to public decency. If a person persists in breaking such unwritten (or written) rules for social conduct, it is assumed to be a signal or symptom the person is a *counter-revolutionary*, a *political dissident, insane* or *asking for help*. Such *help* is more likely to help the embarrassed families, colleagues or government functionaries since it means removing the gay person from the community and keeping her or him in an institutional setting such as a mental hospital, jail or detention center. The non-gay community is thus reassured that such feelings and behavior are indeed rare and *wrong*.

If we could view this social phenomenon as science fiction, it would seem incredible. I ask the non-gay reader to consider your own feelings in a few hypothetical situations. If you are a heterosexual woman, imagine that you are with a woman friend in a public setting, such as a restaurant in a conservative community. While you are waiting to be seated, she tells you that her life has been difficult lately. Her daughter has had a miscarriage and her brother has been diagnosed with a terminal illness. You see tears in her eyes. You touch her elbow and tell her how very sorry you are while she attempts to control her tears. She tells you how much she has needed to talk with you.

Your natural impulse might be to reach out and draw her to you. But because you are two women together in such a setting, you might feel restrained and unable to express yourself as fully, and instead anticipate misunderstanding and disapproval from those around you.

You may suggest that the two of you go to a more private place. Thus, the meaningful moment of compassion expressed with comforting close physical contact is lost to the social conditioning of *appropriate* behavior for two women together in public. The invisible line surrounding *permissible* physical contact between two women varies from one community to another, but it is there—always.

If you are a heterosexual man reading this book, imagine that you and a trusted, loving male friend are alone together while on a holiday or a business trip. He seems distracted, sometimes not hearing what you say. When you ask him about it, he says that when he is with his wife, he concentrates on comforting her, but that when he is away from her, he thinks constantly about the recent death of his daughter. He confesses that he sometimes feels as if he is losing control and perhaps losing his mind. He grips your arm and closes his eyes in an attempt to choke back tears that begin to escape.

You are alone. There are no furtive glances of disapproval to worry you. If your friend were a woman, you might take her in your arms. You might sit down with her, perhaps easing her head to your shoulder or against your chest—rocking, patting and holding her as she cries, trying your best to share her burden for the moment and comfort her.

But your friend is another man, like you. It probably required great trust for him to grasp your arm and cry in your presence. For the two of you now to embrace, pressing bodies together for comfort and feeling mutual tears on the soft skin of your faces, is nearly unthinkable. You can talk but not touch intimately. Your wish to help, your natural human impulse to share and comfort with physical contact at such a moment is rendered impotent.

Neither of these examples include any sexual thoughts or behavior. They involve deep human feelings which our gender training discourages, and we are all the poorer for it. For a gay person, feelings of caring affection for someone of the same gender come easily and need not be stirred by such dramatic events, but are they any less respectable because they surface with less extreme provocation?

In 1972, a group of gay psychologists formed an organization. We called ourselves the Association of Gay Psychologists. Our primary objective was to force the American Psychological Association to see us as responsible, if oppressed, members of the profession and to support us in our struggle for the same full civil rights due any American citizen.

At the end of 1973, the American Psychiatric Association removed homosexuality (and gay identity) from its diagnostic list. The organization declared itself ready to view homosexual interests as *different from* but not *better or worse* than heterosexual interests. It was an admission that the belief held throughout the twentieth century that people should be considered emotionally disordered and in need of treatment and/or be institutionalized because of gay identity had been a mistake. The organization deserves respect for that monumental admission, although the enormity of human suffering caused by the mistake is incalculable.

But prejudice, self-interest and oppression do not yield quite so easily. A remarkable series of events followed. Some politically powerful physicians within the organization caused the issue to be reconsidered by the entire membership. Each member of the Association was invited to *vote* on whether he or she considered it natural and normal to be gay or whether it might be considered a mental disorder. The membership voted, drawing upon professional experience, personal values and *personal prejudice*. Consider how unusual such an event is! It was a close vote, but gay people were voted sane unless we present the same symptoms that a non-gay person might present for a psychiatric diagnosis of an emotional disorder.

A year later, in January of 1975, the American Psychological Association issued the following statement:

The governing body of the American Psychological Association (APA) today voted to oppose discrimination against homosexuals and to support the recent action by the American Psychiatric Association which removed homosexuality from that Association's official list of mental disorders.

The text of the policy statement, which was submitted to the Council of Representatives by APA's Board of Ethical and Social Responsibility for Psychology and recommended by the Board of Directors, follows:

1. The American Psychological Association supports the action taken on 15 December 1973 by the American Psychiatric Association removing homosexuality from the Association's official list of mental disorders. The American Psychological Association therefore adopts the following resolution:

Homosexuality per se implies no impairment in judgment, stability, reliability, or general social or vocational capabilities.

Further, the American Psychological Association urges all mental health professional to take the lead in removing the stigma of mental illness that has long been associated with homosexual orientation.

2. Regarding discrimination against homosexuals, the American Psychological Association adopts the following resolution concerning their civil and legal rights:

The American Psychological Association deplores all public and private discrimination in such areas of employment, housing, public accommodations, and licensing against those who engage in or have engaged in homosexual activities and declares that no burden of proof of such judgment, capacity, or reliability shall be placed upon those individuals greater than that imposed on any other person; Further, the American Psychological Association supports and urges the enactment of civil rights legislation at the local, state and federal level that would offer citizens who engage in acts of homosexuality the same protections now guaranteed to others on the basis of race, creed, color, etc; Further, The American Psychological Association supports and urges the repeal of all discriminatory legislation singling out homosexual acts by consenting adults in private.

The council also amended the Association's 'Statement of Policy Regarding Equal Employment Opportunity' to include sexual orientation among the prohibited discriminations listed. APA's employment practices in its various professional placement programs and advertisement in all Association publications will comply with this policy.

Psychoanalysts fought with great vigor to continue to have gay identity viewed as pathological. *Two decades* after the American Psychiatric Association removed gay identity from their diagnostic list, the American Psychoanalytic Association grudgingly issued a statement in 1991 indicating that it would no longer oppose admission of lesbians and gay men to its institutes of training. In 1992 it finally appended an amendment to that statement allowing gay men and lesbians to teach in their institutes and act as senior analysts!

Both the American Psychiatric Association and the American Psychological Association have a great deal of influence in professional mental health work far beyond the United States. The position statements from both organizations represented a major step forward but oppression dies slowly when a prejudice has been ingrained in a society for many generations.

In the late 1970s, gay characters began to appear in plays, films and on television, but their characterizations were usually limited by stereotype. Gay men and lesbians did not appear in TV commercials. The fears of the advertising executives are particularly telling. They know that advertising is generally more successful it if carries a mild shock. But the impact of two women, or two men, trying on engagement rings, picking out a new home or test-driving a new car together remained taboo. The travel industry, some clothing manufacturers and a few liquor and wine distributors did realize a handsome profit by advertising in gay publications but dared not present us in mainstream advertisements.

Public disclosure of a gay identity once meant automatic exclusion from a partner's position in a major law firm. Today, an especially capable law school graduate who is openly gay may be recruited by a major firm with the hope of grooming her or him as a showcase partner representing *diversity*. In the corporate world, however, there is a glass ceiling for women executives and a ceiling embedded with iron bars for anyone who is openly gay. Survival in the upper echelons of business and industry depends, in large measure, on the individual's political clout *before* coming out publicly. Among the lower ranks of the workforce there continues to be little forward movement or support for the openly gay employee.

Educational institutions, ever looking to the future while tied to the social habits of the past, easily tuck prejudice into costumes of progress and conveniently fail to notice that many of their students are being harmed. But college and university students more easily ride the waves of social change than do the faculty and administration of these institutions. They continue to force recognition of gay students and, to the confusion of the their elders, form not only Gay Unions but Gay and Straight Alliances which grow in political strength and will remain as long as they are needed to spread tolerance and appreciation for diversity. These students know, if their elders do not, that survival in a newly small world depends on getting along with your neighbor whose customs and tastes may differ from your own.

Administrators of schools who manage students below college or university age watch the trend with anxiety. They know that this awareness is coming to younger students also. The youngest student may have one or more openly gay parents. If he or she does not, they may know a classmate who has a gay mom or dad.

Religions also find themselves caught in the tides of social change. A few embrace the changes that have come and are arriving still for women, gays and others who are *different*. Other religions notoriously dig their heels into their mud and fight change imagining that centuries-old dysfunctional traditions will see them through future centuries.

Gay men and women perplex these religious rule-makers. They are willing to receive our financial, volunteer and participatory support as members of their congregations but they insist that we are sinners eligible for *compassionate* oppression but not eligible for leadership as their priests, clergymen or policy makers unless we remain closeted and are very quiet about our affections. Their pious platitudes offered with smiles suggest one must "condemn sin but love the sinner." Convenient. Oppressive.

Some nations arrogantly flaunt their hypocrisy by making full use of gay people in their armed forces while denying them full recognition. In 1996, a committee within Britain's Department of Defence came to a startlingly self-serving conclusion. After a four-month review that consisted of canvassing opinions from within the military itself (where homosexuality is forbidden and honest opinion, therefore, highly unlikely), the committee was able to agree with itself to continue its policy of prejudice and oppression, maintaining its ban on homosexuals in the military, and ignoring the rights of gay people under European equality laws.

In the United States, a hopeful presidential candidate named Bill Clinton, following the earlier example of Jimmy Carter, courted gay votes by promising that, if elected, he would issue an executive order banning discrimination against gay people in the armed forces. Instead, after winning the election, he sought the approval of the military leaders for whom he was supposed to be the commander in chief. Since the very same people had kept the policy of discriminatory oppression in place, it was not surprising that they failed to approve the change. The surprise was that a civilian commander in chief would set the dangerous precedent of bowing to the wishes of the military and pander to popular prejudice.

The newly elected president and his staff then helped to fashion the infamous, so-called "Don't Ask, Don't Tell" policy, which stated that it was permissible for lesbians and gay men to serve and give their lives for their country provided that they did not ever say that they were gay! Imagine the public outcry if Irish-American Catholics had been told that they could serve and die for the United States, as long as they never said they were Catholic or had Irish ancestry, since this might bother the Protestants of Irish ancestry, or some other ethnic group, with whom they were serving.

What a shame that President Clinton failed to take the opportunity to do what was right rather than what seemed politically expedient. He might have taken courage from another of his predecessors, President Truman, who in 1948 took the highly controversial step of finally ordering racial integration of the military.

In 1996, the president of Zimbabwe publicly described gay people as "worse than dogs or pigs" and had his government block a Zimbabwean gay organization from opening a stand at an international book fair. With financial help from a Dutch group, the battle was fought to the nation's supreme court and, ultimately, the gay organization opened a small stand with only flowers and volunteers to answer questions at the fair. In the aftermath, the government issued warnings of anti-gay violence that were clearly designed to stir up more trouble and further intimidate the gay population.

In too many parts of the world, we are one of the last minority groups required to pay taxes while not enjoying the same civil rights enjoyed by other citizens. Crimes against gay people are common in areas where prejudice is sanctioned. If we are forced to hide our identity, we become easy prey for extortion and blackmail. A lesbian or gay man may be robbed, beaten or killed with the excuse that he or she stepped out of line, was sexually provocative or morally insulting. It is amazing that such excuses could even be considered, unless you accept the premise that we are not equal citizens under the law and, as inferiors or outcasts, we must behave in a subordinate manner.

Most of us are, or have been for many years, invisible. This is an important fact to remember. It is during these "invisible years" that real damage is done. Physical wounds to the body heal. Irrational hatred and abuse can be understood when it comes from intellectually limited and socially damaged people, but when the wounds are inflicted by family, friends, trusted counselors and civic leaders, the wounds go deep, our concepts of ourselves are heavily scarred and self-esteem is seriously damaged. Almost every gay person has endured periods of invisibility. Some gay people remain invisible all of their lives.

We see men and women set up as heterosexual models for expressing feelings of sensuality and eroticism with one another. We see it within our families, on the street, in magazines, in the movies and on television. Thus do we shape our ideas of what is right, normal, natural and good. Yet we know we have loving feelings for certain individuals who share our gender and that we sometimes want to express those feelings sensuously and erotically. Thanks to TV and films we know there are gay people but seldom see loving expressed by two men or two women.

Our inner truth is not validated visibly. Because we are not visible in many parts of the world, we listen to the pointed derogatory jokes and stories about people who share our feelings. These hurtful messages may issue from the mouths of fathers, mothers, aunts, uncles, brothers, sisters, teachers, counselors and friends. Few would think of telling a story or a joke that is anti-Arab in the presence of an Arab or one that is anti-Jewish in the presence of a Jew. But if, by chance, the Arab or Jew is exposed to such an insult, he or she has the comfort of *shared* indignation or resignation from family and a larger community of relatives and friends. Not so for the gay person. She or he is invisible. Too often, not only can we not turn to family or friends, but it is these very people who insult and traumatize us throughout the invisible years of development.

The gay person can easily begin to think of herself or himself as wrong, bad or defective. The one hope is that no one knows, no one sees. The secret must be protected—sometimes with lies that reinforce the bad self-evaluation. "Not only am I sexually perverted," we may reason, "but I am also a liar." Energy goes into a personal civil war fought against natural gay feelings.

We grow up during the invisible years suspecting that there must be many basic things wrong about us. Why else would loved ones say such things about people who share our feelings? The seeds of self-doubt and self-hate grow and flourish every day. Only the fortunate find ways to excise them.

Though individuals continue to suffer with the need to be invisible during formative years, gay people are becoming more visible to the world as a group. We are appearing more often as characters on TV and in films. Like other *foreign* people integrating in a population, we are presented as stereotypes, thereby a source of laughs. But gradually more three-dimensional gay characters appear, peculiar or *bad* ones first unfortunately, but our portraits become more complex. We are losing our collective invisibility.

As the AIDS virus attacked the international gay male subculture, average citizens were shocked to learn how many famous, talented or otherwise highly valued men were gay. Many of these men had their sexual orientation exposed as a result of the illness. Others, both male and female, not infected with the virus but emotionally ravaged from care-giving, grieving and loss, revealed their own gay identity also as an act of solidarity.

One man I know said, "All of my friends are sick or dying. I am the only one who was not infected by the virus. Could I possibly dishonor them by hiding and pretending to be different than they— other than I really am?"

And a lesbian friend who had worked herself to exhaustion as a caregiver, told me, "Seeing how we all came together so quickly to handle this crisis has made me want to be right out there in everybody's face. I wear my gay identity as a badge of honor and anger. We earned our pride in the trenches and nobody's going to make me hide ever again. They can just get out of my way."

4

PRESSURES
TO CONFORM

C ONSIDERING THE UNENDING bombardment of negative messages, the resulting injuries to self-esteem and the exhausting efforts required to hide true feeling, it is no wonder that so many gay people give in to the massive pressures and try to conform to a popular image of the *normal* person. More often than not, these first efforts to conform go on for many years.

Usually, gay people are aware of their gay feelings long before considering themselves eligible for the label. Much effort goes into rationalizing and explaining to oneself why the feelings are there. The attempts at explanation are usually extracted from the anti-gay mythology of the surrounding culture.

The conclusion may be that the gay feelings stem from having had a strong mother and a weak father, or a cold mother and a loving father, or an absent mother and a disagreeable father—thus drawing on one of the many pseudo-scientific psychological caricatures of family situations that are the lingering residue of a generation of ambitious psychoanalysts who thought they were smarter than Freud. These "theories" have never contributed to understanding but instead have served only to pathologize homosexuality and make people feel bad about themselves.

Religion can be a powerful influence and it is not unthinkable for a gay person to believe that the gay feelings are being sent by evil spirits or by Satan. A person may believe that she has inherited a defect: Because Aunt Joan was committed to a mental hospital, gay feelings are a mental problem; or because her mother's brother committed suicide, she may believe that she is "genetically predisposed" to do "bad things." A young person may feel that he is being influenced by the wrong crowd at school. Or it may come down to something as simple as a belief that "gayness" is due to masturbation.

Whatever the presumed genesis of the feelings, the next effort in the struggle to conform is to guard against the expression of gay feelings in behavior. This is a time when the full use of willpower is called upon. It is also easy to become too vigilant or overly self-conscious—watchful of every word, tone of voice and casual touch. Even the strongest use of willpower, however, usually seems insufficient and more vigorous efforts to disown the feelings may be called into play.

A common and nearly transparent ploy is to announce intense anti-gay feelings and to behave accordingly. The person who puts a peculiar amount of energy into baiting and hating gay people is likely to be doing battle with unacceptable feelings hidden inside himself or herself and those feelings are probably homosexual in nature. A person trapped in this stage of denial is dangerous, not only to themselves, but also to others. He or she may succeed in putting the unacceptable desires out of *conscious* awareness, but the feelings and impulses remain in the shadows of the mind, always threatening to reappear. This can drive the person to vehement verbal tirades and acts of gay bashing that seem, to any reasonably sane observer, strange and puzzling in their strength and lead to precisely the sort of speculation that the behavior was intended to avoid.

While this war to disown feelings rages, control over having the feelings is, ironically, apt to be least efficient when translated into behavior. The openly gay person is able to decide when to act on her or his feelings, but the person torn asunder with internal conflict cannot. He or she is like the person obsessed with a weight problem who is constantly confronted with cakes, candy and other irresistible but fattening delights. He is the soldier or sailor who gets drunk, wanders into a gay bar—accidentally on purpose—and swears he remembers nothing the next morning when he awakens in bed with another man. She is the woman who arranges a weekend away with a woman friend whose admiring glances have supposedly gone unnoticed, picks a hotel room with the best view—that happens to have only one bed—and awakens during the night outraged to find that the other woman has just finished committing a rather lengthy sexual act with her. He is the macho man who goes on extended hunting expeditions, fishing trips or to other places where there are no women and then lets a *queer* have his way with him because his virility requires a release of sexual tension, and he somehow mysteriously has forgotten how to masturbate.

The homosexual feelings are there, along with hidden feelings of gay affection that are strangely covered by hatred. The inefficient controls fail on such occasions. The distorted mixture of feelings are expressed in behavior that is not loving, followed by a slight memory loss, black-out or a long bout of unattractive rationalizing designed to hold off the crushing guilt. That guilt, of course, is the result of having given in to the unacceptable feelings and, worse, having blamed others while distorting the satisfaction of needs made bad and ugly.

Homosexual rape of an adult outside of prisons is rare. People involve themselves emotionally and sexually with others of the same gender usually because the involvement is desired. A person who is aware of his or her homosexual desires while pretending that such desires do not exist is said to be in the closet. Since most gay people started out *in the closet*, we are sensitive to the symptoms and understand their meaning.

Though we may react with sympathy or irritation, remembering our own dark days shut away from the truth, we are likely to spot the phenomenon quickly. A fading bit of gay folk wisdom dictates that "today's trade is tomorrow's competition." Someone described as *trade* is a person who invites homosexual attention while remaining so deeply in the closet that homosexual desires are not admitted to others or to themselves. Such people are relatively easy to recognize. The folk wisdom simply confirms that someone who invites homosexual attention or seduction is, of course, eager for homosexual experience.

It is a phenomenon that is fading in most parts of the world now as we see how self-degrading it is to involve ourselves with people whose current prejudice combined with their unacknowledged feelings devalues both the gay experience and gay identity. The gay person of today is more likely to decline the invitation to seduce but may offer helpful counsel to the self-proclaimed *straight* when he or she is ready to come out of the closet.

A gay person, out of the closet and comfortable about it, is able to decide when to express erotic feelings in sexual behavior, just as the person who does not have a serious weight problem is able to decide when to have a sweet, testing the strength of the desire against such reality factors as appropriateness of time and place. If there are no complications of self-concept, one can decide whether the sweet is apt to spoil an upcoming meal or increase the likelihood of indigestion. One can likewise decide whether it might complicate current interpersonal relationships or add unwanted demands to an already satisfying sexual life to partake of the erotic temptation. If one's intellectual and emotional evaluation is that it will be an affordable and rewarding treat, why not? However, if it appears that the experience is likely to cause more trouble than the pleasure is worth, it will be declined.

I do not mean to imply that all gay feelings are sexual feelings. That is a part of the mythology that has been perpetuated by anti-gay propaganda. Gay feelings run deep. They encompass love, compassion, sympathy, respect, empathy, understanding and altruism. Sexual interaction may help to express some of these feelings in ways that cannot be expressed in words, but gay people do express gay feelings non-sexually as well. The internal struggle with gay feelings is likely to focus on sexual feelings and sexual behavior, because sex has been made the tangible center of the taboo.

Often there is a kernel of truth to be found in a stereotype. A gay man described helping his grandmother prepare for an eightieth birthday celebration. Her seventy-nine-year-old sister was also helping out, but was overwhelmed when the sixth bouquet of flowers was delivered. She turned to her grand-nephew (whom she knew was gay) and said, "Oh please do something with all these flowers. Your people are so good at things like that. I just don't have your touch."

One by-product of the difficult internal struggle with gay feelings can be increased creativity. Necessity being the mother of invention, the desperate need to find any new patterns of understanding and/or behavior that might alleviate the awful anxiety accompanying the struggle pushes an individual to be more receptive or open-minded. He or she is likely to try on new ideas or juxtapositions of ideas viewed from a variety of unaccustomed intellectual and emotional vantage points. Like the prisoner of war obsessed with the hope of escape, new and unusual possibilities are entertained in a manner that could only be understood by a psychologist as an increase in creativity. Whether it shows itself in original flower arrangements, solving a crime or building a better airplane, it is the gift of heightened creativity. For those who survive the period of attempted integration, the increased creativity is likely to be an added asset that lasts for life.

During that inner struggle with gay feelings, it is easy to lose a sense of balance and perspective, however. Before seeking professional help, we may turn to a loved and trusted family member or friend. Family, particularly parents, may feel fearful and guilty of the blame that the community may place on them for having fostered the development of this *deviant*. Friends and siblings can become fearful of guilt by association. In rational moments, family and friends are apt to fear that their loved one will be treated harshly in an unsympathetic world and urge outward conformity at least, and inward conformity if possible. "Be discreet." "You don't need to advertise it." "Don't tell your father."

Sometimes the loving friends and relatives waver, sensing a basic human responsibility to encourage integrity. Sadly, over the years I have heard many variations on a too familiar story from clients.

Recently I was consulted by a young man and a young woman who genuinely loved one another. They had been close friends since elementary school. They began dating as teenagers and the relationship became sexual. It was assumed by both families and by them that they would marry one day.

The young man, however, began to be increasingly aware of his attraction to other males. He saw the need to be honest and tell her about his gay feelings. She was mildly surprised but not shocked. She had known him as best friend, intimate confidant and lover for years, after all. They decided, however, that she might benefit from talking with a counselor. Unfortunately, she was advised to break off her relationship with him as soon as possible and begin dating other men, not only by the first counselor she met with, but by a second counselor as well.

Neither of them had known any gay people well. But a friend of a friend who was gay gave them a few gay-positive books to read. "They really came at the right time," the young woman said. The seemingly "professional" advice she had received troubled them both. All of the stereotypes, bigotry and prejudice to which they had been subtly exposed throughout their young lives began to surface. They knew they needed help in deciding how they would tell their families and how they might best go about keeping their feelings of mutual caring and respect intact. More than anything, they worried about being separated by traditional conventions and circumstances that were beyond their control.

When the internal war against gay feelings is being fought, the controls against expressing these feelings in behavior become unreliable. After repeated homosexual experiences, we must eventually choose either a somewhat schizophrenic existence with dual identities or begin to view ourselves as one of *those people*. Often the self-confrontation is harsh and we apply ugly labels in a hurtful way: "I am weird." "I'm a dirty queer (lesbo, pansy, dyke, fag—or other sexually explicit and derogatory names)." It is a step toward personality integration but at the cost of self-hatred—one step forward and two steps back.

With the failure of the first prolonged attempt at conformity, more than a few homosexually oriented young people commit suicide. Having cut deeply into an already injured self-esteem with the hurtful internal confrontation in which ugly labels are assigned, a part of the previously valued self is, literally, murdered. Feeling alone and worthless, we become easy prey to the unflattering anti-gay bigotry that we may have once actively supported in earlier attempts to maintain our distance from homosexuality. Weakened from the mutilation of a valued part of self and haunted by visions of a bleak, distasteful future, it is not too difficult to imagine the final hours before giving up.

Hope for self-respect may be vanquished. The only chance for peace may lie in completing the process of self-murder by drawing on the energy of the non-conscious rage at a world that seems to make it impossible to be our true selves and also have self-respect. The rage turns inward, and one can believe in a final, crazed moment of loyalty to society that "*they* are right and I am *bad*." The misdirected rage provides the impetus to pull the trigger, tie the noose or jump from the bridge. This lonely act of self-murder is a shame that we who represent that society must bear. It should be cause for any parent, brother, sister, friend or acquaintance to re-examine personal values, prejudices, conscience and past behavior very carefully.

Gay people who do not kill themselves after this awful self-confrontation and attempt at integration often seek professional help. We turn to counselors of all sorts. Once again we may try to change ourselves. We try harder to conform. We pray, take pills, enter psychotherapy or submit to painful electric shock therapy designed by behavior modification professionals to *recondition* our feelings. Brainwashing and other atrocities of medical experimentation may seem mere words used to describe phenomena that have taken place in distant and brutal times and places. Yet the ingredients of these distasteful, inhumane practices exist in respected hospitals and expensive private clinics around the world. Some gay people make considerable sacrifices of time and money and willingly subject themselves to these physically and emotionally traumatic experiences because they are given hope. They have been told by authoritative, respected professionals that these experiences will change them into socially acceptable heterosexuals who can be admired and respected by family, community and God. At the very least, they are told, they will be rid of part or all of their shameful homosexual *tendencies*.

The first massive effort to conform is motivated by a reluctance to admit to a socially deviant identity. It ends in failure. The second struggle to conform is motivated by the hope that this identity, while true and privately accepted, can be changed. After this second struggle toward conformity, most of us are left emotionally and financially drained with seriously decreased self-esteem, confronted with despair. It is at the end of this second try that a large number of people seek an end by turning their rage inward and completing the process of self-murder. It is a harsh weeding out of those with less than superior emotional stamina and reserves. The strong and well-defended survive. It is a quiet, internal war not required of conforming heterosexuals or any other category of the population. The final solution for those who choose death must confront the conscience of *all* who remain.

How do those of us who survive cope with anguish and despair? Some choices are heartbreaking. Some people settle for a zombie's life of work, food, television and sleep. Some enter an institution that will take care of them for life. Some try to kill the pain with alcohol or other drugs. Some give in to the stereotypes and become the devalued, laughed-at eccentric—the males perhaps lisping, mincing and giggling; the females perhaps shaving their hair, sporting warrior tattoos and wearing male clothing. They are laughed at but tolerated, permitted to exist now that they fit into a recognizable niche.

If others are made uncomfortable, it may be because the extreme behavior displays a kind of integrity that brazenly flaunts the lie of the stereotype in the face of the bigot. The behavior says, "You knew me once as a person like yourself. And I know you too may have these bottled-up feelings. But I have decided that my honesty about my feelings is more important than any respect that I might get from people like you. I will not pretend that I am like you." These are deeply hurt but brave people. They are surviving and refuse to go under or to go unnoticed.

An increasing percentage of gay people are able to choose a path of integrity and truth without giving in to caricature or conformity. They are able to find their anger and use it as a key to freedom. They transform their despair into support for one another. They are the ones who manage to grow stronger in the struggle. Most of them are young but they come in all ages and from all walks of life. These survivors have chosen to close the closet door behind them forever and to let the doomed conformists of the world find a way to live with it.

5

COMMUNITY

I T WAS NOT UNUSUAL in the late 1960s for a gay man to register for a workshop or other gay group experience that I was facilitating by using only his first name and last initial. It was an expression of reasonable fear. To have one's homosexual orientation revealed could mean being fired from a job, losing a professional license, or receiving a dishonorable discharge from the military services. It also might involve being publicly humiliated in newspapers, hounded by scandal, divorce and automatic loss of one's children. In the United States there was no shortage of reminders of the ruined lives left in the wake of the rumors and fears that fueled the witch hunts for homosexuals and communists led by Senator Joseph McCarthy just a decade earlier.

Sad but true, mental health workers of that time used the product of these circumstances to bolster assertions that homosexuality was associated with pathological paranoia, thereby helping to construct a general picture of homosexuality itself as pathological. In such an environment how could anyone not have been cautious, worried, secretive, vigilant and suspicious?

There was another level of fear operating also. We were easily inclined to distrust one another, having absorbed the anti-gay stereotypes, myths and prejudices that permeated the world in which we had grown up. As the first level of fear has eased with each passing decade, I notice by contrast how the second level of fear persists.

I remember one young man who, during the first evening of introductions for a weekend retreat, said, "I've heard so much about all of you for so many years, that as I was climbing those stairs this evening and walking toward the door, I realized that I was totally prepared to distrust and dislike each and every one of you before I even laid eyes on you or heard a word from you. It's amazing. I guess these are the judgments I've been carrying around about myself. Why would anybody trust *me*—if they ever found out about the real *homosexual* me, that is?"

There is also a very positive phenomenon that I have seen repeated again and again in workshops, psychotherapy groups and retreats. A group of gay men, strangers to one another, gather together with some anxiety. They are careful with one another in the beginning, using tried and true defenses that have worked for a lifetime. But these defenses are soon shed. Smiles, laughter and tears become frequent and by the end of the experience the group bathes in the warmth of caring brotherhood. They have found community.

In the decades that have passed since those days when the courageous few approached gay growth experiences with trepidation and first names only, there has been tremendous growth in the number of gay organizations and support groups. In those parts of the world still dominated by prejudice and superstition, much of the contact and community building is, of necessity, underground, but even in those places community exists and grows.

Computer-generated communication has made it easier than ever before in human history for lesbians and gay men of all ages, social classes and nationalities to reach out to one another. Ideas can be explored and feelings can be expressed in anonymity. There is an amazing sharing across ancient barriers such as national, racial, economic and social boundaries. Friendships begin, arguments without harm are possible, assumptions are questioned and support can be found.

Loneliness is no longer a necessary part of gay identity. Paranoia is no longer the expected alternative to conformity and self-destruction. Gay people not only survive but thrive and grow strong in the struggle for integrity and freedom from oppression. They do so by increasing their awareness and developing a sense of community. Increasing conscious awareness involves being increasingly alert and sensitive to all facets of oppression. It takes work.

If you do not see the arrows coming, it is easier to get wounded. Much oppression is perpetuated by otherwise decent people who do it, not out of malice, but from ignorance and insensitive, unconscious habit. They must be educated. It is up to those of us with increased awareness to help our unthinking oppressors to open their eyes and see what they are doing. Once aware, most people are willing to alter their behavior so as not to offend or harm another person.

Increased awareness and developing a sense of community go hand-in-hand. It is possible to increase awareness through the honest exchange of thoughts and feelings with a friend, or through reading or observation, but the most efficient method is by participation in discussion groups. Wartime research with small groups in the 1940s consistently demonstrated that attitudes change most easily in small groups. Changing attitudes help to pave the way for new awareness of feelings and, consequently, new behavior. Honest, probing, searching group discussion facilitates increased awareness of previously unquestioned assumptions.

Open, honest discussion of feelings with other gay people can be a liberating experience in itself, but it also lays the foundation for honest feedback or verbal reaction from other group members, helping us to see our own attitudes, feelings and behavior more clearly. We begin to observe ourselves constructively and to observe other people more carefully.

Women have helped us to see how words like *man* and wife, chair*man* and *man*made encourage the exploitation of women with the psychological suggestion of male superiority and consequent male rights to power. Such usage provides the psychological foundation for exploitation. We must expose the use of language that supports the limiting ideal of heterosexual male and female images and degrades homosexual images. Consider the possibility that a he-man (real man) can kiss another man, hold hands with him, do needlework, cook a meal, nurture children and appreciate art. Or the possibility that a real woman can fill another woman with desire, change a tire, balance a checkbook, run a corporation, build a house and support a spouse. These images are peeking through in films and television that travel the world and change public perception, but most producers are reluctant to show overt same-gender affection, not daring to use the same intimacy and body contact that suggests the affection of women with men or boys with girls.

Increasing conscious awareness is not only a matter of becoming more sensitive to words and pictures. The gay survivor learns to be wary of solicitous people who ask such questions as, "Do you have any idea why you've had trouble developing fully satisfying relationships with members of the opposite sex?" Such a seemingly innocent line of inquiry reinforces the prejudicial stereotype that gay people are running away from half the population—which is more likely to be true of an exclusively heterosexual person, since homophobia is much more the style of the day that heterophobia.

As gay awareness increases, we see the need to protest victimization of others, even when we are not involved directly and personally. We see the need to write a letter to the editor when a slur against gays is printed as if it were part of a reported news story. We see the need for a telephone call to the television station when we see the one gay person in a drama portrayed as less desirable than any of the other characters for no reason that has anything to do with the story. We see the need for picketing a business where the employer discriminates in the hiring or advancement of gay people for no reason more substantial than that "it would harm morale." We see the need to mourn openly and send contributions to help survivors of attacks on gay establishments.

No gay person has the time and energy to tackle all of these wrongs, but we learn to take on as many as we can because each time we take action, we are making a statement of our right to be who we are and of our determination not to give silent assent or support to thoughtless victimization. As the scope of our vision widens, we find one another more easily and recognize our need for mutual support in order to survive and mature. As a group we are but another in the long line of oppressed peoples who have come to understand the truth that united we *stand*, divided we *fall*.

This does not mean that because we are gay we must love all gay people. We are too varied for that. It does mean that each of us must honor the bond of gayness and offer support to other gay people who are threatened with oppression, whether they happen to be individuals we might like for friends or not.

Lesbians and gay men of the twenty-first century are riding the crest of a wave of surging social change that followed the Second World War and led directly to the Stonewall Rebellion in New York City in June of 1969. This was a watershed in our history. From that time forward, those who had been ridiculed and punished because of natural erotic preference seriously began to question the right of others with a presumed superior heteroerotic orientation to place them in positions of social contempt.

Though the pace of the gay movement for equal rights has continued to accelerate since the Stonewall Rebellion, the path of change has been and will continue to be unpredictable. You may actually hear someone who is describing the plight of gay people in the first half of the twentieth century begin with words such as "Once upon a time..." but we know better than to think that any of us will live to see a time when the story ends with "... and they all lived happily ever after."

Collectively, we have had a period of maturation that has been intense, rapid and brief. It followed closely on the heels of another force of change called the human potential movement. This was a marriage between the philosophy of humanism and the rapidly expanding field of psychology. The human potential movement was able to move forward only with determined experimentation and permissiveness, questioning all time-honored articles of social faith and human limitation. That inherited orientation was helpful to gay liberationists. We, too, became determinedly experimental and permissive, questioning any assumed reason for prohibition. If that sounds adolescent, it is worth remembering that it represented a major leap forward from the second-class, child-like position in which we had been held.

The human potential movement set the tone, asking some of the questions we needed to ask and others that were subtly related. Why should a man wear a suit and necktie instead of a comfortable, loose, embroidered shirt with sandals or bare feet and beads? What was wrong with a woman breast-feeding her baby in public? What would be the harm in seeing a totally nude adult male in films? Why should a woman marry in order to have children? For that matter, why should a woman feel obliged to have children? Why should people live in small family units rather than in chosen collectives that served as family? Why not make use of marijuana or other substances that added joy and comfort to life and dance in the streets rather than drink whiskey and dance in night clubs filled with cigarette smoke? Why should a man not choose another man as his sexual partner for the night or for life? Why should a woman not choose a woman as her life-partner? Why should a person not form a marriage with respectable, loving multiple partners?

Truth seekers, gay or not, wanted to be all that we could be and live life as fully as possible. We wanted to learn more about the positive nature of our human potential. It was not a new phenomenon in human history, but it was new for most of us within our lifetimes. And the technological revolution in communication that had begun permitted questions and visions of freedom to spread like wildfire. We were as determined in our permissive exploration as any army engaged in a holy war—with one difference. An emerging ethic at the time was that while gaining more, it was important not to take away from another person. The lust for power and property, so evident in warfare and its subsequent civil variations, had been tried and found not only wanting, but plainly wrong.

Lesbians and gay men, along with other people, made important gains during that period of questioning that moved us all along the path of self-understanding. It is hoped that the world will never again be as smugly ignorant of its propensity for damaging prejudice. The right of any group to subjugate or limit the lives of another group is more easily and quickly called to question as a result of that period in human history. The hard shell of shame that kept gay men and lesbians from demanding their full civil rights had begun to crack.

Our eagerness to conform to a new code of strident permissiveness would have a price, of course, and many of us had a vague premonition of it at the time. Clearly, it would be difficult later to establish new codes of personal integrity and group morality. But we had to sample widely before knowing when and where restraint might be helpful.

The problem we encounter again and again is our human propensity to conform to a current code, even when that code prescribes nonconformity. In the mid-1980s an exhausted male client said, "There didn't seem to be any time then to stop and take stock when all that fun was going on. There doesn't seem to be time to stop and take stock now either. Then I was running to the next party or political meeting. Now I'm running to the next sick friend or memorial service. What's going on at the moment always seems so urgent. I want to remember that it wasn't the parties and the sex that was bad, it was our naïve belief that medical science had made it possible to cure any disease passed from one person to another. Who used condoms for anything except to prevent pregnancy? It's been a hell of a wake-up call. But I don't want to shut down and hide from life. I know now that I have to take the time I need to get perspective."

During that quarter century following Stonewall, the gay community went from hiding and subjugation to insistent free-wheeling permissiveness, questioning and exploring as it grew more visible. It showed itself to be a highly diverse community, strong and focused in its ability to respond to any threats to its well-being. When the AIDS crisis struck, we showed the world a remarkable ability to rally together quickly and effectively. In that brief twenty-five years, we made enormous gains in understanding ourselves as a group and as individuals, continuing tirelessly to demand our full civil rights in diverse communities and nations around the world.

The AIDS epidemic and our response to it not only showed us our own strength and our capacity for caring, it showed us our own capacity for violence when pushed too far. We had discovered our power and were discovering the various forms it might take. There had been a hint of the potential for violence contained in the Stone-wall Rebellion.

It was demonstrated more clearly the following decade in the United States when San Francisco's mayor and its first elected openly gay city supervisor were assassinated. The assassin's name was Dan White and he was also a member of the Board of Supervisors. His murder trial concluded in a conviction, but with a mere five-year prison sentence. The full impact of this shameful insult was deeply and dramatically felt. Within hours a spontaneous protest rally exploded into what became known as the White Night Riot at City Hall. Police cars were overturned and burned in a frustrated, angry and anguished response to oppression.

And later that same night we learned the difference between our potential for violence and the potential for violence by police, the peacekeepers charged to protect us. The White Night Riot was followed, within hours, by another riot during which uniformed police rampaged into the center of the gay section of the city, smashing property and people they found in their path. The White Night Riot had registered protest by damaging the property that was symbolic of unfair laws and enforcers. The police riot damaged not only property, but attacked its own citizenry.

It was a very painful reminder that our greatest power resides in the strength of our convictions combined with the pride that comes from our willingness to continue moving forward in nonviolent ways. Nonviolent protest is a newer way in the world, still finding its following in contemporary times, but we are learning that, ultimately, it is the only way to effect lasting social change.

It is important that we not harm one another, as individual members of any oppressed group may be tempted to do in moments of impotent frustration. We have had our share of forming circular firing squads in the early years of our social revolution, targeting comrades whose ideology did not exactly match our own. It is easy to be too quick to pick a truth and shout it louder than the person with whom we do not quite agree, but whose goals are basically the same as ours. It is also stupid—a glaring symptom of inexperience.

We have had to learn to cooperate and take care of one another because we can only move forward together.

A community is not a group of people with whom one always agrees. Instead, it is a group of people within which it is safe to disagree, knowing that together ways can be found to live in *harmony* rather than *sameness* while still achieving common goals. The growth of gay people as individuals and as a group has been astonishing. It is not possible to guess how exactly we will grow from our experiences in the years ahead, but it is possible to predict that growth will continue, one way or another. A diverse and strong global community has been established. We are here.

The warmest reward that comes as a result of developing a sense of membership in community with other gay people is that we are no longer alone. The nightmare of isolation ends. Unlike other minority groups, we were not reared in gay families. In our earliest years, we grew up feeling alone and different. As our vision embraces an ever-broadening spectrum of the gay population, we know beyond doubt that we are no longer alone. There are heroes and heroines to be found. There are people who share our personal values and lifestyle. There are people to learn from and models to emulate. It is a sense of coming home, familiar only to members of other minority groups after having been separated from their people for a long time.

More and more gay women and men are emerging from their closets, pulled by the powerful magnets of liberation and community. Since so many of us have been invisible, we frequently have the opportunity to witness the emergence of someone we admire—an Olympic athlete, an elected government official, a respected teacher, a military commander, an actor, an author or a philanthropist. It comes as a surprise and delight: "You too?" There is that sudden warmth of kinship. And beyond the momentary joy there is the assurance and emotional support that comes from simply knowing that there are so many who have been there too—where we once were—people who share our feelings.

6
REWARDS

For many, perhaps even for most of us, being gay is not easy. It is natural, but not easy. We do not choose it. It is simply there, within us. The foregoing attempt to portray the gay experience from an insider's point of view, while discussing some of the dynamics of gay identity and oppression, may have presented more of the sorrows than the joys of being gay. Hopefully, it is clear that the sorrows need not be there, since they are no more than the result of interaction with a hostile environment. As the hostile environment becomes friendlier, those sorrows will go. It is a testimony to the good sense and goodwill of surviving gay people that our joys survive and bloom even amid the toxic pollution of rampant prejudice.

The question is asked, again and again, in one form or another. "If it's so much trouble, why do you stay gay?" It makes us weary to hear that question. Why continue to have blue eyes, be left-handed, have dark skin? Because it is who I am.

Trying to conform to a non-gay image represents an impossible compromise. It would be an unnatural choice for us. The unhappy consequences of such efforts are not hard to find. We can change feelings, attitude or desire if circumstances force the change. We can change behavior too when we must, but we *cannot* change the ultimate direction of our strongest affections. It is not humanly possible.

Do people actually enjoy being gay? Yes, indeed. It is impossible to make generalizations that fit every gay individual, but pleasure in gay identity abounds. I enjoy knowing that so many other men are potential partners in affection rather than worrisome competitors or enemies. I know that it is really better to make love than to make war. I hope that I, and other gay people, may one day persuade the rest of the human population of this truth. Re-examining past behavior and investing in retraining toward global cooperation rather than feeding the loathsome habit of competitive slaughter may become a reality someday.

There are simple pleasures that come with being gay. I like walking down the street anywhere in the world and exchanging a quick glance and a smile with another gay person, acknowledging that we are related and we know it. And I enjoy the *camp* humor that we have developed as a means of spotlighting the silliness of most conventions. Our ability to laugh and keep afloat on tides of insanity stirs a deep pride in me.

As a gay man, I feel privileged to be able to share sweet tenderness, touch and compassion with other gay men. I know that we are showing the way for non-gay men who have been denied access to these simple acts of humanity but are watching, willing and wanting to throw off their own oppression and learn. I like the democracy that permits people to flow across the social barriers of income, education, ethnic identity, nationality and religion.

I like the way women, gay women in particular, relate to me as a person, an equal, and not as the *opposite* sex to be flattered, feared or manipulated. Gay women and men know that females and males are anatomically, physiologically and biochemically different in many important ways But our perceptions are not as extreme as the non-gay men and women around us. Their more extreme perceptions of differences are the result of training, attitudes and expectations which can and do change from one century to the next or from one part of the planet to another. We gay folks accept and appreciate biological differences without losing sight of all that we share in values, beliefs, goals and abilities.

One of the fringe benefits of being gay is that, while we are outcasts, we are *outsiders* easily mistaken for *insiders* (like the Jewish person who "doesn't look Jewish" or the person of color with very pale skin). Contrary to prejudicial expectation, we can appear in any social setting, at any moment, to the considerable surprise and discomfort of any bigot present.

Circumstance once placed me at a fashionable cocktail party in Washington, D.C. Two men with whom I was chatting for a moment were talking about golf. One of them mentioned someone at their club whom he thought to be "a little light in his loafers." I smiled and said, "Perhaps it's because we gay men are not as weighed down by prejudice as so many non-gay men are. We usually keep our feet on the ground, though." I smiled and excused myself, leaving them with their dropped chins and a gap in their conversation. Gays do not intend to mislead—usually. It is the bigot's own blindness that creates our invisible condition. He or she deserves momentary embarrassment when we respond with honest indignation or amusement at their lifetime's worth of social blunders.

The problem that we present to conformists can be a boon to us. Since we are already a puzzlement to the Establishment, we have nothing to lose. We may even gain in our self-respect by questioning the presumed sacred moral tenets of our society. This provides us with more flexibility in sorting through personal values and establishing a satisfying code of personal ethics than is available to the average non-gay person.

For example, I must decide whether it is satisfying and right or hazardous to my emotional health to retain contact with my biological family. Or, when politicians panic at the prospect of two men or two women wanting to make a legal, state-sanctioned commitment to marriage and make such acts illegal, we are forced outside the usual guidelines, rules and laws. We must decide if monogamy and fidelity are suitable and satisfying options. In any serious relationship we must see the value of it day by day in order to continue if the state does not license the relationship and thereby makes it very easy to dissolve it. The flexibility inherent in the status of *outlaws* is at once both a privilege and a responsibility. It is a gift most of us would not have chosen, however, since it is born of pain.

Perhaps the greatest joy in being gay is that it permits one to be fully human. By definition, you do not fit your society's picture of the *normal*/real man or the *normal*/real woman. Once the program is thus flawed it makes it much easier to go ahead and explore options supposedly reserved for the *opposite* sex. As a man you can be tender, intuitive, warm, sensitive, spontaneous, uninhibited, colorful, emotional or even flirtatious. As a woman you are free to be strong, determined, reliable, forbearing, dependable, tough, smart and even aggressive.

Nor is there any need to give up any of the attributes ordinarily reserved for your own gender when and if you find them attractive and satisfying. The same holds true for behavior. A gay man can whip up a great dinner party and a gay woman can patch the roof of her house and not fret about what the neighbors will say. They are saying it already, anyway.

The gay man may continue to be a home handyman just as the gay woman may continue the pleasures of cooking and sewing. I must, in fairness, add the refreshing note that, thanks to increasing gay visibility and women's liberation, more and more heterosexual women and men also are daring to explore the wider world of occupations and tasks previously denied them by restrictive gender roles.

The range of relating is increased for gay people. We're free to relate in depth to anyone, regardless of gender. Of course, popular anti-gay mythology stereotypes gay men as not liking women and gay women as not liking men, but it is not true. Most of this *heterophobia* is the projection of homophobic heterosexuals. Gay men are likely to relate to women more fully without dragging along the male superiority games played by unenlightened heterosexual men who have been programmed to try to dominate women. Gay women can and do relate to men as friends and equals without any need to play at appearing less intelligent, less responsible or the subservient coquette. From equality in relating can grow fine friendships and loves. Nor is heterosexual sex excluded. The gay person may be more attracted to persons of the same gender in general, but a particular sexual relationship is based on individual attraction, not general attraction. It is true that there are some gay people who have not yet questioned the mythology fed to them and have kept a distance from people they were trained to see as the *opposite* sex. Increased awareness eventually exposes the programming inherent in that myth.

Being gay is not *anti*, it is *pro*. We are not against people, we are for them. We have learned to appreciate individual differences the hard way. *We have a stake in everyone's freedom because it is the only way we can be assured of our own.* And we cannot survive without our freedom. We have been hated because we are people who have dared to follow our own truth about love in times and places where our affection has been forbidden.

There are so many advantages to being gay. Many of them are difficult to communicate joyously because they have been earned at considerable cost. The gay person is apt to have had more experience with both reality and fantasy than he or she would otherwise have had. The realities may have been as harsh as hearing your own young daughter say, "You know, Mom, most lesbians are so disgusting that I think it might be okay to have some kind of program to exile them or exterminate them."

The pain of such a moment may be difficult for a non-gay person to understand. The reality, however, is not new to a lesbian mother. She can understand that her daughter has learned to hate an image, does not fully know her mother, is struggling with her own sexual impulses and can be helped to develop tolerance—all of this while bearing the pain and not missing a stroke in the brushing and braiding of her daughter's hair.

Experience with fantasy can be intense. Imagine spending years in an army surrounded by men, developing deep feelings for one of your comrades while listening to him talk about a girlfriend back home. You stay emotionally alive with fantasies of your comrade discovering his love for you and celebrating it sexually together on a three-day pass, then settling into a quiet life on the farm you will buy together if you are both still alive when the war is over—all of this while cleaning your rifle and encouraging your beloved friend to be patient with his girlfriend for not responding or writing often enough.

This daily experience with reality and fantasy builds a wider and deeper internal emotional capacity, though it may not be visible to everyone around you. It is a quality that the more sensitive non-gay people feel and wonder that they are so often drawn to people who turn out to be gay. It is an asset also in terms of flexibility. Our increased experience with reality and fantasy makes it easier to take life's surprises in stride, maintain balance and take care of our responsibilities in everyday life.

Then there is physical attractiveness. It seems unlikely that *most* gay people are born with genes that make them more attractive, yet a disproportionate number of us do seem to be more attractive—or become more attractive once over the hurdles to self-admitted awareness of gay identity. Almost certainly it is due in part to having faced fears and let go of a lot of tension. People are more attractive when they are honest with themselves and more relaxed. It must be admitted, however, that it is probably due in part also to hypersensitivity to the media's concept of beauty and to the proportion of money and time willingly spent contributing to that image so as to be found worthy of desire.

I suspect that most of the extra quota of attractiveness is due to the positive aspects of awareness. One is aware of physical attraction to some people of the same gender. Unlike the non-gay man who is not supposed to notice other male bodies, the gay man enthusiastically notices the bodies, mannerisms and attributes of other men and sees what is naturally most beautiful about a male who cares for and respects himself. The gay man is more likely to watch his diet and less likely to get paunchy. The gay women is less likely to preen with a palette of paints and artificial devices designed to disguise her true form since she is appreciative of the natural beauty of other women.

In parts of the world where we are ruthlessly subjected to prejudice, gay people have had to develop a benign, self-protective alertness that can be viewed as something like a positive form of paranoia. We must try to be aware of how other people are seeing us and reacting to us emotionally. It is necessary lest we be hit unexpectedly with a stroke of bigotry based on someone's suspicion of our gay-ness. This gay pseudo-paranoia acts as an early warning system that helps us to make the adjustments that smooth social interactions. It is not the malignant sort of paranoia that makes a person tense with the suspicion that the whole world is out to get him or her and makes social intercourse tempestuous or impossible.

The gay early warning system is costly in energy, but it pays dividends. It provides plenty of practice in noticing vocabulary, into-nation, posture and facial expression. In other words, it provides the experience that increases sensitivity. It builds not only greater sen-sitivity but also greater self-awareness. When you are alert to how other people are responding to you emotionally, you naturally corre-late the information with your feelings and behavior of the moment. Gay people are more likely than their non-gay counterparts to know that a fixed smile will not cover unsunny feelings and that it is bet-ter to stay home when you are feeling unsocial—or at least let your social companions have some clues as to what is bothering you so that they need not feel responsible. The combination of sensitivity and self-awareness, though costly, is a strong social asset.

There is also something wonderful about being part of a group that has survived and brightened the world under the most adverse circumstances. We're like that beautiful orange flower called the Cal-ifornia poppy. We are apt to pop up anywhere—beside a railroad track, in the wilderness, in a pampered floral display or in a long for-gotten garden covered with weeds and trampled by careless foot-steps. We keep blooming with a beauty that is there to be seen by anyone willing to appreciate it.

Most of all, I suppose, from the long list that could be drawn of the rewards that come with being gay, I like being able to be myself. Being gay has given me a self that is respectful of differences in peo-ple. It has granted me the ability to look on the human world with a greater sense of compassion.

It is not easy to be gay in many, many areas of the world, though it is easier than it once was. Once you realize you are gay, you know that you are likely to experience pain and struggle. The cards are stacked against you. You will face discrimination and prejudice—

some of it from people who love you. The emotional pressures are enormous. At one time or another you even may be tempted by suicide as a way out. Painful wounds increase chances of falling into alcoholism or other drug abuse. But none of this is due to your being gay. It is due to the prejudices of a society that has used gayness as a scapegoat for a bewildering variety of ills.

Despite the enormous weight placed on you by an oppressive environment, it is possible to join hands with wonderful people who appreciate gayness, especially other gay people, and celebrate both the pain of the past and the potential of the future. While others struggle with their assigned gender roles, we are released by our gay identity. We know we can love anyone worthy of our love, including people of our own gender. We know that we can be complete human beings. For those of us who survive—and there are more and more of us who do—our world can be very rich and full. And we know enough to appreciate all of the richness and fullness granted to us.

[PART TWO]

Gay and Growing

7
THE GIFT OF GAY

Z ALMEN SWEEPS FLOORS at night and is a part-time helper in a florist shop in the afternoon. "I didn't tell people much about my life or how I got here. Almost nobody knows I speak five languages. I'm not the best looking forty-year-old guy, not handsome, but people like me. I thank God for one thing every day, starting with morning prayer. I thank God I am gay. It is my life. It is why I am here and not dead. It is my gift. It brings me love and lets me give love. I know I will marry the man I love most one day."

He smiles often, a smile that causes others to smile. "My other job is to take care of my gay gift and use it to make the world a little bit nicer. That's my *thank you* to God. But I've still got a lot of learning to do in this life and I got to get rid of the bad stuff I learned once."

Much of Part Two of the book has to do with unlearning and relearning. It takes considerable effort to unlearn negative associations relating to gay identity. Subtle negative messages we receive are so constant that we fail to notice that they are being absorbed as a part of our understanding of the world and our place in it.

This section also deals with becoming conscious about how we live our lives as gay people. Being awake and aware of our behavior makes it possible to be responsible for our thoughts and actions and therefore able to develop real pride. Gay pride is earned.

Gay identity comes with the acceptance of your homosexual orientation and awareness that every area of your life is influenced by that orientation. Gay sexual orientation is a gift granted by life. Some people, like Zalmen, would say it is a gift granted by God. In any case, one is learned, one is earned and the other is simply given to us.

It took time and effort for me to own the wholeness of my gay identity. It takes time and effort for everyone. But we help one another by passing tips along about how to enjoy the *self* that you happen to be. Sometimes a professional can offer special help.

The gay-affirmative professional is someone who, in addition to relevant professional training, has located homosexual and other affectional gay feelings within herself or himself. Such a person may choose to act or not act on these feelings at any given time in life, but awareness is gladly accepted. This is someone, gay or not, who values gay identity. Because it is not foreign, there is an emotional understanding and appreciation of our oppression and how related life experiences influence an individual's psychological development. The gay-affirmative professional understands that while gay identity may add difficulties to life, it is a gift to be developed.

Gay-affirmative professionals offer service in such a way that gay clients retain and gain self-appreciation, self-respect and pride. A professional who is not gay-affirmative, though he or she may indulge in homosexuality in private life, cannot be considered gay since this person is not responsibly appreciative of gay identity as a gift. Such a person is likely to reinforce the covert belief that heterosexuality is superior or better. Gay-affirmative people understand and appreciate the richness of gay identity.

Gay people who come to a gay-affirmative professional for psychological service come for the same wide variety of reasons that people everywhere seek psychological help. When the precipitating factor is an affair of the heart—a woman may have just ended her first lesbian relationship or a man may have just discovered that his lover/spouse/domestic partner/husband is having a fling with another man, and feels as if life has lost its worth—it is likely that the person is processing emotions with two sets of guidelines. We learn one set for living in the heterosexual world and a slightly different set for the gay subculture. It helps to have a therapist or counselor who is familiar with both and appreciative of their complex interaction. Thus equipped, the counselor is less likely to sabotage a gay client's self-esteem.

Beyond matters of romance, sex and love, people have the same sort of human troubles whether or not they are gay. The death of a parent or a sibling can produce profound feelings for anyone. But gay people are better served if the work is done within a framework that appreciates gay identity and is sensitive to the experience of being a gay person in a prejudiced world. How did that parent or sibling relate to the sexual orientation and subsequent gay identity of this daughter, son, brother or sister? Were there resulting complications in the relationship that make the mourning process more complex?

A special kind of learning comes to the gay-affirmative professional who chooses to specialize in work with gay people, whether or not she or he is gay. I feel very fortunate to have been enriched by that learning. Gay people are the same as other people, *and* we are different. We have grown up in the general culture and we have been influenced by the gay subculture. Both cultures are changing.

Gay people have some special coping to do to balance the influence of two changing cultures coexisting in a sometimes subtly, sometimes not so subtly, hostile environment. Usually we are better for having to make the efforts in response to these special challenges to our integrity. We may learn greater alertness, sensitivity and strength but the struggle is long and difficult and deserves to be respected, not minimized.

A woman who was in the grip of a terrible internal struggle came to my office, She was happily married, had two grown children and a first grandchild. Her family insisted that she seek help because she seemed unhappy. She told me that she knew her unhappiness stemmed from the realization that her life was passing and she had never exercised her secret yearning to share passion with another woman. She said, "Even if it's not too late for me, though, I can't imagine upsetting the whole family by letting them know that I might be a lesbian."

A very young man wrote to me asking if I would be willing to contact him at a temporary Internet address he was using because he had read one of my books and was desperate to talk with someone about his feelings for men. "I am deeply ashamed and have tried everything to make myself normal but the feelings don't go away."

You are no less worthwhile for needing help in accepting your sexual orientation and developing your gay identity. If you are currently in conflict, struggling *against* your natural orientation and unsure about developing a gay identity, know that almost all of us have gone through the same struggle. One day, hopefully, you will be proud of yourself as a gay person.

There are outstretched hands in many parts of the world today, ready to help if you ask. Many universities have a Gay Students' Union or Association of Gay Students and Alumni. A telephone call or letter to such a group can put you in touch with local gay groups or individuals who are very willing to talk and help. Phone books often have listings for PFLAG or FFLAG, the organizations of parents, family and friends of gays.

Cities often have a Gay Community Service Center or a local Gay Information Service listed in the telephone book. A Gay Community Service Center may have *drop-in* discussion groups, possibly including a *coming-out* group that could help answer questions, offer support and quell uneasiness. Telephoning a nearby reputable health center or clinic can also yield gay-affirmation referrals. Suicide Prevention Centers and AIDS hotlines are likely to have such listings as well. Gay-oriented newspapers have proliferated and usually list *Gay Services* information or will, at least, respond to a telephone call for assistance in finding help. Listings can also be found on the Internet.

But if you are as uncomfortable and shy as most of us are during the initial struggle to find identity, chances are you will not contact any gay organization at first. You are more likely to contact a professional counselor who is not gay (because there are more of them and because you may have been led to believe that they will be more objective). In truth the non-gay-oriented counselor is *not* more objective and is likely to be *less* knowledgeable unless he or she has had some extra training in gay-oriented counseling. Unfortunately, a non-gay-affirmative professional may want to help you down a tortured path toward conformity. If he or she is more enlightened, you will be advised to stop resisting your natural orientation and begin to establish your gay identity.

Beware of help with a plan to change you, no matter how many university degrees are displayed on the wall. And remember that actions speak louder than words. If the counselor *says* she or he thinks it is okay to be gay, but brightens and seems more enthusiastic when happy heterosexual events are discussed, *run—do not walk—*to a genuinely gay-affirmative counselor. Double messages really can cause you more trouble. If you are emotionally, intellectually and physically attracted to people of the same gender, you know it. You may be far from wanting to admit it, but you have a homosexual orientation. Efforts to convert and conform will be costly in time, effort and money and are likely to leave you scarred, lonely and feeling even worse about yourself.

For the time being, until you are ready to reach out for some gay-affirmative help, the best thing to do is to read. Go to the library and find books that deal with being gay. If anything describing the book or in the book itself suggests that being gay might be immoral, or pathological, *close the book*. You have been exposed to a lifetime of that poison already. Look for good news about being gay, preferably written by a gay person who knows from personal experience. Reading can help you begin to free yourself of the belief that you are bad if you admit to your gay identity. No matter how large the obstacles seem now, you can and will be even more yourself and create a life of dignity and warmth. Once you begin to understand that, you will be ready to contact gay people who may be a little farther down the path. At least they can listen and know what you are talking about.

I do not mean to present all gay people as angels and all non-gay people as the enemy. Some gays, having accepted a stereotypic picture complete with anti-gay mythology during their developing years, may now act out some part of the stereotype by being the unkind *bitchy queen* or the *predator* ready for the next conquest on their promiscuity menu. But this sort of gay person is disappearing as we are increasingly able to re-educate and reclaim our individual identities.

Gay organizations make great efforts to be staffed with counselors who are both responsive and responsible. They are there to help you rather than use you. They are people who have traveled some rocky paths and are interested in helping you to travel yours with less difficulty. If you happen to run into a gay person who seems ready to misuse you emotionally or sexually in order to meet his or her own needs, the problem presented is no greater than in a comparable heterosexual interchange. It should be enough to say, "Thanks but no thanks," and move on to another, more responsible and sincere counselor.

You cannot afford to believe the advice that comes from any one person. If you expose yourself to many points of view from a number of gay people, you can piece together advice in ways that make personal sense to you. If you are uncomfortable with feeling indebted by permitting someone to help you, please remember the debt is automatically canceled: As the more experienced gay women and men help you, you are helping them to question, review and reinforce their own understanding. It is a phenomenon well-known to members of twelve-step programs such as Alcoholics Anonymous and Alanon.

A former roofer who is a member of both organizations told me how he came to seek help. "Everybody knows how awful it smells when you're putting a new tar and gravel roof on a house. I told myself that's why I needed a drink every now and then during the day. Then I fell off one of those roofs and had a few weeks of not very pretty detox while on my back in a hospital. But it gave me a chance to take a look at myself and my life. I used to think that I couldn't do anything about my interest in other guys until my Papa was dead. I'd tell myself it wasn't killing me to wait and he deserved to have the kind of sons he wanted. Anyway, once I fell off the roof, then went to A.A., I came to realize that while it wasn't exactly killing me to put it off—like nobody was putting a gun to my head or cutting me with a knife—I was letting my life go as if it wasn't worth anything, as if I had the right to do that, as if I was God making that decision. I wasn't playing the cards I was dealt, just letting the game go by. Nobody has that right—nobody. All the cards I was dealt—including the gay card? That's my business to use them well and not miss the enjoyment of my life. I was killing myself. Now I'm sober, gay and myself and guess what? Papa's glad I went back to school. He admires me. But even if he hated it, I'd have to play my own cards."

8

RIGHT, WRONG, GOOD AND BAD

H IS FRIENDS CALL HIM HONI. "It means 'kiss' in Hawaiian and it's something I like to do with other guys. I got the name growing up on the Big Island near Hilo. We've got lots of different kinds of people there, all kinds of how you're supposed to be with each other. The sun still comes up from that ocean each morning so we have to learn to relax and let people be who they think they are."

For many years zoo keepers were puzzled by chimpanzees who were *different*. They were quieter and more gentle and, when possible, settled disputes and made other necessary social arrangements by using friendly sexual contacts rather than the chimpanzee's usual noisy aggression. We know much more about these gentle, love-making bonobo cousins of ours now and appreciate their natural ability to enjoy love-making and avoid war. Unlike the chimpanzee, they have a female-centered culture and little conflict.

Bonobo, chimpanzee and human had a common ancestor six million years ago. The chimpanzee and bonobo had a common ancestor still until about three million years ago. There is no doubt that some humans today clearly show that they are more related to chimpanzees while others of us show that we are more related to the bonobo.

In studies the bonobo continue to surprise researchers in their differences from chimpanzees. While chimpanzees are described as coarse and hot-tempered, bonobo are found to be sensitive, lively and nervous. The chimps raise their hair at the slightest provocation or pick up branches to challenge or intimidate anyone perceived as weaker, while bonobo rarely do so. Physical violence is rare among bonobo but common among chimps who bite one another and use full-force hitting. Bonobo are more vocal and "comment" on minor events. While both chimps and bonobo are capable of language and empathy, only bonobo display altruism. The chimps are status oriented while bonobo are tribe oriented, so group welfare is most important. Bonobo are described as "extraordinarily sensitive and gentle creatures" who soothe tensions with sexual or erotic interactions unlike the "demoniacal primitive force" of adult chimpanzees.

"It's all there, references easy to find on the web or in the library," Honi tells everyone. "Gay guys remind me a lot of those bonobo, lesbians too. Me, I'm bonobo all the way. Too bad we got so many chimps running the world, running around making their wars, killing and scaring everybody and then leaving their mess for us to clean up. I'm glad that chimp software don't work in my computer, man."

Computers and their software were designed as complex *thinking* machines that would *behave* or produce results in a variety of ways. Each type of computer has its own character and personality, determined by its design and construction. But the thinking and behavior of computers are shaped by the interaction of their internal program and software programs that are added. A program is a complex set of instructions fed into the machine, telling it to operate (think and behave) in certain ways that are good or bad, right or wrong, according to the definitions of the persons who constructed the program. Should a software program be fed to a machine which cannot follow the instructions, because of technical limitations or differences in design, the computer will not compute. If its design permits it to handle similar tasks but not exactly those on this program, it might behave in a *neurotic* fashion, trying its best to do the job with unreliable results, or it might fail to function at all. Computers and their programs of software were designed as simplified copies of how humans think and behave.

Each of us is programmed from the day of birth to the day of death. We are told what is right and wrong, good and bad. We are told how to think and how to behave. These instructions come not only from parents, teachers, religious leaders, friends and relatives but from television programs, political campaigns, newspapers, magazines, movies, billboards and cereal boxes. We are bombarded with instructions. From them we build a general program that is harmonious because its parts fit together. Dissonant instructions are discarded or not taken seriously because, like the most imaginative advanced software programs, adult humans can screen instructions and decide which ones do not fit our overall basic program.

The basic program, however, made up of many thousands of bits and pieces of information fitted together, is forced upon us. We do not select it; it happens to us—its fundamentals having been put into place before we were old enough to reason and sort. If the basic program does not fit our own basic individual nature or psychological makeup, we are apt to behave neurotically or fail to function at all. The overall program for each of us is unique, since each of us has fitted together the thousands of pieces personally. But the fundamental building blocks of that program are similar for all people in a given society because they are constructed from and inserted by the values of that society at such an early age.

Although there are promising signs of change in the world, the program fundamentals in too many societies still do not fit the natural orientation of a gay person. You are too often instructed to follow a strictly heterosexual path that ignores feelings of attraction to people of the same gender. If this conflicts with your psychological makeup or natural orientation, what can be done? We might try taking the computer apart and rebuilding it in such a way that it will accept the program, or we can make a new software program. For too long we have attempted to take gay people apart and rebuild them. It is past time to create a new customized program that works well for us.

Futuristic fiction, such as *Stranger in a Strange Land*, *Brave New World* and *1984*, portray the extreme difficulty encountered when human beings are forced to unlearn a program and then are reconditioned to accept a new one. The guilt and anxiety are intense. It can be done more easily with the aid of a support system made up of similar people who are also working to deprogram and reprogram themselves. Their support helps allay the fear associated with the unfamiliar. Their ideas point to possible directions for a more personally satisfying, more responsible and less destructive program.

With near superhuman efforts, the deprogramming and reprogramming can be accomplished alone, if help from others is not available. Certain parts of the process must always be done alone. With or without help, this process is essential—your life depends upon it if you are gay. You cannot trust your life to a program based on the assumption that your most natural loving feelings are wrong and make you a bad person. A lifetime of such programming almost guarantees a short, narrow and unhappy life.

If there is one available in your area, or if you can find other gay people to start one, you would do well to begin your deprogramming and reprogramming with a gay discussion group, gay support group or gay psychotherapy group. A discussion group might pick a different topic for each meeting. Each member would share personal experiences and feelings related to that topic—often saying things she or he has never said aloud before. In a feedback period, members can share their thoughts and feelings about what they have heard in the meeting.

A psychotherapy group is usually led or facilitated by a paid psychotherapist who has been trained in group dynamics. The style is determined by the therapist, but it is an arena in which each person is free to say what is on his or her mind and expression of feelings is encouraged. Such a group permits the luxury of hearing honest feedback from other members in a safe environment. You can learn how your behavior, thoughts and feelings impact others. Not only the things that you say, but things that fellow group members say, will provoke you to re-examine basic beliefs, assumptions and behavior.

A gay support group is somewhere between a discussion group and a psychotherapy group, since some amount of discussion, psychotherapy and support are inevitable in all three formats. Whether or not there is a designated facilitator, it offers an opportunity to talk about your thoughts and feelings while recounting current events in your life. Group members agree to listen respectfully and speak from their own experience. A support group's mandate should be to review rather than criticize.

Choosing a gay support group, discussion group or psychotherapy group will depend on whether you will feel more comfortable knowing that a qualified leader is in charge, or whether your goal is simply to increase awareness or to make difficult changes in your life pattern. If you choose a psychotherapy group, make sure that the leader is a gay-affirmative professional and not simply a therapist who has assembled a group of gay people with the covert or overt assumption that conformity to heterosexual norms can be equated with increased mental health. In any of these groups, it takes only a few meetings before you begin to be more aware of the ways in which you have been taught to think and behave. You will begin to see the thousands of *rights*, *wrongs*, *goods* and *bads* that you have accepted without question.

Reading is both stimulating and informative. Of course, the standard magazine rack selections will not help because they merely reinforce much of the old program. But books and articles coming out of the worldwide gay movement and the *alternative press* are sure to make you think and re-evaluate. These books, journals and magazines are increasingly easy to find, particularly online or in large bookstores in large cities.

If you are trying to work through the reprogramming process without a group support, writing autobiography can be extremely helpful. Weigh *right*, *wrong*, *good* and *bad* evaluations you have accepted along the way and do it on paper. The physical act of writing forces you to be specific and more articulate. Value-driven omissions or temptations to alter the truth become noticeable.

It also helps to write about the future, trying out new, more personally satisfying values as well as any of the old ones you have decided to keep. You might want to venture into science fiction and place your future in a world that has changed. But beware of telling yourself that you cannot be yourself and be happy until the world changes. Instead, get down to the more difficult job of looking at what assumptions, beliefs, attitudes and behavior you would have to change *in yourself* in order to be yourself and be happy in the world *as it is now*. Use the future to show yourself how you can make your life more satisfying and how you can increase your feelings of worth.

A necessary exercise is to examine your stereotypes about gay people You can use paper and pen or it can be done as a project in a support group or discussion group. Write down every generalization you have ever heard and even partly believed to be true of gay men and lesbians. When you believe that you have put them all down, you may see when you read them over why you have resisted accepting your gay identity. Who wants to be like that? Understand that for years these stereotypic generalizations acted as self-fulfilling prophesies for many gay people. We thought that was how we were supposed to act, think and feel if we were gay and knew that we were gay. For many years, many of us tried to squeeze into a mold because we were told it was the right and proper mold.

Looking at a comprehensive picture of the stereotypes you held to be true at some time, it becomes possible to re-examine the belief that you have to fit that picture in order to honor your attraction to people of the same gender. You can then construct another set of generalizations about the excellent, super-good gay person. How close do you think you can come to living up to that ideal? Looking at who you are and who you may become as a gay man or woman you will see that the road to change lies comfortably and comfortingly somewhere between the two.

Once begun, deprogramming and reprogramming is never really finished. Each day brings fresh insight about some behavior or feeling that comes from the old program. One of my personal favorites was the day that I noticed something odd that happened too frequently in routine flurries of polite social greeting. I would hear someone who was addressing a lone member of a gay couple say, "How are you and Joe doing?" or "How are you and Nancy doing?" It was subtle.

There was a slight note of reserve or concern. The questioner was not asking the standard, "How's Joe?" or "How's Nancy?" Asking how the *couple* are doing is an inquiry about the well-being of the relationship rather than the well being of the missing member of the couple. There is a hidden assumption that betrays a value.

The assumption is that the gay couple may not be doing well together because, unlike the heterosexual couple who are supposed to be together, the gay couple represents an unnatural union that should not succeed. To cover the hidden hint of programming, all that I had to do was imagine the same greeting when addressed to a husband: "How are you and Anne doing?" or to a wife: "How are you and Albert doing?" It would seem rude unless something had been said to indicate that there was a possible problem in their relationship.

After some practice, you look forward to such discoveries because each one offers another opportunity to change yourself in the direction of the new program, designed by you to fit your own personality, character and personal needs, in the changing world *as it is*. Since that moment of discovery, it is very clear to me that I have no right to ask that question in that way. And I suggest that if asked the question in that way, any lesbian or gay man would do well to simple ask, "What do you mean?"

You might actually find that it is fun to keep an account of old hidden assumptions as they appear, perhaps recorded in a personal journal—the better to contrast them with newly learned information and personal hopes for the future. Looking back through such a journal after a few months can give a lift by reminding you of how far you have come in the course of personal liberation and growth.

Asked once to read through a jargon-filled psychiatric report written about a gay man by a non-gay professional, I was shocked. The report urged the reader to see the man as having a *narcissistic personality disorder*, but it did not make sense. The author of the report had noticed the enthusiasm with which this man, who was in the early stages of coming out, compared himself with other men—both gay and non-gay—the way one was "just like me that way" while another was "very different from me and very attractive to me." The recent loss of a sister along with the recent loss of his job had pushed him into a psychological trouble zone, but it was not due to a personality disorder.

The author of the report had happened upon his subject while the latter was discovering and building his gay identity. At this point in life we often actively compare self with others and match up the evidence with feelings of attraction. Talking with this gay man, I could hear the process. "When I came out last year and told everyone I was gay, I was being attracted to guys who were my opposites. I'm dark, and they were fair. A lot of my life is about music, theater and reading; they were jocks or construction workers who watched television in their spare time. It helped me to expand my interests, and now I see that I'm starting to like men who are more like me—or have mostly the same values and interests."

A lesbian or gay man often starts the love-search being attracted to people who seem to be the opposite of the self, as if seeking to incorporate that which is different and admired in a kind of growth-by-association. It is a seeking for completion through integration of that which has not yet been developed in the self.

The phenomenon may have to do with anti-gay training that taught you to devalue yourself because of your natural sexual orientation. The irrational inner assumption involved would be that the more different the other person is, the less unwholesome or bad the other person is. She or he "just seems to have what I lack." It may also have to do with a lifetime of training which told you that you should be attracted to the *opposite sex*, so that while you cannot help being more attracted to people who share your gender, you are on the lookout for opposites. Whatever the dominant facets of the programming involved may be, they are almost certainly related to a society's obsession with categorization and with the seeming opposites and dualities such an obsession is bound to produce.

As the process of deprogramming and reprogramming proceeds, the facets of self that have not been much exercised in the world or have been held out of awareness and are now invested in *opposite* love objects come more clearly into focus and demand integration in your self-concept. As the integration continues you find yourself feeling stronger and more worthwhile. The strong person is not a half-person but a whole person, androgynous and rounded, able to choose to exercise those facets of self that are most satisfying in any given situation. You learn that most presumably *male* and *female* attributes are a product of human imagination based on a few genuine anatomical or physiological differences between the genders but blown far out of proportion by a need to see categorical opposites.

As we relearn by way of deprogramming and reprogramming and become more whole and self-respecting, we are apt to be increasingly attracted to individuals who have similar values and views, truly as lovable as our own newly evolving self. There are always sufficient individual differences to give pause and assist in achieving momentary distance or perspective. It is a necessary part of coming to better understand our self and the beloved other.

People who love one another over a long period of time, socialize together, eat together and sleep together are living together—whether or not they have the same official address. They begin to borrow bits and pieces from one another. Manner, tone, inflection of speech, posture, gait and smiles become more similar. After a time, other people notice and sometimes comment on the similarities. If the two people are of the same gender they may be mistaken for one another over the telephone, or they may find themselves wearing very similar clothes though they may have dressed in separate rooms. It represents a sweet, touching merger of two individuals.

Learning to value individuals who are more like you as you grow and become more who you are does not mean that you are seeking exact copies or clones, however. It is the internal qualities of character, personality and values that are recognized and appreciated. It actually facilitates overcoming once difficult, potentially divisive differences such as nationality, socio-economic level or age. Two loved ones can appreciate that they have come from different places, or are at different developmental points on the same life path, and that the differing experience of each enriches the experience of the other.

"I'm dating a guy from Scandinavia," Honi said. "How's that for different? He's all pale and blond. But he's bonobo all the way, like me. We're getting political. No war. No more Mr. Chimp getting elected so he can make more war. We want more kissing."

9
EMOTIONS

A s WE GROW FROM CHILDHOOD into adulthood, we usually become less and less aware of our feelings. We know what we *think* more often than what we *feel*. The intellect is efficient in problem-solving, but we need the balance of our emotional side if we are not to end up imitating the logic-driven computers that were built to imitate us. It is our emotions that add depth, beauty and color to life, that make it worth living. It is our feelings that lead us away from the ill-fitting programming of the society into which we happen to be born, and it is our feelings that guide us toward building new, more personally satisfying programs. Feelings are of little use without intellect, and genius is of little use without feelings. The loss of awareness of feelings is a problem for adults.

Gay people face an additional risk: We are more vulnerable to the loss of awareness of feelings because some of our feelings are firmly invalidated from the first day we become aware of our homosexual desires and related gay feelings. It is not only the awareness of gay feelings that becomes dulled, but *all* feelings.

It happens in a process of generalization, usually when we are too young and uninformed to fight it. We become aware that we have feelings of attraction for some people of the same gender but few, if any, of the people around approve or encourage such feelings. A shift happens, beyond conscious awareness. Feelings that seem so unlike other people's must be wrong. But they do not disappear. The emotional conviction grows that these strange/wrong feelings must be changed. After all, you want to be a good person—like the good people around you. And so the process of generalization begins.

Once you have begun to view some of your feelings as wrong, others become suspect. It is guilt by association. You begin to dislike your feelings. You do not trust them because they might get you into trouble. A few minor episodes in which your feelings do get you into trouble (and this happens to everyone) are all that you need for proof. You are now severing diplomatic relations with your feelings and paying as little direct attention to them as possible.

Feelings are necessary to life, however, and they have sufficient strength and authority to reassert themselves into your consciousness now and then. Their reappearance can be disturbing. You disown them in the hope that they will go away. They do not go away. They live underground, beneath awareness, occasionally erupting in seemingly inexplicable behavior. "I don't know what's gotten into me," you say. "I can't imagine why I did that." Had your feelings been living in the light of conscious awareness where they could be accepted and honored, you would have known why you did it and had far more choice about whether or not to do it.

We are apt to lose sight of our feelings because we may well have learned to associate them with discomfort, having tried to disown those that were homosexual or gay. The process of generalization spreads the alienation to the rest of the family of feelings. Add to this the realization that we need access to our feelings more than the average person because we need their help in getting free of standard programming in order to establish new personal guidelines, and you can see our dilemma.

Once the gay feelings are accepted and begin to accumulate some respect, other feelings begin to reappear. But it all happens slowly. The feelings have been in hiding for years and are likely to remain timid about emerging in the daylight of consciousness. Sometimes it is useful to speed up this process.

The key to the reclamation of emotions is one of the feelings that went underground almost immediately. This key feeling is anger, and it probably has been partially submerged every time it has tried to reappear. Some people are able to divert and express anger in other areas of living, but most of us who are gay have been busy pushing it away out of sight, throughout our gay lives. This presents an added danger, because swallowed anger is notorious for contributing to depression as well as to various physical ailments such as severe headaches, ulcers, high blood pressure and colitis.

This anger appeared naturally in the earliest days of gay feelings because you were being told that a part of you was wrong. You were being told that what was natural in you was bad, a phenomenon guaranteed to generate anger. But you may try to stifle or kill the natural and spontaneous loving feelings that have been judged as bad. This results in more anger at those who have abused, hurt or wronged you by their negative judgments. You may then turn that anger on yourself for having had the troublesome feelings in the first place. This is the course of an *emotional logic* that leaves you intolerably angry at yourself and at the world. All this anger then must be banished from awareness if there is to be any semblance of peace.

A sensible program for reclaiming ownership of your emotions involves self-recognition of all gay feelings and all angry feelings, along with a public testimonial of at least some of the anger. Public acknowledgment of anger acts as an announcement to the world and to yourself that you are entitled to your feelings. It is a call to your feelings to come home because all is now understood and forgiven. The public anger need not be a temper tantrum or a dramatic production of any sort, but you should not be surprised if you find feelings of deep sorrow attached to the anger when it finally emerges.

Dramatic expressions of anger are suspect and problematic. They may make a good show, but they may also generate additional unrelated anger. Only societies that are attracted to violence assume that anger must be expressed in a frightening manner. All that is required is a brief, quiet, sure statement such as, "That makes me angry" or "I am angry." Expressed in this non-provocative way, anger harms no one, rather, it is capable of helping.

Once your anger is located, owned and announced, you are in the clear. If anyone wants more information about the probable cause or circumstances related to your anger, and if you feel comfortable sharing that information, you may choose to do so. But your task, for the sake of reclaiming your feelings and steering clear of depression and physical ailments, is the simple announcement of anger. When to share and when not to share your other gay-related feelings publicly is more complicated. There may be risks involved if you have not fully come out as yet. Also, most of us live in societies where one does not casually disclose any erotic thought passing through the mind. Failure to observe this social taboo can have results ranging from social ostracism to institutional incarceration.

Before you can honor and express your feelings you must find them. The initial search can be difficult. One device that helps is to create a *feelings* diary or journal. It requires an agreement with yourself that you will write about feelings for ten minutes each day, no less. During that ten minutes, you write about any feelings you are aware of having at the moment, as well as any feelings that you may have noticed since the last writing. If the key feeling of anger is particularly elusive, you may need to start by making it an *angry book* and spending the entire ten minutes looking for angry feelings. Once angry feelings appear easily, you can branch out to general feelings. Every month you might review your diary and, with a colored marker, call attention to each word denoting a feeling and rejoice in how many there are.

Be aware that shame and consequent guilt have been used to control you. They are used to control all children and adults. These feelings generate the emotion of anxiety, an emotion people will do anything to avoid. When hidden feelings emerge they may need to be rinsed clean of shame, guilt and anxiety. Time and practice can do that job. Talking to an unjudgmental friend or counselor can help.

Another technique that can help you to locate feelings, particularly those you are shy about expressing, is to write *unsent letters*. It is a technique that I have used for many years as an aid in psychotherapy.

You may have unexpressed feelings relating to another person but find some of the feelings unclear, confusing or difficult to express. Make a contract with yourself to write a letter that will *absolutely not* be sent or shown to anyone. Then arrange some uninterrupted time, sit down and begin the letter with no rehearsal of what you are going to say. Continue to visualize the person to whom you are writing as you remember moments throughout your relationship and write whatever thoughts and feelings come to mind.

As you write, you may risk exaggerating since it will never be seen by anyone but you. The exaggeration will help you get in touch with dormant feelings. If you did not like something that the other person did, say that you *hated* it. If you felt a slight stirring of erotic desire, say that you wanted to touch, kiss, get involved in specific sexual ways, etc.

You may continue to work on such a letter for days or weeks, until you are certain that you have nothing more to say. Then put it away for a day or a week before reading it to yourself. As you read, you will confront awakened feelings that you had during the course of the relationship and may still have for this person. You will have begun to awaken your dormant feelings.

Some days after reading the unsent letter, you may wish to put it away or destroy it and write a real (to be sent) letter to the person. Knowing it will be read, you will naturally tone down some of your expressed feelings, but you will know what you are feeling and how you wish to communicate it. You must *never* send the original not-to-be-sent letter, because the non-conscious part of your mind will record the betrayal of trust and be more guarded if you ever try to use the technique again.

Yet another technique for investigating your feelings is a game that can be played with a friend or in a support group. Take turns describing as many details of your day as you can remember. As you recount your day, following each statement with: "I felt...," "I thought...," or "My judgment was...". See how many times your friend or other participants can catch you in an inaccurate description. "I felt embarrassed" is a winning point in the game because it is a description of a feeling or emotion. "I felt that he was being unfair," loses a point because it is a judgment rather than a true statement of feeling. "I felt that it was quite possible that she might not be home" also loses a point because it is a statement about a thought rather than a feeling, unless the person speaking is psychic.

Before you can become comfortable with your feelings you must learn to identify them. Part of the identification process is learning to not get them mixed up with thoughts or judgments. It is simply a matter of ancient confusion or mislearning. I am reminded of a college roommate who believed that he was partially color-blind until we discovered that he could see each color as a different color but had learned incorrect names for many of the subtler shades.

Gay support groups and discussion groups are great places to try out locating and expressing feelings, if everyone in the group is willing to follow the same rules regarding the expression of feelings. Basic ground rules might include the willingness to listen without interrupting and repeating back what you believe another person has said to you. It can help you to see that a person who is describing a feeling, even a negative feeling connected to you, is sharing information about himself or herself with you. It is an offering of information about what is going on inside of that person. If the person did not care about you, there would be few, if any, feelings to share and little, if any, wish to bother sharing them. That is additional information about the person speaking to you. You are learning about that person.

There is so much confusion about feelings because we are taught to view some feelings as *good* and some as *bad*. Sympathy, for instance, is usually seen as a good feeling while anger is seen as a bad feeling. In reality, there are no good or bad feelings. All are equally valid and all are needed for survival.

Sometimes there is confusion in attaching a name to an emotion, even when it is experienced clearly. Remember that you experienced and learned most emotions before you were taught language. The words you learned to use as labels may be inaccurate when compared to the manner in which other people around you use those labels, and this can be confusing. Parents are notorious for teaching children to mislabel feelings such as anger or frustration. "You're just tired, dear. You need a nap." The nap often lessens the frustration or anger, but the name of the *emotion* is not *tired*.

As you become more adept at identifying, understanding and expressing your feelings, you will find ways to unlock your grip on them and their grip on you. Some emotions are uniquely compounded and complex, and you may not be able to find an appropriate single word in your language to name that feeling.

There is one such compound emotion that I have witnessed many times with gay people. It sometimes bursts into awareness around the time of coming out. It is a combination of frighteningly strong anger mixed with frighteningly strong sadness plus some fear. I have seen it come to the surface unexpectedly and suddenly but only when the person is feeling sufficiently safe.

I recall a man telling me about an all-male gay retreat he attended in a beautiful rural setting. The participants had spent an entire afternoon giving one another massages. During psychotherapy he was describing how deeply healing the experience had been for him. But he was puzzled, he said, by a peculiar thing that happened while two men were giving him a massage near the end of the afternoon. "I was enjoying it so much and it felt so wonderful, and then I began to shake. I was shaking so violently that I almost fell off the massage table. They ended the massage by just holding me and then I started to cry. Maybe they were tears of joy." As he retold the story, he began to weep again. As his sobbing increased in intensity, he began to tremble and shake again and asked if I would hold him.

"They're also tears for all the years when I didn't get held or touched by men," he said finally in a tight, anguished voice. "And I'm angry!" These last words came through gritted teeth as he continued to cry and hold his stomach.

A lesbian told her therapy group about her family reunion. "I left Janet at home but all my brothers and sisters had their married and unmarried partners there. Not one person said anything about my being gay. Not one person asked about Janet. I felt so alone!" She too had found herself getting teary and then sobbing as she told her story in the safety of her group. "I am so damned angry," she told them, "... and lonely." She told me that she had felt as if the emotion was ripping her open, becoming stronger as two of the group members moved closer to hold her. "It was like I had all this heat in my stomach, not nausea, but like there was something in there."

There is no proper name for this compound emotion. I call it a *belly full of tears* because that seems to describe it best. Often the person describes a fear that the crying will never stop or that the anger is so strong that it is dangerous for everyone. Once expressed, it usually leaves the person feeling spent, tired and very much more at peace with himself or herself. Awesomely deep feelings have been tapped, feelings that had been held in and sealed over by the threat of anxiety for many years. The child this person once was must have experienced the full power of this mixture of feelings and was too frightened by the combined strength of the rage, sadness and loneliness.

Depression is a big problem for many gay people. Much of it comes from denial of anger, denial of self-worth and denial of emotional fatigue. A person can feel decreasing self-esteem in the uphill fight against subtle everyday messages that invalidate, and then turn anger inward. It can be an unfortunate downward spiral that rarely permits corrective evidence or positive experiences to have any influence.

A first line of defense that I recommend to people is to decrease the use of alcohol and other optional drugs, increase physical exercise and try using an easy-to-remember **4-N Approach**. It involves pushing yourself to do things that are **novel**, permitting **nourishing** experiences, expressing anger with a simple "**no**," and getting yourself outdoors in **nature**.

It may help to make a small list of things you have been wanting to do and have not done. Friends can make suggestions to add to your list. Then push yourself to do one of those things each day. It may involve a simple novelty like wearing something unusual, or something as nourishing as making a long-distance call to a friend and luxuriating in the renewed contact. It may be as complex as saying "no" when asked to organize a mailing for some event "because you are the only one who really knows how to do it," or as wonderful as taking a walk in the woods, along the beach, in the desert or to the top of a hill where nature is larger than you are.

If you continue to use less alcohol and other drugs, increase physical exercise, and do the *four N's* each day, you give the world a chance to offer you some positive reinforcement. Your own efforts bring you additional self-respect.

If it does not have too strong a foothold, the depression soon begins to lift. If this sort of first-aid does not work, it is time to ask for help from a mental health professional. There are a variety of anti-depressant medicines that can give a needed boost up the first rungs of the ladder also. Talk-therapy, which is what psychotherapy is sometimes called, should be taken with the pills for fastest relief and maximum lasting benefit.

Feelings do come and go. When we are not holding on to feelings, they do so with surprising speed. Most of us have been taught to stay mad or stay happy all day. Unthinking determination to remain unhappy until another person changes his or her behavior is neither productive nor rewarding. The gay person who learns to relocate, appreciate and stay tuned-in to feelings is often surprised to find that he or she is angry one hour and happy the next. Feelings are always present and they are always on the move.

Emotions in motion, constantly changing, consciously or not, are doing their work in balancing the cognitive thought process—thoughts being the other half of the team that is the inner you. Your thoughts move along quite rapidly too. If you are sensitive and *listen* to both your thoughts and feelings, you will find that the resulting self-awareness is the vital ingredient in developing self-respect. Self-awareness truly reclaims ownership of the self. It leads to choice. I can choose how and when to express my thoughts and feelings in behavior, whether they be angry, erotic or less exotic, but only if I am aware of them. Otherwise they tumble out in a jumble of confusion that involves embarrassment and fragile disguise.

10

GAY, STRAIGHT, BI AND OTHER CATEGORIES

P EOPLE LIKE TO KNOW the names of things. In some societies there seems to be a shared compulsion to name things. In the process of naming, categories are created. When those categories contain people, they can be limiting to the people seemingly contained therein. Such categories also limit the thinking of anyone observing the categorized individuals. Even such a seemingly simple and natural categorical division as naming *women* and *men* sets the stage for limitations.

As a psychologist I must say that I believe the naming phenomenon has to do with the human desire to control (or to seem to control), and thereby quiet the anxiety that comes from living in a complex universe whose laws seem chaotic or random. In truth, there is not much that goes on in this universe or on our planet that we can control. Meteor showers happen and sometimes a meteor strikes a planet with enough force to alter its destiny. Hurricanes, tornadoes, earthquakes, floods and famines occur regularly on our planet—often unexpectedly and with devastating consequences. Death comes when and in the ways that it does—often without warning. We crave a sense of control. Creating categories and identifying them with our labels helps us to believe that we have some control.

The scientists who named some of our primate cousins *chimpanzees* made it more difficult to learn the ways of the cousins later named *bonobo* who, like us, were similar to the chimps but different. For bonobo, sex and erotic play soothes, promotes bonding and displaces war games and other acts of aggression. The bonobo could not be seen and we could not learn needed insights about human potential because they had been put in a limiting category.

Labels must be applied to individuals with great care. Beware of the labels you accept. Labels that encourage you to think of yourself as someone with wider horizons or greater competence can be helpful but there are more labels that limit than there are labels that liberate. Think twice or three times before applying a label to yourself and be prepared to define any label that you do assign in ways that will facilitate your own growth.

Individuals who retain conscious awareness of their physical attraction to people of the same gender are often labeled *homosexuals*. The word "homosexual" is more accurately used as an adjective than a noun. It can be used to describe a sex act or a feeling, but it is not appropriately used as a representation of a person. By referring to us as homosexuals, a society can create social distance and lessen the discomfort of non-gays who do not honor feelings of attraction for people of the same gender. If we are placed in a separate category with a label that has anxiety-provoking, unattractive connotations, those non-gays feel safer because they do not belong to the same category. But the label must be used regularly in order to keep us *over there*, at a distance lest we get too close.

A sad example of this sort of irrational fear was on full view during the 2004 elections in the United States. As had been true four years earlier, candidates from the major political parties felt it necessary to pander to prejudice by pledging allegiance to a federal statute called the *Defense of Marriage Act* which proclaimed that a state need not recognize and honor homosexual marriages recognized and honored in another state.

The major candidates for President and Vice President embarrassed themselves by endlessly mouthing the simple-minded mantra, "I believe marriage is between a man and a woman." None of them could say why they thought heterosexual marriages needed to be defended from homosexual couples marrying. No one wanted to talk about the inequality of civil rights, tax benefits and social status involved.

The Republican candidate for President managed to shame himself additionally by asking the Congress and the state legislatures to approve an amendment to the nation's constitution that would forever ban gay marriage. It was clear to all that no such amendment could be passed. The U.S. senate brushed it aside. He and his aides knew that it was no more than oratory but they wanted to make it clear that he supported this prejudice.

The data painstakingly presented in the Kinsey studies of half a century ago (Kinsey, A., C., Pomeroy, W. B., and Martin, C. C. *Sexual Behavior in the Human Male*. Philadelphia, Saunders, 1948) has faded from view. These studies clearly supported the observation that humans are like all creatures in nature. Human attributes are not a matter of categories but of continua. The categories are manufactured by people. The data clearly demonstrated that it was *not* possible to separate *homosexuals* from *heterosexuals*. While some people are able to restrict their sexual behavior to only homosexuality or only heterosexuality throughout their lifetime, many (perhaps most) change the balance of their interest from time to time—at one point being more interested in homosexuality, at other times being quite interested in both, or neither.

When the Kinsey studies were first published, charges were made of sloppy research and manipulated statistics. The work was eventually successfully defended, but the data were subsequently overlooked and have largely sunk into oblivion. People (including social scientists) have ways of avoiding that which makes them uncomfortable.

The social device of categorizing and labeling us in a way that creates social distance from the majority of the population worked well until the second half of the twentieth century. Global communications and economics have virtually ended cultural isolation around the world. Too many people have been exposed to different social customs and mores. Circumstance and determination caused gay people to question the negative mythology that had kept us out of sight for so long.

A colleague said, "I think I am really confusing my children. It's a good thing they're adults now and can take such things more in stride—and even offer Dad some advice now and then. First they had to get used to the idea that I was gay and really did like men. It took a little while but they're comfortable with it. Now, I've been seeing more and more of this woman I met—and the sex is wonderful! I don't think any of us were quite prepared for this turn of events. Especially since I continue to feel physically attracted to many more men than women. They're teasing me about whether they're going to get a second mother or a second father."

Yet the mythology and categorization persists, suggesting that one does not step out of a sexual category easily—if at all. Since the end of the nineteenth century, some mental health professionals have lured us with the promise of a *cure*. With our effort and their help, we were told, there was hope that we could change from the homosexual category to the heterosexual category. These professionals were repeatedly confronted with evidence of people moving back and forth from one category to another. A heterosexual who indulged in a period of homosexuality was said to have experienced a short period of emotional disturbance, dissociation or regression. A homosexual who indulged in a period of heterosexuality was experiencing spontaneous remission, miraculous recovery or may have been misplaced initially into the wrong category.

Religious leaders also offered first-class redemption—some continue the offering today. If the sin of being a homosexual was confessed with true remorse and the sinner prayed and worked for the miracle of salvation, it was said he or she could become a heterosexual. Heterosexuals who only temporarily became homosexuals had yielded briefly to the devil, while homosexuals who temporarily became heterosexuals were nearly saved before their willful or spineless, sinful backsliding. Research and education do not count for much in such a system.

In recent decades people have been more and more open about moving from one category to another. Our faithful keepers of the categories and their labels, rather than consider decategorization, created a new category and named it *bisexual*. If the homosexual is someone over there, the bisexual is someone who is in another territory altogether—way *over there* in the realm of exotica. She or he is said to have *confused sexual identity*, which in behavioral terms means that the person will not stay in one of the two provided categories. What it means in mental health jargon is that the person has not developed *normally*—has not grown up to be a heterosexual or even a homosexual but is emotionally somewhere back in very early childhood, sitting on the fence, unable to make the choice that permits first-class maturation or to admit to the alternative preference. Currently they are scratching their heads and wondering what to do with the self-described *metrosexuals* who happily bounce around and through the categories as if they do not exist.

Even within the official, enlightened view of the American Psychiatric Association, the American Psychological Association and the better-late-than-never American Psychoanalytic Association, having declared homosexuals to be not emotionally disturbed, per se, there is professional concern about the person considered to be suffering from *confused* sexual identity. Most religions are decades behind the mental health organizations and consider anything less than one hundred percent heterosexuality to be unacceptable. They just will not put up with it! The homosexual can only be pitied, prayed for and advised to remain celibate. The bisexual is willfully unrepentant, sinful and disobedient and the metrosexuals are beyond the pale. While clearly capable of heterosexuality and therefore capable of walking a *straight* line, they choose not to do so. Such is the fate of those who refuse the demands of the superintendents of conformity.

Periodically there is a popularization of bisexuality—it is exotic and can be considered chic. The media turn on the spotlights and see people moving between the two most familiar categories and declare it a fad. Then they turn out the lights and report that the fad is fading.

These most frequently recognized categorical labels attempt to describe human sexuality while disregarding the fact that it continues to defy categorization. Unfortunately, it is not simply a harmless amusement. It is a destructive process. People are taught to believe that they must choose one of the two original categories and stay there or be otherwise classified and considered emotionally immature or mentally disturbed. For those of us who have remained aware of our attraction to people of our same gender, there is pressure to call ourselves homosexual—with all the stigma attached to that label. We thus may come to believe that we are incapable of having satisfying emotional and sexual involvement with a person of the other gender. It is a stupid game that nobody wins.

The custodians of names, categories and conformity have been kept very busy. Now there are *transsexuals* or *transgender* people—a man born into a female body or a woman born into a male body. Once relocated in the body that fits their psyche, such people are usually heterosexual. This is terribly confusing to the conformists. I remember the distasteful look on the face of a mental health professional I encountered some years ago as he said, "You mean you've got this man who wants to have sex with other men but first he has to become a woman with all the right equipment and everything—or a woman who wants to have sex with other women but first she has to have a man's equipment?"

My very quiet, "Yes," did not help. Nor was he cheered by my more elaborate explanation that it is about far more than sex. It is the overwhelming need to actually be the gender they need to be in all ways. He was not having a good day and I had the impression that he had stayed in his field too long.

Transvestites are often mistaken for homosexuals or transsexuals. In fact, transvestites are simply women who like to dress in men's clothing or men who like to dress in women's clothing and it has nothing to do with their sexual orientation. Most transvestites are heterosexual in orientation. It can help to have more understanding of people who do not share one's gender and facilitates glimpses of hidden aspects of the whole self. Of course, they upset the keepers of categories and conformity quite a bit.

Gay is, at best, a self-descriptive label that simply means "I am a man who is physically attracted to other men and who is able to love another man with body, mind and spirit" or, likewise, "I am a woman who is attracted to other women and able to love them entirely as well as to make love with one or more of them." It signifies a sexual capability rather than a restriction or disability. It may imply a frequent or nearly constant sexual preference or attraction for people of the same gender, meaning that I (a gay man) might notice more men than women on the street or might notice my attraction to men before I notice attractive women.

But the self-assigned label does not limit us. A gay man can love a particular woman and a lesbian can love a particular man. *Homosexual* and *heterosexual*, when used as nouns, are naïve terms that carry destructive nonsense in the form of labels that limit.

Perhaps it is best to refuse to permit other people to assign you to a category. It is you who must decide when to drink red wine, when to drink white wine, and when to refuse wine altogether and drink soda, water or juice. It is you who must decide the relative strength of each of the speakers in your sound system if you have one. It is you who must pick your own descriptive label, if there is to be one, and only you who can know with which individuals you touch the wonderful mysteries of sex and love.

Perhaps, after all, *queer* is the best label. It represents anyone who honestly refuses the categorizing demands of the conformists in our societies.

11

TELLING

"TALK ABOUT COMING OUT! I know about coming out. I've been on both sides of that stove and I know about the heat."

Millie is a widowed mother of one adult gay son, one adult non-gay son and an adult non-gay daughter. She is also a grandmother, a person living with AIDS, and a warm, outspoken person with a generous sense of humor. "It's really all about heart. When Jamie told me that he was gay, I thought my heart would break. He was my firstborn, wonderful, handsome, smart, perfect son who could have anything he wanted from life. When it was my turn to tell them all that I had tested positive, I could hardly get the words out because my heart was in my throat. I didn't want to change in their eyes or to lose them or to cause them pain."

Wayne, a gay male friend of the family who met Millie at an HIV support group, said, "For me it's been one coming-out after another. First I had to announce I was gay and then five years later I had to announce that I was living with AIDS. At least I had an intermission. Some guys I know had to do a double coming-out because the discovery that they were HIV-positive pushed them out of the closet."

"It's crazy that it's harder for Wayne to come out about the infection than it is for me but that's the way it goes in a crazy world,"

Millie said. "He got infected while he was making love with someone in a bedroom. I got infected while I was having my gall bladder taken out. One is better than the other? I'd have preferred the making love route, I think."

The repeated question is, "Who should I tell first and when should I tell?" Letting people know that you are gay (or living with AIDS, a transsexual, or have unexpectedly inherited a huge amount of money) takes practice. In the beginning it is likely to be frightening or embarrassing. As Millie would say, "Your heart is in your throat." You want to share information about yourself that may cause people to see you as a different person. You are exposing yourself in a way that makes you vulnerable. You could be inviting hurt.

Naturally, you are concerned that people you care about might abandon you or misunderstand you. You could lose your job, marriage, children or even your gay lover who might not be able to afford the exposure and guilt-by-association. But guarding your feelings and hiding your identity is emotionally draining and ultimately self-defeating. What to do?

Years ago, a despairing friend said, "I think I'll just put an announcement in the newspaper and leave town for a month and get it over with." I have seen people wearing various *announcements*, such as a red ribbon lapel pin to signify AIDS awareness or a small American flag to signify unity following the 9/11 terrorist attack, patriotism or because they are politicians. Many automobiles now sport a small rainbow decal on their rear bumper. "My car tells the story," a woman told me. "If someone doesn't know what the rainbow bumper sticker is, they ask. I answer. They asked—so they can deal with it. Besides it makes a lot of lesbians and gay men more forgiving of my less than perfect driving when they are in the car behind me."

In deciding who, how and when to tell, you must sort reality factors from fantasized fears. My friend's bumper sticker would put her in danger in some parts of the world. If you work for an employer who displays prejudice about gay people, telling anyone who might leak the information directly or via gossip could be a real threat to your career.

In the long run, however, it might be best to leave a job where you suspect that you would be punished if people found out that you are gay. It may be too costly to stay there. But practical considerations and economic responsibilities may keep you in it. If you decide to change jobs, you may need time to save some money to put toward the change, and that could mean holding off on any announcements for a period of time.

But if keeping the secret erodes your self-respect, your emotional well-being or physical health, it might be better to risk telling the boss now and collecting any unemployment insurance funds (if available) while you look for a more suitable job environment. There are places in the world where legal protection is available if you are terminated for no reason other than your sexual orientation. Such cases may be quickly settled in an administrative hearing but some involve protracted, expensive lawsuits.

If your career calls for a security clearance of some kind, no matter who the employer, the best course may be the choice to be openly gay. The usual excuse for denying a security clearance to a gay person is the person's susceptibility to blackmail. This explanation does not hold up very well if you are already openly gay. Another choice is to retrain yourself for work that is similar but does not require security screening.

Fortunately, many employers are becoming sufficiently enlightened to realize that they cannot afford to lose valuable employees because of prejudice. It may take a bit more effort to find such an employer but it definitely is worth it. Unfortunately, gay people still face discrimination in the job market and careers are less often permanent or long-term than in the past. It is wise to develop the discipline to put money aside to help in times of unemployment related to prejudicial discrimination.

It is best to proceed on the assumption that you cannot hold the secret of your gay identity forever. Each time you pretend to be non-gay when you know yourself to be gay, you give yourself a quiet, irrational suggestion that it is wrong or bad to be the person you are. Your intellect may know better and you may have ready rationalizations handy, but the primitive emotions inside of you accept each act of hiding as additional proof that the gay feelings are wrong or bad and that you are therefore wrong or a bad person. Also notice that a lie of omission, such as not correcting someone's presumption that you are non-gay, weighs every bit as heavily upon you as a lie of commission, such as actually stating that you are, in fact, totally heterosexual in orientation.

Accumulating such emotional evidence (that you are a bad person) over the years leads to serious trouble. It leads to self-destructive behavior. As a matter of habit, you may choose the wrong partners who will treat you badly (as you secretly believe you deserve to be treated). You may abuse your body in ways that help you to become a regular customer of your physician or a surgeon.

Many serious physical problems result from muscle tension in the body which was induced by wariness and lack of ease associated with a distrust of self. You may misuse alcohol and other drugs as a means of momentarily dulling emotional pain while punishing yourself. Or you may simply drift through life, never reaching your goals because you secretly believe you do not deserve to reach them.

If you are not thoroughly proud of yourself, it will show in your body and your behavior—one way or another. If you feel like a bad person, you will punish yourself. Eventually, you must discard the secret. You cannot afford to hide being gay for too long. It is too costly.

But beware, *failure to prepare for disclosure experiences can be a mistake.* I was ill-prepared for one of my own first experiences. After a few very positive experiences, I was riding the crest of a wave of open, honest, good feelings. I invited a long-time and much valued friend to lunch in an Italian restaurant in Greenwich Village. We had been in the army together, had seen one another through graduate schools and the earliest years of our training as psychologists, and we lived near enough to one another to share the pleasures and difficulties of the first years of marriage and child rearing. I disclosed my secret with some anxiety, looked at the red checkered tablecloth and waited for his reaction.

He smiled and reassured me that he had half guessed it long ago, said that he admired my courage in making the choice to be honest and that it would make no difference in our friendship. He leaned back in his chair and mused aloud about how it had crossed his mind at times during our army days, when we were off on a weekend pass together, that we might try to express our feelings for one another sexually. I told him, honestly, that I had not been having those thoughts or feeling those feelings.

After a walk through Washington Square and more trading of memories and mutual admiration, we parted. The air was cold and the winter trees were without leaves but I felt warm inside—and free. I have not seen or heard from him since. It took time to realize how hurt and abandoned I felt. It has taken longer to realize that I had unintentionally wounded his male pride when I said that I had never been sexually attracted to him *after* his admission that he had thought about sex between us while we were in the army.

It is possible to prepare yourself for the disclosure. It need not be so painful or frightening. It helps to sit down with yourself or a trusted gay friend and think through who you need to tell and why you want that person to know. What do you want that person to know, how do you hope the person will respond, how do you fear the person might respond and what will you do and feel after either a positive or negative reception?

A good example is parents. Think how often you have heard a gay person say, "I haven't told my parents—it would break their hearts. I want them to grow old and die in peace. They've had enough troubles. My father has a bad heart and it would kill him. My mother has no way of understanding it and it would only destroy the picture she has built up of me as someone she feels proud of. I could never go home again. Anyway, it's really none of their business."

Why might you want them to know? There is, of course, the mystical parent-child bond that humans have. Parents know so much about you during the important early years of childhood. If you knew something about yourself that they did not know during those years, you were probably withholding the information because you thought it was bad. Withholding this information about being gay now is sure to bring up those childhood feelings and may contribute to bad feelings about yourself today.

You might want them to know because you love them and have shared everything else with them, and you feel guilty for holding back this important information about your identity. You might want them to know so they will stop badgering you about getting married. You might want them to know because you fear they will find out from another source and it would be better to tell them yourself. You might want them to know so that they can arrange their wills accordingly and leave what they wish to you rather than to children you do not plan to have. You might want them to know so that you can freely participate in political activities without the fear of unwelcome publicity. You might want them to know because you are angry at them and hope that the information will hurt.

All but the last reason are positive. All but the last are signals to go ahead with the disclosure, because you could accomplish something that will make you feel less hampered and better about yourself as a person.

What do you want them to know? Do you want them to know the details of what you do sexually in bed? Unlikely. People do not usually entertain parents with details of heterosexual sex, either. You might have the kind of relationship with your parents that does include open discussion of such intimate information and they may have had little experience with gay sex and want to ask detailed questions to satisfy curiosity. If so, prepare yourself to deliver the information gradually—at your own pace. But if you do not usually have that level of intimacy, there is no reason why you should feel pressure to respond to requests for homosexual information any more than a brother or sister would feel called upon to respond to a request for detailed heterosexual information.

Probably what you want your parents to know is that you are gay and how you define that; that you have been gay for years; that you are responsible for your *self* and intend to feel good about being gay; that it is not something they are entitled to feel guilt or responsibility for; that you want to be able to present a lover, partner or spouse to them as someone deserving the same respect as a heterosexual wife or husband; that you have gay friends whom you respect and are proud of whom you would like them to meet, and that you love them no less because you are gay even though they are not. Take care to make such a revelation when you have arrived at a place in your life where you really do feel good about being gay. If you announce that you are gay in the same tone of voice that you might use if telling that you were thrown out of school, lost your job or that the building you live in burned down, you can hardly expect them to rejoice with you.

How do you hope that they will respond? You probably hope that they will be pleased and honored that you have shared this difficult and important information about yourself. Perhaps you hope that they will be eager to meet gay friends and welcome them into the family home. Perhaps you hope that they will be interested to learn more about what it is like to be a gay person and will want to know what they can read or where they can go for more information. Perhaps you dare to hope that they will join an organization such as PFLAG (Parents, Family and Friends of Lesbians and Gays) and help to fight for their own and the world's understanding and for gay civil rights.

How do you fear that they might respond? You may fear that they will literally or figuratively throw you out of the house and tell you not to return until you have changed. You may fear they will cut you out of their wills or ask you not to tell your brothers, sisters, aunts, uncles and cousins. You may fear that they will insist that you enter a mental hospital or pray for your release from sin. You may fear that they will simply say they do not want to know about it and to please keep such information to yourself.

What would you do and feel? Sort it through for yourself *ahead of time*. If their response is positive you do not have to do much more than feel good and celebrate. (Though an initial positive response can be followed by a later shock wave of caution, question and homophobic doubt. Remember, they have lived a long time in the same world as you!) Another weight has been lifted from your back if the response is generally positive. If they respond negatively, I hope that you will find your own anger, hurt, sadness and loneliness and communicate those feelings. The feelings were there all the while, hiding behind the fantasy of how your parents might respond.

You will not lose your parents in such a moment of disclosure. If it is their true reaction rather than expression of initial shock, you lost your parents long before. They did not love you, they loved an image of you that they and you invented together. Confronted with the real you, they admitted their unavailability as parents to the person you are by nature. You mourn the loss of your parents, parents who were lost long before you confronted them with the truth. I hope you will admit the feelings of loss, including the anger, get through the mourning and permit yourself to grow, parent yourself and have your own good life.

The disclosure need not be made in one dramatic announcement. Often the best strategy is to simply be gay and let people draw their own conclusions, or ask questions if they must. You can act as if everyone already knows. That means not making any effort in the presence of a particular person to cover your tracks, disguise your feelings and attitudes or otherwise misrepresent your true identity.

I remember riding up a mountain in a high speed, four-person ski lift with friends. The non-gay man seated next to me said, "Did you guys see those two women in the line behind us? Man, I have never seen such well-developed women, if you know what I mean! I think I'm in love."

"I didn't notice them," I volunteered. "I was trying not to fall over or step on the skis of those four guys ahead of us—outstanding looking guys! They must be gymnasts or models. Their ski clothes fit like gloves."

There followed a thoughtful moment of silence and then all four of us had a good long laugh with no discussion. There was no need for speeches. I had simply told the truth, been my gay self and made sure there was room for all of us with no need for subterfuge, dissembling, opposition or hiding.

The timing of a disclosure is especially critical if the person to whom you are disclosing is likely to be emotionally threatened by the revelation. This is very likely with husbands and wives. If you let go the floodgates and deluge your spouse with everything you have always wanted to tell her or him about your gay identity, do not be surprised if their reaction is like that of a drowning person—thrashing and fighting to stay afloat.

Be sensitive. If it is going to be a big surprise, let it come more slowly so that your spouse can begin to prepare for it. Letting it be known that you enjoyed a book or a film with a gay love theme is one good beginning. Letting it be known that you notice the attractiveness of some people of the same gender at the beach or on television is another step. These are statements of general attraction rather than attraction to the person who lives next door, which might well set off an alarm bell.

Talking about deep and real feelings of affection for same gender friends in the past and the frustration of never having fully revealed those feelings can be another large step. By now your spouse is probably aware that you are not conforming to the usual cultural code and is alerted to the possibility that you are an individual who is different. Your spouse may also begin to appreciate your willingness to share intimate feelings. If you continue to be open in confiding these relatively unspecific feelings, your spouse is likely to become more direct in asking questions that you can answer truthfully. You are permitting your husband or wife to set the pace.

The rule of thumb is to *answer only the question* asked and not give more information than is requested. If a husband asks, "Do you mean that you feel as if you want to be sexual with another woman sometimes?" the truthful answer is probably, "It depends upon the woman, but I do feel that way sometimes." He can take the information and digest it more easily than if you respond with "Yes, I am a lesbian and have been for years and I'm glad it's out in the open. Not only did I feel that way about the heroine in the film, but I also feel that way about Sarah and I can't bear to hide it any longer!"

The gradual disclosure with someone like a spouse who might be emotionally threatened does require caring, restraint and effort. It would be easier perhaps to spill it all at once. The slow, gentle disclosure is an act of love. You know your spouse has been trained to react to such confrontation with wounded pride and perhaps passionate, even savage, hostility toward you and the invisible enemy. This is an attempt to safeguard their territory or save the marriage. The training can be so thorough that it seems like second nature. The true act of love is to present the information with sensitivity as a sharing of yourself and your secret feelings, rather than a sudden, explosive confrontation that can easily be experienced as an attack.

Your spouse may react negatively no matter how caringly and carefully the revelation is made, but you will know you did all that you could to soften the impact. The usual course of events is for the spouse to respond with rhythmic waves of alternating anger and increased intimacy. The disclosure promotes more intimate sharing between you two but also presents a dilemma. Can he or she trust or rely on you to care and receive such intimacy as much as before? And so come the waves of anger, closeness, anger, closeness. Riding those waves will often bring the couple safely to shore with an expanded relationship and ability to communicate. If the rhythm becomes a habit, however, it may be time to seek help from a gay-affirmative counselor.

A general rule in selecting the people you need to tell is to consider how much emotional energy you are spending by *not* telling them. If you find yourself repeatedly fantasizing a disclosure with a particular person or that you go to some lengths to cover your tracks in order to not have the person discover that you are gay, the secret is costing you too much emotional energy. For the sake of your own well-being, you would do well to tell her or him sooner rather than later.

Having heard many tales of disclosure experiences, I know that there is no way to predict the reaction. So much depends upon the inner psychodynamics of the person being told. She or he may have a secret personal agenda that may surprise everyone.

One man told me about gently preparing his parents for the announcement for a year. All of their responses to gay topics had been positive and he expected no real difficulty. He went to visit them in the home in which he had grown up. Over a drink before dinner on the first evening, he told them that the reason for his visit was that he wanted them to know more about himself so that they could have an even better relationship than the one they now enjoyed. He revealed his gay identity. Both parents were silent for a few moments and then his mother stood and went upstairs.

She returned with an enraged face, dragging three empty suitcases. She told him that she wanted him to put anything of his that he wanted in the suitcases and leave immediately because she did not want a homosexual son in her home. He was shocked, as was his father who had been quietly assimilating his son's disclosure—but there was no reasoning with her.

His father contacted him a few months later and began to visit him and to write to him, but his mother remained furious and would not discuss it with him or his father. The son attempted to visit a year later, having made prior arrangements with his father. But when he arrived at the home by taxi, his mother was in the automobile in the driveway, about to go to the grocery store. She actually drove purposely toward him as he walked up the driveway, narrowly missing him.

Unhappily, the resolution that usually does come, did not start until after he told his parents several years later that he had tested positive and that the HIV infection had progressed to AIDS. The full reconciliation of mother and son occurred only in the final months of his life.

As surprising is the story of a woman who, after some preparation, told her aged mother. "How long have you known?" asked her mother.

"Mama, I'm almost sixty years old and I've known since I was an adolescent—more than forty years. I can't imagine why I felt I had to keep it so secret this long."

Her mother was angry but in a quite different way. "No grandchildren, no truth, and no son-in-law even. But you could at least have given me another daughter! Now I see. There was Shirley, Maria and that girl whose name I never could pronounce—all pals. We could have had more of a family."

But, more often, there are the stories of positive reactions. There is the wealthy widowed grandparent who had been planning to give half of his fortune to a museum but decided, instead, to put it in a trust for his grandson and his partner to administer, "to do something to help other good men like yourselves find your right place in this world." He told his grandson that he too would have been gay and proud if the world had been more enlightened when he was a young man.

One of my happiest stories is about a woman who had to write many letters, hire a private detective and travel half way around the world in order to locate the aunt who had disappeared from the family twenty years earlier. "She was more fun and had more spirit than all the rest of my family put together and I had missed her terribly all those years and feared that she might be dead. For some reason, I just knew I had to find her and come out to her." There was a joyous reunion when she was located and, after the disclosure, her aunt introduced her to her own lesbian partner with whom she had been living all those years. "I really liked her too. We didn't speak the same language—but we managed somehow. We communicated. So I got a double reward."

A final thought about disclosure. It is best to disclose your identity to someone close and have years to share thoughts and feelings with one another in the light of this information. An increasingly loving relationship can be built. But there are times when this is not possible. Unexpected accidents and disease may suddenly threaten the life of someone important to you whom you had been preparing to tell.

People are sometimes reluctant to tell a loved one who is seriously ill or near death. Remember, it is your last chance. If you wait too long you may find yourself talking to the deceased person for years, trying to complete a relationship across an abyss that is impossible to bridge. It can be daunting if the person is in a coma. But it is possible to lean close, be brief and speak softly into the person's ear. It is very likely that somewhere inside of that exquisite human mind that records everything, you are being heard.

But why trouble the dying person with your disclosure? You must use your judgment. If you're merely presenting trouble, restrain yourself. But if you believe it is good news and have been very important in this person's life, it can be a gift—a sharing, an offering of yourself. It can be for the sake of the person dying as well as for your own sake, a completion.

It may be a gift that is not wanted, but there is no way to be sure unless it has been offered. You are demonstrating that you care enough for this person to try your best, right up to the last moments, to communicate something that might be of value. If you were dying, would you prefer to leave someone you love, sensing that an important secret had been left unspoken, wanting to be said, but hidden? Or would you rather have heard it?

The person near death may be too occupied with his or her own process of dying to offer much of a response. But you will know that you did not withhold your final, truthful communication. Should the dying person happen to have a negative response, you may take some comfort in knowing that you used your best judgment and did what you could to strengthen the bond between you in the time that remained and that it was the dying person, for whatever reasons, who was unable to accept your offering.

12

ATTRACTIONS

MARC AND I WERE POSTED in Prague for six months. That's when we came out to each other," Sara said. "That was a terribly big event, a turning point in both of our lives. It might sound foolish but the other big event was the woman we saw in the Metro there. Our subway car was stopped for some minutes and she stood directly opposite me. She was a plain and ordinary middle-aged woman and yet she was very attractive."

Sara explained that the woman was neither thin nor overweight, not pretty, not expensively dressed and wore little make-up. "But her posture was good and I could see that she had given some attention to which shoes, bag and earrings she chose for that dress. More than anything it was the very slight smile, as if her inner thoughts were contented, pleasant or happy. Marc mentioned a French expression that says someone goes well in their skin. That was definitely her and it made her very attractive to me."

Sometimes on a first appointment with a psychotherapist, clients bring their body along, filing complaints against it for behaving badly. They seem to have a troublesome relationship with it, not quite realizing that they *are* it. The division of mind, body and spirit is an artificial human invention that permits us to talk about various aspects of the living self, rather than the self as a whole.

It is not unusual for someone who is battling a disease to feel unattractive because her or his body is not looking and acting healthy. It is also not unusual for someone to feel uncomfortable in their otherwise healthy body, displaying their discomfort or disrespect in an eating disorder or other form of self-inflicted damage.

A woman client was painfully thin. "I eat every chance I get and I cannot gain weight," she told me. "My doctor has run all sorts of tests and says there is nothing wrong with me." What was wrong was that she had begun to have sex with several women and had hidden feelings that she was doing something wrong. She was unconsciously trying to make herself less attractive and flirting with a risk of serious illness.

A man of thirty found another way to deal with lingering discomfort about his homosexual desires. He appeared for a first appointment wearing shorts and a tank top. He admitted using steroid drugs to build bulk, though he knew that the drugs were not good for him. He worked out in a mostly gay gym every evening and had built a massively muscular body that kept him busy with its maintenance program and fending off admiring men who were not as well developed as he. His presenting complaint was that he feared he would never find a man who would love him for himself rather than for his body.

And a college sophomore told me that he was "tattooed almost everywhere," also pierced and ringed in more places than are usually contemplated. "I'm out there," he told me. "I've got plenty of friends and I get plenty of action but I keep having accidents. Last week I fell off a skateboard, the week before that I fell down a flight of stairs at school, and the week before that I drove my best friend's car into a ditch I didn't see and almost broke his axle and my nose."

What these three people had in common was a feeling of discomfort with their own body-associated erotic impulses. All three were expressing a need to disrespect or disown their bodies, suspicious of anything having to do with self or others from the neck down.

Disowning your body can be attempted in many ways. One person may ignore or neglect it as a vague nuisance used to house and transport mind and spirit. Another may take revenge on it by caus-ing it to have repeated accidents and illnesses, or simply by over-feeding or underfeeding it. Or one may reconstruct and redecorate so as to obscure and hide it behind an artificial façade that looks just like people in magazines. Whichever path, the body is rejected and disowned, becoming *it*, not *me*. It is an attempt to be rid of the respon-sibility for unacceptable feelings.

Gay people who discover the richness of their gay identity also discover a need to claim their bodies and become attractive. It begins with an understanding of the fact that every body is different. Accom-plished actors understand this and they learn how to make them-selves attractive at one time and unattractive another time with little or no help from make-up, wardrobe and lighting. Posture and attitude are important as a start.

Whatever the natural size and shape of a body, the person is most attractive when neither underfed or overfed. Regular exercise that produces healthy tone to one's muscles rather than an unnatural shape suggests self-respect. Clothing that is clean and fits comfortably suggests that the wearer is conscious of her or his appearance in the world. Attention to grooming—personal cleanliness, hair and nails, sends the same message. Like the woman in the Prague subway, one can easily make a statement—"I am attractive, appreciative of my good home in my body."

If you find that you do not know about a part of your body and how it works, consult some books, ask friends, or see a sympathetic and competent medical doctor, masseur or anatomy teacher. It is your body. It is you. And you are learning to know and claim your-self fully.

Another way to become better acquainted with your body is to learn to give yourself a loving massage, not the sort given to athletes after a game which is more like the kind given to a horse after a race. A loving massage is done by stroking every part of the body with sensitive care. Any kind of stroke that feels good is the right one to use, taking care not to omit any part of the body lest it feel neglected and unworthy. The genital area deserves its share of the stroking. Parents too often neglect this part of the baby's anatomy early in life and thereby send a quiet message that it is *untouchable* and, therefore, unlovable. If masturbation becomes part of the massage, it is done with the same gentle loving respect given to the whole body.

Becoming comfortable with your own body leads to appreciation of the bodies of friends. Reaching out to touch friends more often tells them that you appreciate the attractiveness of their bodies.

No body has the muscle tone at sixty that it had at thirty. Some abdomens are more round than others but all adults find theirs naturally rounded when relaxed. A relaxed smile that betrays positive feelings invites more lasting respectful attraction than a jawline that has been sculpted to perfection. A body is beautiful if it radiates self-respect. It is attractive to others.

Victor, a man in his sixties, met a man thirty years younger. "He's bright, fun, well-educated, kind-hearted, financially stable, has a great sense of humor, is dedicated in his work, and, as if all of that isn't enough, he is extremely good-looking. When he touches me I have to concentrate so that I don't forget what we're talking about. I'm probably too old for him but how wonderful it would be if he had some of the same feelings for me. He feels so good when we hug, touch or even shake hands! I really like his hands. They're strong and perfectly shaped. I know he likes me but I'm terrified that I'll say or do the wrong thing and drive him away."

Sally, a woman of thirty-one, was attracted to a woman a year older than she. They met standing in a grocery line, learned that they lived in the same neighborhood, worked near one another, and they made a date to meet for lunch. "I was attracted to Cynthia right away. Maybe it was the way she speaks and the things she's interested in. We have many of the same interests and always have more to talk about than there is time for. At our first lunch, I made sure to let her know that I'm a lesbian. She is too but she's only been out a couple of years. She comes from a socially prominent family and is trailing a lot of stuff about it that slows her down. She's never had a real relationship but she's had sex with other women.

"So last evening we had dinner. Talk, talk, talk—all of it fun and interesting, but I had a second track going in my mind about how good she hugs, looks, smells and touches. I drove her back to her car and she says to come over to her place so we can finish the topic. Then later she walks me out to my car and gets in because we're still talking. Finally we hug goodnight again and I just spill it and say, 'I'd like to sleep with you sometime, Cynthia.' She looked shocked, so I said, 'It doesn't have to be tonight or this week or this year... Never mind. Erase it. Forget I said it... blah, blah, blah,' backpedaling. I was so embarrassed and ashamed that I just wanted to get the hell out of there. She could have her pick of plenty of women. Whatever made me think she'd have any interest in being with me?"

Craig, a young man who had gone to a public swimming pool on his day off, is a very attractive professional athlete with a sunny disposition. "So I'm in the showers and there was this guy there soaping himself up way too much so I just avoided any eye contact but said 'Hi' to another guy who came in who I see there sometimes. Then I'm getting dressed at my locker when Mr. Super-soaper appears in his towel at the end of my row and stares at me again. I avoid eye contact and he finally goes off to wherever his locker is. I hurry up dressing, but when I'm leaving he's ready to leave too. I go to the front door and turn around suddenly, like I forgot something, and go all the way back to the rest room that's inside the locker room and pee, figuring it will give me time to lose him. But in he comes and plants himself at the next urinal. I zip up and hustle out to my car, but I have a feelings he's on my heels—which he is. As I'm unlocking the car he comes up to me and tells me very explicitly what he'd like to do for me sexually. I told him I'm in a relationship and he said, 'Yeah, I am too and I really shouldn't be doing this but how about it?' So I shook my head 'no,' got in the car and drove away feeling like one of those women who complain about guys yelling sexual stuff at them on the street because they're wearing a short skirt and have nice legs or whatever."

Any kind of human interaction requires good communication if it is to be a positive interaction. But people with excellent communication skills very often forget them when they are experiencing a strong attraction, anticipating rejection, or are being intrusively victimized.

The most basic rules of good communication are to say thoughts and feelings clearly and briefly, listen carefully when the other person is speaking and say what you believe you have heard before offering a response. You try not to infer meaning that has not been stated in the spoken words and to confess any inferences that you do make so that the other person can correct your addition if two plus two are adding up to six, twelve or a hundred. It may slow down the process to continually ask "Do you mean...?" but it is much more efficient in the long run because there is clarity in the communication rather than a tangle of misunderstandings.

The truth underlying these guidelines is that you can only give the other person information about yourself, not about him or her, and the other person can give you only information about herself or himself, not about you.

Perhaps someone who is clearly attracted to you says, "You're breathtakingly beautiful. Your eyes are gorgeous, your voice is music and your body could stop traffic in any major city on the planet." If you understand that people can only give you information about themselves rather than about you, there should be an internal voice behind your smile that prepares you to say, "Thank you for telling me about you." Because, indeed, all that you have been told is that someone is very taken with you. You have been given some information about someone else—not about you. If you understand that, there is no reason to blush, tremble with gratitude or be terrified. Your overt response will be determined by your feelings about the other person and what has been revealed about him or her. You may say, "Thank you. What's your name?" Or you may say, "Beauty is in the eye of the beholder." Or you may say, "Well now that we both know what interests you, perhaps we can move on to another topic." Or you may want to simply move away.

It is helpful to remember this underlying truth about communication when someone says something negative, such as "You are the most conceited person I have every met." The interior voice begins its mantra: "Thank you for telling me something about *you*." This person has told you that he or she is bothered and believes the bother is about you not being sufficiently responsive or being too involved with yourself and therefore unavailable. All that you know is that he or she is bothered. If six people have told you that they think you are conceited, it is something that you should be considering. But if you've been told by only this one person, your response could range from "Well, thanks for letting me know what bothers you," to "Excuse me, do I know you?" The information given to you was *not about you*. It is information communicated about the person speaking.

Quiet attraction can put cheer in your day, like walking through a garden and noticing beautiful flowers. Attraction that is more active can be much more unnerving. There is always the possibility of rejection and rejection does not feel good. Anticipation of it can produce feelings ranging from uncomfortable to terrifying. Since attraction often contains some amount of sexual desire, that desire can add shame and embarrassment if there is a hidden assumption that homosexual sex is a shameful thing people do to one another rather than an emotionally powerful, positive sharing.

There is a nearly universal fear of rejection. The fantasy is that your open interest in the other person will be met by disinterest or distaste. This points up the vital need that lesbians and gay men have to construct sturdy self-esteem. Sally was attracted to Cynthia. We do not know what was going on in Cynthia's mind when Sally said she would like to sleep with her. Indeed, we do not have any idea what connotations *sleep*, in the context of the moment, had for Cynthia. Sally's fear-fantasy was that Cynthia was rejecting her. It is one of those classic crisis moments that cries out for more communication.

One or both of the people may feel shy and awkward but there must be clarifying communication as soon as possible because there is real risk that all will be lost. Sally may back away in humiliation while Cynthia backs away in confusion because of all that is imagined rather than what is said aloud and clarified. At the very least, lack of communication risked losing what might have been a friendship, perhaps one that would grow intimate and include vacations together, sometimes sleeping in the same bed. At worst, lack of communication might destroy what could have led to a beautiful, fulfilling lifetime partnership or marriage.

Victor's story indicated that he needed to take communicative steps also. The steps can be taken one at a time. Step one: "I really like you." Maybe on the next meeting: "You are really a very attractive man"—volunteering information about himself (I am attracted to you). A meeting soon thereafter: "I am having romantic fantasies about you." By then the cat is out of the bag and it is time for courageous, respectful, clear communication with the often repeated "Do you mean...?" because it is easy to hear something other than what is being said when emotions are running high and the talking is difficult.

Victor would learn that the younger man is interested or he is not. If interested, Victor must learn what this person's boundaries are and what the relationship possibilities are. Is the other man romantically interested? Is sex a possibility? Are they both on the same path? Is it a path that may lead to lasting friendship, romance or a spousal relationship? What are the known limitations at present, if any?

When a person falls in love there is a great internal change in feelings and perceptions. The whole world looks better and the beloved looks *fantastically wonderful*. A large amount of what is seen in the beloved is, indeed, based on fantasy and wonder that comes from within the person who has been struck by Cupid's arrow. That *in love* state is wonderful and terrible. Every moment with the beloved and every action of the beloved's that can be fitted into the fantasy picture are sublimely reassuring, bolstering the bliss. But any moment separated from the beloved can turn suddenly dark with unexpected doubts that torture the want-to-be lover, and every action of the beloved's that does not fit the elaborate fantasy picture can be as piercingly painful as a knife wound.

For all of the *highs* associated with the in *love* state during a developing relationship, there are guaranteed *lows* to follow, as if in payment. The other person must be reduced to realistic dimensions sooner or later, offending the perfect picture and thereby seeming to hurt and disappoint—almost as if causing the hurt on purpose. "Why are you doing this to me? Why are you not the person I imagined you to be—the person I created in my desire-colored perceptions of you?"

Good communication cannot counteract the pain entirely, but it can prevent much of it if conversations are clear from the start. Good communication can also lessen the degree and frequency of the pain as the beloved shrinks to the normal dimensions of her or his real self.

If communication is neglected and an obsession is permitted to develop, it can be a nightmare for the presumed beloved as the object of the attraction and an ongoing torment for the person owning the obsession. It is essential that the obsessed find a way to face the fact that he or she is talking about an it (my *obsession*, that I created and *own*) rather than about Nancy, Tom, Helen or Patrick, whenever they find themselves pronouncing the name of the other person. It is the crucial first step before going on to recognize that the obsession that has been covered over by the name and face of a person is a substitute for unacknowledged or avoided anxiety. It is a good time to seek help from a psychotherapist. It is a very difficult job to get rid of such an obsession without help.

All of that notwithstanding, we would not wish Victor to forego this or any other opportunity to experience love. But he has to pay his dues like everyone else. He must subject his blossoming feelings to conversation with the beloved. If it is about only one person, it is an obsession. A loving relationship involves two people.

Craig's story represents a situation that is familiar to many women. No matter how strong the attraction or *presumed* invitation, none of us has the right to victimize another person by intruding in that person's life without permission. Craig was being used as an object—an object of sexual desire. His lustful pursuer knew nothing about him except the body that he saw in the showers. It was an imaginary relationship that contained only one person. It was a moment of intrusive insanity—when desire overcomes the usual testing or awareness of reality. Because the pursuer is not sane in such a moment, it feels dangerous to the pursued. When desire is motivated primarily by a need to seem powerful it can lead to rape—a pathological intrusion that no sane society can afford to condone.

It is not possible to confuse the victimizing pathology of such an intrusion with the simple expression of attraction. Attraction to another person that is more than passive and visually pleasant must involve concern about what the other person feels and thinks. Craig's story would have been quite different if someone had noticed him at the swimming pool, or in the showers or locker room and smiled and said "hello." If the smile and hello are returned there can be a next step—perhaps an attempt at brief conversation, the response to which either does or does not indicate a willingness to interact further. Encouragement could lead to a more bold *getting-to-know-you* next step, such as "Would you like to go for a cup of coffee?" But when the observed avoids eye contact and avoids being in the same area as the observer, it is a clear signal that he or she is not interested and is unavailable for further interaction.

As to the fear of rejection that so often interferes with a simple expression of attraction, it is possible to tackle that fear directly. The more experience you have in not being rejected, the more sure of yourself you become.

There is a *rejection game* that I have suggested to people and it gets results if you agree to its rules and play fairly. Your goal is to learn how many social rejections you can earn in a single day. The first rule of the game is that your attempted interaction with another person must be based on your own genuine feelings of attraction, whether sexual or otherwise. The second rule is that you must anticipate rejection from the person. The third rule is that you must be both respectful and genuinely honest in your words and actions in the interaction, no matter how brief or lengthy it is.

You notice that someone is attractive to you, anticipate that this person will reject you and then indicate interest by saying hello or making small talk. If the person turns away or is polite but brief or in some other way indicates she or he wants nothing to do with you, it counts as a rejection. The goal on the first day is to get one such rejection, the second day you must get two, the third day three, and so on.

Interesting things happen. You begin to worry less about rejection as you focus on earning your increased required score for the day without spending your entire day doing it. Not everyone you thought would reject you does reject you and your self-esteem improves. As you have more contact with individuals who are attractive to you, your social skills in interacting with such people improve and it becomes more difficult to find rejection. Finally, you reach a saturation point when you realize that the game is annoyingly time-consuming rather than the anxiety-provoking task it was at the beginning, since the rejections you experience no longer matter to you as much.

You must take care not to be intrusive or to knowingly damage the self-esteem of anyone else while in this game. If someone indicates that they are not interested, take your earned rejection and leave, with a smile and a kind word if possible. It is guaranteed way to meet people and do some relearning that can build self-esteem.

Every gay man and lesbian can make a wonderful contribution to our community very easily. Since everyone fears or dislikes rejection, learn to be more *inclusive* rather than *exclusive*. Be as attractive as you can be and be willing to attract. Smile and say "hello" when you see another gay person. Develop it as a habit. Be welcoming. Be more willing to touch and be touched if the touch is not intrusive. It can all happen in a few seconds. It need not be an invitation to complicated interaction. You can be clear in your communication and protect your true boundaries. Do not invite intrusion but do demonstrate inclusion by being yourself and being generous.

13
RELATIONSHIPS

HUMAN BEINGS ARE SOCIAL ANIMALS. Some of us are more gregarious, some less, but all of us need reassuring contact with others. Without it we are inclined toward loneliness and accompanying anxiety. Gay people growing up in non-gay environments are sure to experience loneliness.

Vivid examples emerge in gay psychotherapy and support groups. "I was always the kid picked last for the team," one person will say. "I've spent my whole life feeling alone," another may add.

I remember a young man sitting on a cushion one Sunday morning, sobbing as sunlight poured in through the windows behind him. Two others whom he had not known two days earlier were sitting on either side of him, holding him as he cried—their faces covered with their own tears. "I don't want to let you guys go," he said, looking around the group. "After all these years of having friends but feeling alone, it feels like I've found my own gang—the one I couldn't have when I was a kid. I can be myself with you. I feel strong and wanted and safe with you guys!" The room was filled with the mixed laughter and tears of others nodding agreement.

In the process of attempting to break free of non-gay and/or anti-gay programming to which you have been exposed since birth, it is likely that you will experience guilt and anxiety that will slow your progress. As a gay person you try your best to grow and develop in a non-gay environment. Non-gay people have their own troubles getting along with the directives that surround them, especially during their early years of growth and development, but they can find support in the general community as well as models who have traveled a similar path. They can select bits and pieces from those models and plot a course that suits individual needs. A gay person needs growth models too.

You need people you like, respect and admire, people who are glad to make themselves available to you for a phone call, a chat or for physical holding when you are feeling unsure and alone. As you grow, non-gays who are unfamiliar with the path you are developing may tell you that what you are doing is wrong or bad. Sometimes it is implied so subtly, you may wonder why you feel guilty or anxious. These may be biological family members or friends who love you but who simply do not understand the experience of being gay in a non-gay world. It is at these times that you need to check in with members of your own personal gay support system and ask their opinions.

There will be times when you feel uneasy or depressed, when it feels good to be held in the arms of someone who understands or cry on the shoulder of someone who has shed similar tears. It is no disgrace to weep or rest or seek comfort, but in the past all too few of us have known where to seek such understanding and comfort.

Perhaps only half of the gay people in your world are visible but with each passing year there are more. Friends can be found at events sponsored by a local Gay and Lesbian Community Service Center, at an LGBT (lesbian, gay, bi and transgender) fund raiser, a college Queer and Questioning Union, a book club, a theater event or via the Internet.

As you look over feelings and decisions—yours and theirs, from present and past—you begin to see how to use these people as models. You may base your decisions or behavior on what they tell you they have done in the past because it makes sense to you. Or you may clearly see a mistake one of them has made and save yourself from doing the same. It requires careful sifting and sorting on your part, but it is easier to make a cake from six different recipes than with no recipe at all.

As the months and years pass, your support system will grow larger, though at any given time, you will be most interactive with only a few. If you find, however, that you are not asking for any support at all, something is wrong. It can sneak up on you because people have relocated or died.

Add people who are older and younger than you are. Every young gay person needs the love and assistance of trusted older gays and every gay elder needs the affection, touch and fresh views of much younger gays. Isolation by age group is damaging to us as individuals and to our community. It leaves us more alone and inflexible as individuals, weaker as a group.

No one becomes so strong or so sure that he or she does not need at least a sounding board or a reassuring hug. One supportive friend is never enough to give balanced support. If you go for a year without shedding tears, you probably are holding back on awareness of feelings, perhaps because you do not feel safe. The more you are willing to be honest in your need for support, the more other people can be honest in their need of you also. You are much more certain to survive and thrive with a little help from your friends.

True intimacy is the grand prize in human relationships. It is earned only with caring communication, however. Respectful touch and honest, clear talk are its necessary ingredients.

Responsible erotic contact, offered as affirmation, welcomed and gladly received, is a form of communication. It lowers defenses, builds self-esteem, and strengthens the bond of intimacy. But conversational communication is vital to clear away ambiguity, uncertainty and fear.

I teasingly tell friends who are about to become parents that they must be prepared to face a future in which they cannot know if or when they will be permitted to have a full night's sleep. "Someone other than you is going to be in charge of that," I say. But the truth is that one of my most cherished memories is sitting in a rocking chair, looking up at a dark sky filled with stars, rocking slowly and holding a precious infant close to my heart—able to bring peace and comfort to both of us with that simple sacrifice of sleep—a gift rather than a sacrifice.

I also remember a dear friend nearing the end of his life, in the hospital again, saying simply, "I'm scared," and asking me if I would spend the night there with him. We held hands and talked until he slept. During the night his temperature rose and he visited altered states of consciousness, in and out of a fevered sleep. At one moment in the middle of the night he looked at me with bright, burning eyes that might have been seeing me or someone else, perhaps his lover who had died several years earlier. He said, "I want you to get into the bed with me—now, without your clothes—skin to skin..." and then he darted quickly back into his troubled sleep.

A few moments later, the nurse came in to check the monitors and the tangle of tubes to which he was attached. I had gotten onto the side of the hospital bed and was gently stroking his skin with my hand and a cool cloth. "He wants me to take my clothes off and get into bed with him," I said with a wry smile, making comradely contact with the other caregiver who was helping him through this difficult night.

"I don't have any problem with that," she said quietly as she adjusted one of the monitors, "but you might have a problem with some of these tubes," her smile matching my own—a weary compatriot of the night telling me that she had seen it all on this battlefield.

I managed to get more, but not all of me, onto the bed and to provide more skin contact. It has been my sad and lasting regret, however, that I did not use my ingenuity to better answer his request. I could have slipped out of my clothing and found my way carefully into that forest of medical equipment so as to comfort my friend in his troubled night. You never know when the end is near.

Two days later, he was alert early in the morning. We talked as only intimate friends can talk until he tired and asked if I would read to him. He dozed, lost consciousness, and that evening, I held his hand and talked to him softly as the dark of night approached and he took his leave.

We social animals depend on the caring and generosity of others. Your personal sense of well-being and your degree of health from birth to death depend in no small part on your interaction with a communication program that contains touch, talk, sex and intimacy. It is sad and puzzling that we have made it so difficult for many of us to receive the basic gift of touch.

Scientific studies of infants, the sick, the wounded and the elderly make it quite clear that surviving, thriving and healing is enhanced with a generous amount of caring touch from other humans. Some researchers suggest that physical contact with our pets also is beneficial and may contribute to increased longevity.

Touch is something that everyone needs. Some people need more of it than others. A humane theorist and generous American social worker, the late Virginia Satir, sometimes referred to it as *skin hunger*.

It is dangerous to ignore skin hunger. Caring touch calms. Frustration of this basic need leads to physical and social illness. We become irritable and sick.

Discovery of our bonobo cousins and their very different approach to life than our chimpanzee cousins has caused many gay people to reexamine the value of touch, erotic touch in particular. Too many of our human cousins fall victim to their warlords' demands that conflict be "resolved" with the ancient war tools of killing, torture, rape and plunder. Such habitual aggression is the chimpanzee way. The bonobo way is to ease conflict and decrease tension with generous erotic play and sex.

In cultures that follow the chimpanzee path, aggression is valued. The males are considered powerless, weak, *womanly* or feminine if they resist opportunities to display aggression. The females are expected to support aggression, urging their sons and mates to be aggressive. Gay people are seen as odd, queer or not of value in such cultures. Yet, we may offer the best hope for human survival by calling the destructive way of the chimpanzee into question now that there are war toys with the power to eliminate human life on our planet.

If friends do not provide enough nourishment for your skin hunger it is easy to form a habit of putting yourself in the path of strangers who will touch you. If you are an attractive person, you may find many strangers are eager to get their hands on you, some willing to pay money in exchange. If you wander into this without conscious intention, you may not feel very good about yourself after the encounter. You have been used. Your skin has been touched but the contact did not come with the desired message of caring, so it is off to another stranger with the same probable result.

Each time the need for caring touch intensifies, and each time you are less trusting that you will receive it. Infrequently, you may receive a little tenderness from a sensitive stranger. It acts as the same kind of *intermittent reinforcement* that brings people back to the slot machines or blackjack tables designed to take their money. You may find yourself in contact with stranger after stranger, cued by a look of desire in their eyes. Your own hunger grows stronger and stronger and along with it grows your distrust of people who want to touch you. Gradually you become less and less able to feel the genuine caring when it is offered.

Working with such individuals in gay groups, it is extremely difficult to help them reopen their sensitivity to touch. The *prettier* the person is by current standards, the greater the likelihood that he or she has been used and discarded often, and the more difficult it is to restore trust.

The first step is verbal reassurance that any person reaching out to touch you will be guided by *your* permission and *your* need and will do nothing that primarily satisfies his or her need. There will be the pleasure of touching you because you are attractive and because they care about you, but the touch will be intentionally given to you, for you and be guided by you. You will be touched only as much as you wish and in the way you direct. The amount of touching proceeds in small increments. Caring, sensitive friends can help if you share your feelings of need with them.

Such remedial exercises would be unnecessary if we could remember that everyone—young, old, sick or well—needs to touch and be touched. The act of caring touch should communicate and may feel erotic, but is not intrusive. It is offered, welcomed and received as a gift that is naturally enriching. It never steals from one of us in order to meet the needs of another.

Fantasies to the contrary, *talk* is an essential part of any human relationship. Some people carry with them into adult life the infantile belief that "if you really loved me you would know what I'm thinking, feeling, wanting and needing." Caring for infants and preverbal children requires patience, good will, love, intuition and a willingness to play a guessing game until language development allows the child to express his or her needs. Sometimes the guessing games are carried on too long, planting the seed of an unfortunate fantasy that impedes development of love relationships later in life.

Communication has its risks. Sharing thoughts, feelings, judgments and experiences can generate disagreements. Unlike the infant whose only task is to have his or her needs met, older people must face disagreement, solve complex problems, compromise and use the art of communication more skillfully. Fear can get in the way. Fear of disapproval from a loved one causes some people to retreat to an infantile state of waiting expectation—waiting to be guessed over, cared for and adored. Most adults have limited patience with playing that sort of game with an adult-sized person, however.

Talk is a great gift. Not only can we tell one another stories that impart history and wisdom, we have the ability to tell our feelings, thoughts and needs to any person with whom we have a relationship of mutual caring—be it a relative, teacher, counselor, doctor, partner or lover. It is a privilege *and* a responsibility. If verbal communication is difficult because of impaired hearing or other reasons, other forms of *talk* must be used, such as signing, writing or any agreed upon signal system. If you measure another person's caring by their willingness or ability to correctly guess what is going on inside of you, you lose most of the benefits of shared communication. You also risk losing the relationship itself.

The words *sexual* and *erotic* are sometimes used interchangeably in English. It says something about how this "lingua franca" has both served and shaped the needs of people in places that use it to convey their thoughts, feelings and experiences.

The definition of *erotic* can be expanded to encompass sensual soul-mind-body experiences such as bathing in the awesome colors of a tropical sunset while swimming naked in the still water of a peaceful lagoon at the end of a long, hot day; luxuriating in a loving, sensitive massage in a flower-filled garden surrounded by the soulful music of nature; watching two beautiful lovers approach one another, embrace and pleasure one another with a deliberately slow kiss that contains their passion; or witnessing the aura of glowing skin, fresh aroma and tender touch of a contented, cooing baby being lifted from her warm bath to be wrapped in a towel by loving arms and hands.

The drama of orgasmic, ejaculative genital intercourse involving two individuals building toward a grand moment of climax would be both erotic and sexual, while masturbation made too hasty by the limitations of momentary privacy in an overcrowded, squalid refugee camp could be thought of as a physical release that is sexual without being erotic.

There is more to gay identity than sex. A good share of our communication needs for touch and talk are erotic, without being specifically sexual. But both the sexual and nonsexual erotic aspects of affection in gay relationships may be difficult to recognize and enjoy if you believed it was necessary to hide your gay feelings for a long time.

Many people were trained to play an interactive but manipulative heterosexual game and were told that it was the way of the world—"that's *reality*, get used to it." Women learned to view other women as competitors and men learned to view other men as competitors. It takes some practice to learn how to treat people of the same gender as potential recipients of affection. Women have to learn to trust and respect one another's strength and honesty, while men have to learn how to express affection with something beyond a relatively sanitized handshake or backslap and to respect one another's vulnerability. It is difficult in the beginning, and the learning curve is a long one.

First you have to discover what needs fixing. Look for modes of relating that seem acceptable and comfortable with people of the other gender, yet feel awkward or uncomfortable with someone of the same gender. As soon as you locate one of these trouble spots (like two men kissing hello or two women taking a few minutes to talk shop in the social presence of men), start practicing by performing the uncomfortable deed if it holds any promise of future satisfaction. The best way to take the scare out of the situation is with experience. Then you can re-evaluate it and decide how often or under what circumstances you want it in your behavior repertoire.

Learning to relate sexually is somewhat the same. Learning to relate erotically is more difficult. If you are gay, you have a head start in sexual relating because people of the same gender are put together the same way you are, so you already have a very good general idea of what feels good, what responds to pressure and what responds to a feathery gentle touch. The best way to learn more with a particular individual is to explore one another with an understanding that there is no expectation or demand that either of you do more than you want to at any given moment. Sex should be pleasurable, not a contest or a reviewed performance.

We have learned the hard way that sex is only safe when it is made safe. It need be no less erotic or alluring, however. There are many diseases that are transmitted sexually from one person to another. Syphilis was the sexual plague in previous centuries, promising its victims painful symptoms and, finally, madness. Just a few decades after a cure for syphilis was found, AIDS replaced it with even greater virulence. It is not the act of making love, or being erotic with someone, that transmits these diseases. It is the thoughtless rush to sexual intercourse without taking care to protect yourself and your partner from the exchange of anything from a common cold to a ruinous disease. You must care enough to learn how the diseases of the day are transmitted from one person to another and prevent contagion, while heightening your erotic and sexual pleasure together.

As is true in other social behavior, there are plenty of taboos attached to sex. Using your mouth may seem appealing but you may have been taught that it is appalling. With gradual and sensitive experimentation, you may learn that it is possible to give and receive more pleasure with the use of your mouth.

There are certain preferences that take a little more time for some people. The hurdles may be even higher for men than for women. Men have been trained in all sorts of ways to resist being the open recipient of another man's penis, possibly because of the symbolic conquest or surrender involved. It may, therefore, take some practice learning to relax sphincter muscles in the anus or calm the gag reflex in the throat. Women may also have trouble being assertive and insertive. Purposeful working at releasing such inhibitions will not succeed. Gradual acceptance of your own natural desires *will* permit increased relaxation of your body and your inhibitions so that you may enjoy an increasing variety of genuine erotic and sexual pleasure. Forcing yourself is a violation against yourself.

Learning to play with gay friends can help. You can use a costume party or a romp on a beach as an excuse, if you need one. Gay play is important. When we were children we played in order to grow and learn. We watched our playmates and studied their behavior during play so that we could expand our own behavior vocabulary. We also watched their reactions to us as we expressed feelings in the safe guise of play. We pushed the limits with our playmates and learned how far we could push and which forms of expression were safely tolerated. Learning from play forms the foundation of our individual expressions of self or personality in relation to others. It can be a lot of fun to find one or more gay friends who are brave enough to play together as adult-children, consentually exploring new and changing selves. *Dress up* parties are fun for a start. They are always good for a few laughs, allow the participants to express themselves creatively and usually produce some surprising, if temporary, changes of persona.

Anti-gay mythology tells us that we are freaks whose lives are dominated by unnaturally powerful sexual and erotic desires. It is all too easy for a gay person to believe the mythology since we know our sexual and erotic feelings to be strong (as they are for all people) and we have few role models to study. By definition most of us are breaking the established rules of our culture by honoring our gay feelings, and this appears to support the idea that sexual feelings rule our lives. If we begin to behave as if that assumption were true, it may become distressingly close to the truth.

We are required, therefore, to make a concerted effort at establishing self-respecting patterns of erotic appreciation and gay sexuality. Previous generations of gay people have done it but, for the most part, they were not permitted to pass along their experience and wisdom to us. So you are once again a pioneer, cutting your own trail through the jungle of possibilities. Try to remember that we have lessons to learn from the bonobo.

First there is the matter of defining for yourself the nature of the erotic or sexual satisfaction that you are seeking at any given moment. Is it for recreation or affirmation? Recreational sex and erotic pleasures are available with strangers who may be found in gay bars, baths, the streets, in parks or even in line at the bank or supermarket. In order to keep self-respect intact, however, it is important to ascertain whether both you and your newly found partner are looking for simple fun and physical pleasure or are engaging with one another because of loneliness, a need for comfort, respect, or any other need that is less likely to be satisfied in this manner. Try to be clear in your communication so that you can be good to one another.

There are some hazards involved in sex with strangers in public places. In some cases there may seem to be no alternatives, however. It may be that parks, restrooms or the one local gay bar on the edge of town are the only places where you can meet people who are interested in a homosexual interchange. Often, that is not as true as it seems when you carefully evaluate your situation.

If, however, you do indulge in sexual activities in parks and restrooms, be aware that you are increasing the chances of contracting a sexually transmitted disease, possibly one that is life-threatening, if you do not use a condom and other safe-sex precautions. It could also involve an unpleasant experience with thieves, gay bashers and/or the police. Attractive *vice officers* who act as decoys are aptly named. What begins as a surprising adventure may end as a shocking tragedy with police who feel it is their duty to inform employers, families and newspapers.

Gay bars are socially safer because the people you meet there are less likely to turn out to be vice officers. It is always wise to try to get to know new potential partners (perhaps with several meetings, meeting his or her friends at the bar, going out for coffee, etc.) before going home together. If you do leave with a stranger, however, it is a good idea to make sure that he or she is known in the bar and/or that the bartender has a good look at both of you and knows that you are leaving together. Such precautions slow down but do not prevent the actions of criminals whose motives are less than loving.

Many cities have professional escorts or consorts working through agencies or freelance who, while possibly prevented by law from advertising sex for a fee, are professionals who are paid for their time. They advertise their services in gay newspapers, ordinary newspapers, gay guides and the advertising pages of the telephone directory. The more professional they are, the more willing they should be to be interviewed by phone or in person—giving you an address as well as a telephone number.

Likewise there is a cadre of trained fee-for-service *erotic masseurs* developing worldwide. Some who advertise erotic massage are simply using a code to indicate that they offer sex with or without massage. It is necessary to telephone in response to such advertising and learn the details that interest you, such as whether the person has professional training in massage and/or in a type of erotic massage, whether a massage table is used or it happens on a bed, and so on. Again, the more professional the person, the more willing he or she is to answer questions.

There are many nice gay strangers to be met and I do not wish to increase anyone's level of anxiety by making it all seem scary or disgusting. But it is necessary to be responsible when choosing sexual partners, and that includes being aware of increased risks when meeting strangers in public places. Gay baths and sex clubs offer the safest setting for anonymous sex, although these are routinely raided by police in some parts of the world. International gay travel guides that are revised and reprinted each year are helpful resources.

Take care not to undermine the self-esteem of another gay person you meet in a public setting. If you appear to be available and are approached by someone who is not intrusive but who happens to be someone who does not immediately interest you, take a minute to exchange pleasantries in order to communicate that you value him or her even though you are not interested in interacting erotically or sexually. If you do not make this small effort, you run the risk of implying to yourself that any gay person who does not fit your need of the moment is worthless and disposable. It is an arrogance that will come back to haunt you when you desire someone who does not desire you.

Erotic or sexual contact with a friend may lack some of the excitement and mystery of a new person, but it offers the comfort of someone you already know and trust and you may find affirmation along with your recreation. Another old homosexual myth is the taboo that you must never have sex with a friend because it would spoil the friendship. This was based on the assumption that sex is bad and, therefore, you should not do something bad or shameful with someone you value. If you have grown enough to view sex as wholesome and friendly, there is no reason not to share it with friends. If it feels bad or dirty to you, it is not a good idea to share it with anyone.

And remember that erotic or sexual contact is as broadly defined as you choose to make it; it need not be the *performing of sexual acts.* You can rub one another, sleep together, cuddle up or caress each other, taking responsibility for doing only things that feel right and good. Try to stay in tune with your friend so that each of you is doing only what you both want to do together.

An excellent way to ensure that the encounter turns out exactly as erotic or sexual as both you and your partner wish is to take turns giving one another a massage. If the recipient is aroused, a little more stroking will lead to an orgasm if it is desired. The mystique of the orgasm can be demystified. Through friendly exchanges of massage, there can be friendly exchanges of orgasm, or not, with no one having been misused in the process. It does involve being sensitive to one another's feelings and frank in your verbal sharing of those feelings.

There is no need to feel guilty if you and a friend are not sexually interested in one another. It is worth the effort to check your feelings and make sure that it is a matter of taste and that the disinterest in sex is that simple, rather than a disguise covering the *no sex with friends because it's dirty* taboo. But if neither of you are interested, then you are not interested. Mutuality is important in friendship. If one of you is interested and one of you is not, there is going to have to be some give on both sides until you get the level of erotic interaction set just where you both want it. Without a balance—if one of you is in constant pursuit of the other—there is going to be a silent volcano of resentment that is apt to erupt unexpectedly and damage or end the friendship.

Affirmational sex is difficult to find with strangers. It makes beautiful fiction but it rarely occurs in real life. It takes time for you to get to know one another well enough to know what there is to affirm. Affirmational sex is sought when your resources are low and you are feeling unsure and lonely. It is a primitive, nonverbal communication telling you that you are appreciated. The better your friend knows you when offering sexual affirmation, the more reassuring it is. If your partner knows only the look and feel of your body it is his or her lust that is being affirmed, not your worth. So it is best to seek affirmational sex with lovers or friends of long standing.

Finding affirmational sexual experiences with people you already know may be easier said than done. They are so close to you that while you may have shared erotic moments with them, you may not see them as potential sexual partners. To re-view potential partners you may need to talk it over with them.

Some of the strongest affirmational sex and erotic experience can be had with yourself. Only you can imagine all of the ingredients needed to enhance the ritual. You may want particular music or pictures. Perhaps you might like a special scent, flowers, soft lights or bright sunshine, body lotion or scented oil and your own unique body in a state of erotic gratitude as all of it is awakened and pleasured with all the time in the world available. It can be a meditation and a celebration. Your spiritual self most certainly can be present also.

Adam, a man now in his senior years, described his surprise at discovering intimate friendship. "You know my first lover and I had no idea who we were or what we were doing with each other except that we needed the sex and we were imitating all the heterosexual married people we knew for the few years that we lasted together. Then, after seven years alone, it was good to get into a relationship with Raphael. He was kind and we were good to one another. But it wasn't until he was dying that we let all the defenses down, gave ourselves to one another entirely, and learned about intimacy. Now, after six years alone, I've met James on a gay retreat that I was reluctant to join. He lives several time zones away and was born in a different time in history, so he grew up in a different world. Neither of us sees the other as a partner or lover exactly and yet the intimacy started the first day we met. We liked each other right away and there didn't seem to be any point in not telling the truth to one another about everything. I have those last months with Raphael to thank for it. James and I have an intimate friendship that reaches across all those miles, includes sex, and I don't mind being alone so much anymore. I have a friend—a real friend."

It does seem easier to learn about intimacy with someone who is beginning adult life and is entirely open or with someone who is preparing to leave life and finds no reason to be less than open. They can help us to see that the laughter and tears that give voice to moments of real pleasure and pain are not to be feared or hidden.

As gay people, we experience more than our share of the pleasures and pains presented by life; we are keenly aware of the high price of hiding; and we have had to face death on an unprecedented scale—all of which gives us a unique perspective on intimacy. "I think it's the gift of the gods," Adam told me, describing his experiences with intimacy. "I see now that it's got to be earned, though. You have to be willing to let your hair down and put some effort into caring about the other person and let him know what's going on." Well said.

Intimacy, the grand prize in human relationships, is earned with awareness, willingness and effort. You must come out of hiding, use every form of communication available and risk the demons of judgment, rejection and abandonment. Only then will you find the rare relationships in which you give and receive unconditional affection and experience the appreciative acceptance of your whole self.

14
FAMILY

I DIDN'T GET ANY CHOICE about where I was born or the family I was born into," Brian said, "but now I have lots of choices to make about who is in my family and where we live. The where is a suburb of San Francisco, California right now and the who starts with Jake and the kids."

Brian grew up in New York City "with a Puerto Rican type cop Pop and a fourth grade teacher Irish-Italian type Mom who spends off hours on her knees praying for me. All but one of my sisters think I'm weird and Pop doesn't want to know. Jake's Dad is a Methodist minister in Wisconsin. His Mom's a retired nurse. He comes from a long line of pretty blonds, all praying for him."

They adopted their five year old daughter from China when she was an orphaned infant. Their two year old Africa-American son's drug addicted mother died soon after he was born, his father unknown.

"If we were religious types we would say we're blessed. We've been able to buy this big old house we call The Melting Pot. We've told the agencies we're open for foster-care or adoption of any gay kid who might turn up. Brian works half-time as an attorney at a non-profit and half time in a private practice with partners. I'm a half-time writer and a half-time therapist. We have one part-time African-American nanny and one part-time housekeeper from Mexico who cooks vegetarian for us. We also have one dog, two cats and great friends. We're all set. Too bad our original families think we're sinners. They'll get over it or they won't. We were married for six months until the state's Supreme Court forced us to live in sin again when they cancelled our marriage. Idiots."

Brian described their Melting Pot as a "Twenty-first century non-traditional traditional family." He says that half of their lesbian and gay friends have opted for children in their families while half have not. Among those who do have children, there have been a variety of choices—a lesbian couple co-parenting with a pair of gay dads who agreed to artificial insemination, some with offspring from previous marriages, some from adoptions and some from foster care.

"I looked around when I was a kid and saw that I didn't fit. You can really get tortured as a kid and I didn't like the rough and tumble guy stuff but I was attracted to some of the guys. I liked cooking and sewing. I figured I must be a girl with a penis. I liked pretty things. I tried dresses and makeup which sent my Mom to her priest. One teacher was brave enough to say I must be a transsexual. It wasn't until high school that I got a look at gay guys who went to the gym, danced and had nice clothes and nice apartments and I thought 'Yeah. That's me.' I'm not a woman in a man's body but it would be okay if I was and we're open to that for foster care or adoption also. We want this to be a place that's safe for kids to be who they are—parents too."

Nor do all gay families involve children, marriage or domestic partners. LGBT people are keenly aware of their need and responsibility in choosing the members of the family they claim in adult life.

"A few of my friends call me Sophie," Anne said. "You know the old Sophie Tucker song, 'I'm Livin' Alone and I Like It.' Maybe I'll get hitched someday but at fifty years of age I like it the way it is for now. I'm available but not hunting. I like my job and my little apartment. One of my brothers and one of my sisters are in my adult family of people I love. There's also one ex-girlfriend, lesbians old and young, a handful of gay guys I love and call my brothers, and my mother's mother who fits right in with the rest of us."

Finding a friend, lover or life-partner can be difficult but it is not as difficult as most people imagine. It can, and often does, happen in unusual ways. The usual "Where did you two meet?" question can elicit amusing answers from gay couples.

At a dinner party I saw two men answer the question by quickly looking at one another and laughing. Finally, one of them answered. "Lettuce," he said.

"I always say tomatoes," the other answered.

The first partner said, "Both of us were looking at some gorgeous guy who was picking tomatoes at the other end of the produce counter in the supermarket. As I reached for a head of lettuce, I grabbed this male hand instead. Jay and I looked at one another, let go, stammered apologies, blushed, turned away, started to leave, remembered the lettuce and, not looking again, did the same hand-grabbing routine all over again!"

"We each thought the other one was kind of cute but dumb and too apologetic," his partner put in, "but you know—grabbing the same stranger's hand twice has to mean something so when we found ourselves hurriedly heading for the same checkout line at the same minute, there was nothing that we could do except laugh. While we were standing in line I said, 'Nice hand,' and with a very straight face he said, 'Good grip.' We exchanged telephone numbers in the parking lot."

Two women told me they had met at a wedding. "It was my brother's very formal wedding. There were a lot of people. I thought she was involved with the guy she came with and she thought I was the other married sister. But we kept noticing each other and smiling at one another across the room. When the bridal bouquet was tossed, she caught it like a fly ball and looked at me instead of some guy and she winked! Shameless hussy. I knew I was in trouble so I walked right over to her and she handed me a flower and here we are ten years later."

One half of a male couple said, "I was in Paris on business and there he was waiting for me on a Wednesday evening—at the baths near the opera. Of course our parents think we met one another in Notre Dame."

His partner arched an eyebrow and said, "Well, I told my family that he came in answer to my prayer. They jumped to the conclusion it was in church and ask no more questions—and I told no lies."

Humans, gay or not, are social animals who require companionship and community. We need friends and most of us need a certain amount of the complex, intimate sharing that is possible with a lover, spouse or life-partner. Most societies promote some kind of formal, legal marriage. If it is seen as a *privilege* to be sanctioned and controlled by religion and law, it gives rulers a powerful tool that is useful in controlling the population.

Though most gay people are currently denied this privilege so as to keep us in our place as *less worthy* or second-class citizens, we too are influenced by the propaganda that a (heterosexual) marriage will yield security and lifetime happiness. We feel pressure to find our mate as quickly as possible. In the unsure world in which gay people live, it would be nice if one person could provide for all of our needs. Even the chance that it might be true is sufficient reason for many of us to want to win the lifetime-partner contest. But how do I find her? Where do I find him?

There is a Zen saying to the effect that when the student is ready, the master will appear. I think that it is similarly true for lovers, life-partners and friends. First make yourself into the kind of person you want her or him to be. While you busy yourself with this task, your expectations change. They become more realistic and drawn to a human scale because you experience what goes into becoming such a person. Meanwhile, you naturally become more attractive and interesting to exactly that sort of person. And, finally, you are likely to find yourself in places where that sort of person is to be found.

Developing nourishing friendships that may include erotic contact and sex is important. Too many people rush about looking for a spouse or lifetime partner as if such a person were the grand prize in a scavenger hunt. The loved-one sought is not the missing item hidden in the undergrowth, however, but one of the many flowers in the meadow. Learn the names of the flowers in your meadow well and let them take their individual places in a natural order of emotional importance. If one of them becomes most important, he or she is a candidate for lifetime partner. But this process takes time and care.

When the friend, lover or life-partner appears, a relationship begins. It must be tended. The more conscious you are in setting the foundation of your relationship the more stable it will be in the years ahead. Consciously lowering your defenses with one another, one small step at a time, carries you in the direction of intimacy. All intimate relationships require mutual acceptance, but before there can be acceptance, it must be possible to see one another. That does not mean tearing off all of your protective layers immediately. You have learned to keep them in place so as not to get hurt too easily. Removing too much of the defensive structure too quickly leaves a need for protection that the other person may not be able to provide.

The most important component of a solid foundation is clear communication. In addition to touch, there must be talk that reveals and clarifies. It never does any harm to repeat to the other person what you believe that she or he has told you. It offers an opportunity to correct small misunderstandings before they become large misunderstandings. You must also have the courage to say difficult small truths rather than the seemingly innocent little lies that are easier. Each small fib told in the first weeks of a relationship, later revealed in unguarded moments, provides a reason for doubt about anything said in the months and years that follow.

It is also helpful to remember that this special someone is an individual, attached to you perhaps, but a separate being entitled to have his or her separate identity respected. No matter how clear your vision of what is worthwhile and what works best in the world, you have neither the right nor the ability to remodel another person without a specific request or permission to offer that sort of assistance. If you try you will find a stone wall of defense and a creature on the other side of it ready to fight you tooth and nail. She or he has devoted years to integrating the bits and pieces that go into his or her unique makeup.

Your motto might be *respect without neglect*. The other person is a special individual, attached or attaching to the special individual who is you. The reason you are building a relationship together is because you both want the love, acceptance, care and communication that you can offer one another. Offer yourself generously, genuinely and respectfully.

Perhaps the greatest gift you can give to a family relationship is *active listening*. You know from your own experience in life how wonderful it feels to know that you have been heard and understood by someone who cares about you. You're on the same team. Listen carefully. Be supportive. Be accepting. Be present. Listen with care rather than with criticism or correction. When you do not understand how this person could have said or done something, listen again. Clarify what you believe you are hearing. People always have reasons for their behavior. If you understand the reasons, you will usually understand the behavior. Use your empathic abilities to feel what this person has felt and is feeling and then ask if that is truly what the feeling is.

You will have your own turn also. You can and must tell about your own thoughts and feelings with the hope of being heard and understood. You have the responsibility to speak as clearly as you are able about your wants and needs without expecting your beloved family member to read your mind. What magic there is in a relationship begins with truth told aloud. And it never does any harm for both of you to develop the habit of sincerely saying, "Thank you for telling me that"—especially when you guess that the telling has been difficult.

Positive rituals can become an integral and pleasing part of the structure of a relationship. One man I know bakes a loaf of bread once a week on his day off and presents it at the evening meal he prepares for himself and his partner. Two women have a ritual of washing one another's hair. Another female couple reads to each other in bed before going to sleep every night that they are together. Such rituals help to shape the framework of a relationship, making it stronger and more able to weather the difficult times that come.

And then there is jealousy. A heterosexual marriage or otherwise recognized heterosexual union has community support behind it. This does not entirely solve the problem of jealousy, but it provides a certain amount of security to soften the pain of jealousy. Gay spouses, partners or lovers have less support. Settled gay couples are not as visible if they are invited less often *as a couple* to general social gatherings and, like heterosexual couples, spend a large portion of their leisure time alone together or within a small circle of friends. Settled, long-term gay couples must deal with the question of sexual jealousy just as sexually active heterosexual couples must, unless a path of permanent monogamy has been agreed upon and is durable.

Monogamy is an agreement between two people. It can add depth to loving feelings because of the willingness of both partners to turn away from other sexual temptations in order to achieve greater security together.

When one person in a committed relationship feels a need for variety in his or her sexual experience, it is time to re-evaluate the sexual agreement. Monogamy need not be viewed as an identity. It is a tool that couples choose to use because they believe its explicit declaration of priorities strengthens the relationship. But monogamy can do as much harm as good if it is used unquestioningly and without regard for its suitability at given periods in the relationship.

Monogamy works only if both partners believe that they are gaining because of it. If one or both partners become restless and want other sexual experiences, new agreements that continue to recognize the primacy of the relationship while permitting some sexual involvement elsewhere and meeting the needs of both partners, must be worked out as quickly as possible. If monogamy becomes a prison, someone will find a way to break out and keep traveling. Whatever the new agreement, it must apply equally to both partners. An agreement of one-sided monogamy can build terrible resentment.

Jealousy is not to be underestimated. It is probably due, in part, to the biological programming of our species. Your DNA is determined to win in nature's lottery of propagation—even when the parties involved cannot possibly inseminate one another for possible reproduction. There is a simple but persistent urge to merge.

In many parts of the world, jealousy is strongly supported by the rules of society and, of course, it is reinforced by the power of orgasm. The catastrophic fantasies behind it involve possible defeat in a contest of rivalry, rejection, abandonment and awful loneliness. We rarely feel jealousy or panic if our spouse shares himself or herself with others in other ways, but we respond with alarm if sex is shared elsewhere. We need to safeguard all present and future eggs in the nest!

Perhaps you have been taught that sex is always the expression of, or synonymous with *love*. In fact this is sometimes true, but it can as easily be the expression of other feelings including simple sexual desire, boredom or loneliness. Love is expressed by the quality of hundreds of daily interactions, not just during sexual intercourse. But it is very tempting to cling to the notion that love and sex are the same thing and that if my spouse or partner is sharing sex with someone else, he or she is presumably sharing the love that should belong to me.

The enormity of the fear and hurt makes it necessary to find solutions that maximize the comfort of both partners. The special danger for gay couples is that you will yield in pain and confusion to the thousands of subtle messages telling you that it is wrong to be in this kind of relationship. There is always the temptation to give up, but this is especially treacherous for gay couples because there is so little support for staying together unless the couple has surrounded themselves socially with a group of other stable, long-term gay couples.

Sometimes brief loving excursions with other people enrich us in ways that deepen the relationship with a primary partner, but, because it is *forbidden*, you are playing with fire. Many of us have been taught that love is like a loaf of bread: If someone takes a bite out of my loaf, there will be that much less bread there for me. If love were truly consumable it would soon vanish and we would all be very unhappy. One might instead compare love to a muscle and consider that the more you use it, the more it grows.

But in fact, it is possible that we may learn to love more deeply *and* change the direction of our affections. If you are going to share sex and loving with people other than your partner, it is your responsibility to provide adequate verbal and physical reassurance to your partner that he or she is not valued any less, or you will suffer the considerable consequences, which can include loss of the relationship.

When a committed couple agrees to open their relationship to erotic and sexual experiences with other people, communication once again becomes crucial. It is necessary to express doubts and fears and to ask for reassurance. If the two do not live together, doubts and fears are easily magnified. Telephone and electronic mail can be very helpful. Whether or not the couple lives together, a plan that can help in the opening of the relationship is to have the security of a weekly schedule that both can count on but that contains certain evenings or days of the week when both are free to make individual plans without prior consultation with the other. If the couple is living together it helps, especially in the beginning, to declare the home off-limits to amorous activity with other people, since that primitive jealousy process that requires guarding the nest is easily stirred.

Witnessing the AIDS epidemic and the suddenly abbreviated lives of so many friends and loved ones has forced lesbians and gay men to reconsider our basic beliefs and values. We have had to mature quickly as individuals and as a community. We have had to develop in ways that ordinarily would have taken generations.

We have learned that we must beware of tender spots, the unspoken hurts that come so easily in the areas of sexuality, intimacy and privacy. Early twentieth-century sexual and social norms were painful shackles to the gay person. Sexual liberation during the second half of the century permitted the creation of another set of seemingly mandatory norms—especially for gay men. But some people, gay men included, found that the new norms created an equally isolating, painful prison.

Many gay people grow up feeling unwanted. In a family relationship we seek and need peace and security. We need to know that the other person values us. There is a giving of self, each to the other, unfashionable during the early days of our liberation.

This bonding is in some ways as simple and primitive as the bonding of other creatures. It requires that I place *our* welfare on a plane that is synonymous with *my* welfare. I am motivated to help us, protect us, and in all ways see to our well-being. To do this, I must learn continually about my beloved family member and what nourishes her. I must learn what makes him feel safe. I must learn to accept this person as is while knowing that she is also changing in her own ways. I must concentrate on appreciating my understanding of him as is. Only then dare I hope for the same.

The essential bond is formed and developed as two people cast their lots in life together, finding their ways within the relationship to abandon competition and the lonely isolation of self-protection. To do this requires a period of learning and true engagement with one another. In that process resolve is tested, ways found and strength developed.

In a gay marriage we cannot say "forsaking all others." We need our brotherhood and sisterhood. We need to find our ways of acknowledging our appreciation of one another, including our honest feelings of sexual attraction for one another that are both within and beyond the marriage. And we need to do this in our own way, not in the stylized heterosexual manner that has failed. It is here that our heightened sense of humanity can help us to transcend the bonding of other animals. We can, must and do find ways to celebrate the truth of our eroticism while protecting security and the sense of being valued.

Maturity involves willingness to admit mistakes, courage to search for new answers and the inner security that permits one to consider previously rejected solutions that may be worth looking at again. I used to wince when I heard someone talk about "working on our relationship." It sounded like a house or an automobile that needed repair work. But one day someone was in my office speaking lovingly about working on his relationship and the image that came to me was of someone happily at work, lovingly making a comforter or quilt. It was not repair, not a chore, but active, happy creation that he was talking about. It was a sweet, cozy sort of image.

Old-fashioned wisdom is returning. It was missed while it was missing. I think of how gay couples, particularly male couples, are learning to remember to say "I love you" more often when they happen to be feeling it. People are remembering to share private feelings that were once considered too sentimental. A woman friend told me that she had been sitting in the living room with her partner "with a thought going around in my mind for a full four minutes before I could say it." She felt shy about it. "I was stupidly looking at the minute hand go around on the clock on the mantle and I finally had the courage to say, 'I really want to grow old with you. I hope we do.' We both had a good cry, a warm hug and a wonderful kiss."

These thoughts, best said aloud, are vital. They can give your partner or family member a sense of well-being and security. Of course, it is also a good idea *not* to say such things unless you are sincerely feeling them lest you "cry wolf" too often and ruin any chance that your partner will hear the ring of truth when you *are* feeling them strongly.

Humiliation and its connection to wounded pride and damaged self-esteem is a particularly sensitive issue for gay people. You must know your family member well if you are to avoid accidental humiliation. When in doubt, it is best to refrain from possibly embarrassing behavior until you can check it out with the person. Older and younger people and partners from different cultures may experience humiliation in different circumstances. This is not too difficult to understand if some thought is given to it. A younger person may be sensitive to any suggestion that the older person is being patronizing about a relative lack of experience in life. The older person may be sensitive to any suggestion that the younger person is attracted to another younger person. A monogamous person may feel humiliated by a once non-monogamous partner's casual references to previous sexual relationships.

Like Brian, you had no choice about where you were born or the caregivers who tended you early in your life. Now there are choices. Choose your adult family with love and care. Include young and old, gay and non-gay. People from different cultures can add to life. Be respectful, responsible and protective. Take good care of them and let them take good care of you.

15

CHANGE

Humans, like most animals, seek security. When we sense or suspect a lack of safety we go on alert. The emergency systems hard-wired into us from millions of years of evolution get ready. Our fight-or-flight reactions are poised. We are uneasy, fearful. Tolerating fear leads to every sort of problem for our bodies and for our emotional state as well as affecting our ability to interact sensibly with our environment. We become unbalanced.

Change creates opportunities but, because it represents the unknowable future, it can also stimulate fear, especially if it is helped to do so. Opportunistic politicians and religious leaders are aware of this phenomenon. They use the fear associated with change to their advantage, stirring fear while promising security to the loyal and conforming who fall in line behind them.

Throughout recorded human history, different peoples in different times and places have created different gods and sworn loyalty to them. Sometimes it is a variety of gods, sometimes just one. The gods are believed to have superhuman powers. The will and wishes of the gods are conceived, interpreted and communicated by their priests. Rules of right and wrong behavior are issued in the gods' names. Not infrequently people are called to war to show sacrifice, patriotism, loyalty and faith that their god is more right and powerful than another god; also securing and gaining rights and property for current rulers by competitively killing, maiming, torturing, raping, pillaging and plundering along the way.

In the first years of this century the man installed as President of the United States was able to achieve election to a second term by stirring fear while promising security. Gay people in the nation were demanding and gaining equality in civil rights, including the right to choose marriage. Having led the nation into war with the stirred fear that another nation had weapons of mass destruction that would be used soon, he and his political advisors then rallied those citizens who shared anti-gay religious prejudice with fear that their first-class status was being threatened by gay people refusing to accept second-class status.

The logic was correct. If there is no second-class, there can be no first-class since everyone has the same rights. He and his political advisors called for a national constitutional ban on gay marriage. Such a ban would make religious bigotry legal in a nation constitutionally dedicated to separation of religion and government.

Marriage is between one man and one woman only, they said, using religion-toned words such as *sanctity*, spoken solemnly. His opponent felt forced to agree.

Why? Who says? On what authority?

"God says so," the President's people answered.

Oh.

This cynical political strategy was successful, rationalized behind closed doors no doubt with a vague concept of some *greater good* gained by sacrificing an expendable portion of the nation's citizens. Fear was stirred. Security was promised if the proper sacrifice was made. God would be pleased. The President was elected, using war and prejudice instead of the usual promises of peace and prosperity. In a nation strongly divided in that election, eleven states joined others in outlawing gay marriage, some doctoring conscience by allowing *some* second-class rights to people registering domestic partnerships with the state.

Lesbians and gay men demanding equal rights do represent change. We are, indeed, a queer tribe and can be used to stir fear among people who do not know us well. We are born into every kind of family and nation in the world, yet most of us have more in common with one another than with the people of the community into which we are born. Nature sees to it that we persist. Whether or not we are appreciated, we are of great potential value *because* we are different. We are an opportunity.

We are the men who love men and the women who love women. Perhaps we serve nature's purpose less with *procreation* than with *creation*. Nature sees to reproduction for every kind of creature. It is nothing to boast about. But creativity is another matter. What is important is not a human's reproductive ability—not what is reproduced but what is *produced*. Our creativity can, and does, take many forms. Simply by being ourselves—being gay—we create an awareness of the value of people who are *other* or *different*. Our families, neighbors and co-workers are forced to notice us and must try to come to some understanding of our place in their world.

Eventually we may help non-gay people to live in less fear of strangers. We may be able to help the world find the way to peace. Gay men have the musculature and reflexes of the male warrior, but we also have the attractions and desires of the potential lover of male strangers. Gay women have the impulses and strength to fight off intruders and protect the nest but also the attractions and desires of the potential lover of female strangers who, instead, may be invited to share the nest.

We have come to a wonderful time in our collective development as gay people. Thanks to today's modes of information, communication and travel, we can find one another in distant places more easily. We can compare thoughts and feelings and generate a deeper understanding between us. We can separate layers of societal training from our core of inner truth. It permits us to understand our development, our maturation as individuals and to carefully select our elder-guides and mentors, to learn what we can bring to them and gain from them as we become the guides and mentors ourselves.

Most religions have treated us shamefully. Few lesbians and gay men have not been harmed personally in some way by institutionalized religion. Yet we have been drawn to religions of all sorts. Many priests, rabbis, ministers, sisters, brothers and other religious leaders are gay. This fact persists even though these same institutions have persecuted us and shown little understanding, compassion or mercy toward us. Many of us practice the doctrine that many of them merely preach. In a very real sense, we are their contemporary martyrs and they continue to fail to recognize us.

Religious lesbians and gay men searching for alternatives built organizations that could communicate with religious establishments. The Metropolitan Community Church spread from Los Angeles, California, to other communities, states and nations. It famously welcomes lesbians and gay men into the congregation and into its ministry.

Roman Catholics founded *Dignity* and other religions followed with their own representative groups designed to engage in dialogue with their religious leaders. Their work has required persistent persuasion and a willingness to forgive.

Less conservative groups have looked for new forms of worship. *Radical fairies* and *lesbian* witches have been followed by *Sacred Intimates*, *Gay Spirit Vision*, *Flesh and Spirit* Community and many other groups. They have broadened the concept of "church" or "temple" and helped increase awareness of our unmet spiritual needs. As a result, we have seen the establishment of predominantly gay congregations in individual churches as well as the creation of gay synagogues, though loyal believers in several large religions continue to argue among themselves about whether we can be full members of their communities.

The AIDS epidemic brought a merciless confrontation with the fact of human mortality and increased the urgency of our collective spiritual search. Many ailing people returned to the religions of their childhood, some temporarily, knowing that any comfort they found would be mixed with the same psychological punishment they had experienced earlier in their lives.

It is acceptable now to compare one's spiritual thoughts and feelings with others and to ask for help. A muscular, deep-voiced bartender said, "Hell, I don't know how to explain God, but don't push me to explain electricity or microchips either. I thank God I found my way to A.A. and that I have a good job and a roof over my head. There may not be an old man in a dress sitting on a cloud but it sure feels like I'm getting listened to and I don't mind getting on my knees."

Our foundation has become stronger. A three-legged stool is a lot more sturdy than a two-legged stool. We see the value of having intellect, emotions and spirituality in harmony. One can integrate the three while remaining keenly aware of the body and its needs. We are helping the world learn to face up to the challenge of keeping intellectual, emotional, spiritual and physical needs shamelessly together as one moves through the maze of inevitable changes that happen in a lifetime—those anticipated and those unanticipated.

Thanks to the work of anthropologists and historians, we know that there is no standard of beauty that holds true in all parts of the world, nor is there one that has held true through recorded history. The most constant, perhaps, is a kind of radiance that seems to come from within and communicates to other people. It is sometimes called *charisma*.

But shape, height, weight and proportion are seen as beautiful, passing, boring or ugly according to the styles and taste of the time and place. The same holds true for age. Youth is more often seen as pretty to look at and touch, age as an accumulated beauty. Values assigned to the two influence the local opinion of attractiveness.

Getting beyond negative training about age is essential. Each of us is growing older. Too many of us are taught to worship youth. If you follow the dictates of that training it means that, with luck, you will perceive yourself and others as desirable for a fraction of your lifetime. If you live your life with care you should gain in beauty, wisdom, depth and even sexual know-how as the years accumulate. You bring much more than your body to any human intercourse—and that includes sexual intercourse. To permit yourself to be discarded or devalued, or to treat other people that way because they are halfway or more through their lifetimes, is as sensible as throwing away the candy and eating the wrapper.

Youth does have its beauty. The bud is lovely because of the promise of the unspoiled flower soon to appear. Youth deserves respect and admiration for its potential, for its newness and promise, just as age should be respected and admired for what it has accomplished, for the accumulated wisdom and beauty.

Younger people who seem jaded, opinionated and set in their ways have little to offer you except a youthful body with better muscle tone. What the growth-oriented younger person has to offer is a fresh perspective, new questions and new ideas. It is young people who furnish much of the fuel for the emancipation of gay people. Elders of our tribe use their wisdom to point the way but it takes the energy and optimism of each new generation to put into practice what wise elders plan and predict.

We must appreciate both the stimulating promise of youth *and* the stimulating richness of age and remember which way we are all heading. Both young and old can be appreciated as friends, lovers and life partners. Because everyone is growing older, valuing older people helps with the direction of one's own life. Driving down the road looking in the rearview mirror can be hazardous to your health.

Death is part of life. Gay people have had enough collective experience with death to realize how necessary it is to live every day of every relationship as if it may be the last. It is not wise to leave things unsaid or undone, communication incomplete. It makes the grieving more difficult, filled with thoughts of "if only we had... ."

When you lose someone you love the initial pain of grief can be a powerful shock, even though you may have anticipated the death for days or weeks. A death is as awesome to witness as a birth. The impact is usually greater if you are present at this moment of transition, but it is intense also if you are not physically present and receive the news at a later time. In the case of a birth, there is usually plenty of time to see the newborn—to digest the knowledge of this new person in your world. In the case of a death, it may be possible to view the body of the person who was—but the person is no longer here in our world. She or he has departed the body—vanished.

Following the initial painful shock of grief there is the work of mourning to be done. It is as if every memory, thought and feeling that you have ever had and ever will have about the deceased must now be reset in mind and memory. Present and planned future are moved to the past. The current present and new future have to be filled in. People in mourning suffer fatigue, increased dream activity and absentmindedness. They may need reminding that there is emotional and cognitive work being done both while awake and asleep. It takes its toll in time and energy and it has a priority of urgency. If the mourning process is not given the time and energy needed, the mourner may become ill and be forced to spend time in bed, where reweaving of the related past, present and future can take place with less distraction.

Again, though they may fight it or try to ignore it, people usually discover intuitively what will help during the mourning period. One coping strategy is to talk aloud to the person who has died. It is best not to inhibit this impulse because it seems silly or irrational. It has nothing to do with what is rational. There is a kind of communication that needs to happen—things to talk over, unfinished business and the sorrow itself to share. Giving voice to the intuitive need does no harm, it only helps.

There are tears to be shed, sometimes coming at inconvenient moments or times that seem socially inappropriate. Whenever the tears come is the right time to shed them. Death is a part of life others may be uncomfortable with because they are not quite ready to face that fact. Tears at any time are an important and appropriate part of the healing process.

There are thoughts, feelings and memories to be shared—a desire to talk *about* the person who has died with people who knew both of you. Sometimes friends or colleagues, in a misguided wish to help or out of embarrassment at their apparent inability to help, will tell you that the time has come to put the death behind you and move on. "You mustn't dwell on it. You have your whole future life ahead of you."

The last is correct, the first is wrong. You do have your whole future life ahead of you—however long that may be, and you will get to it sooner and live it longer and in better shape if you trust your feelings. Talk about or *dwell* on memories of the deceased for as long and as often as you honestly feel the need. You are tending to your business, the business of mourning. To be forced to keep these thoughts, feelings and memories secret inside of you is to be forced to be dishonest and only confuses and hinders the healing process.

Treat yourself tenderly, with care. A person in mourning is in a delicate condition. Remember to take a deep breath once in a while. Consider taking naps and getting a massage.

You might profit from talking with a religious counselor. If you are a member of a religious group or inclined toward a particular religion, there are rituals and guidelines that can help you through the process of mourning. Or, you may have a need to follow your own spiritual path and create a personally meaningful ritual such as a contribution of time and/or money to a suitable charity, flowers tossed in the sea, a poem read in the woods, a prayer and a stone left in the desert or a handmade monument left on a mountain top. Being outdoors in nature as often as possible helps.

It is also wise to consult an enlightened physician. There are medications that can help to give you a better night's sleep, alleviate anxiety and help you up the first rung if you are at the bottom of a ladder of depression. Make sure your physician has personally experienced the pain of grief and mourning and does not espouse the conviction that the more suffering you endure the better you are. The suggestion that *good soldiers* should just tough it out when it is *merely* emotional pain is needlessly cruel and potentially damaging.

The emotional pain of grief and the process of mourning will surely slow you down. You will not be your normal self. But if you sense that it is going on too long or slowing you down too much in ways that interfere with living, consult a psychotherapist or grief counselor. The need for such a consultation is not a symptom of insanity or weakness, it is a symptom of wisdom.

In addition to death, another unanticipated loss that enters the lives of gay people and the people who love them is the end of a marriage or other close relationship. If the relationship has been based on the understanding that both partners are not gay, when one partner discovers or becomes able to admit that he or she is gay, *it* may mean the end of the relationship.

Some individuals choose to keep the relationship together, altering it as little as possible, making it better where feasible. When this happens in a heterosexual marriage, it can be difficult and painful. It takes enormous generosity to try to help one another meet differing needs. After the disclosure, the gay partner in the marriage often experiences a drop in heterosexual desire. It may be a compensatory reaction to years of having overworked heterosexual desire. It rarely means that the spouse is loved less, only that the sexual desire has shifted. It may be possible for the relationship to accommodate the change. It is one of many hurdles to be cleared in keeping the marriage going. But it is possible.

If one or both partners in a relationship decide that it is time to part, it is difficult to maintain mutual love and respect. We become dependent on a secure, loving relationship. We know it will end someday with the death of one of the partners, but that is in the future and not the result of choice.

It is often too difficult to reconnect until the initial storm of pain and fury is spent. A former wife of a gay man told me, "Now that we're getting to know one another again, some of the old solid love is there. At least I have that and the memories to show for the years. It didn't all just die and go away. We mean something to one another and still care about one another."

A former husband of a lesbian said, "She was willing to try to work things out so that we could stay together. I've wondered, but I think it was right to part ways. She could not be monogamous. It was okay with her if I had affairs. But I need monogamy. It makes me feel safe, I guess. I still love her. It's too bad, but there was a basic flaw in the match."

Another unanticipated loss is the temporary or permanent loss of a loved one to addiction. Outcasts and people otherwise socially disadvantaged are more likely to fall prey to substance abuse. It may be alcohol or some other drug, food, work or sex. At first, it may seem to be only a pleasant distraction that numbs emotional pain. For some individuals the distraction becomes a habit, the point of no return is passed, and she or he discovers too late that they are emotionally and/or physiologically dependent on the distraction in a way that causes pain when it is denied them. By then they are addicted, slaves to the distraction. Addiction interferes with close relationships because it becomes the most important relationship.

Watching this process and trying to interact with the person and his or her addiction is awful. Attempts to help are doomed to frustrating failure as everyone concerned is caught in a web of deception and misunderstandings. In fact, it can become an all-consuming venture that may eventually grow into another kind of addiction. The would-be helper becomes addicted to their continuing ineffectual efforts to help the addict. By then both people are caught in a new kind of relationship, one of *dependence* and *co-dependence*.

It is a vicious circle. The only hope is that, sooner or later, one or both people involved will seek help from a program designed to deal with addictions. For the dependent addict there is help waiting from Alcoholics Anonymous and Narcotics Anonymous as well as other twelve-step and private programs in centers established to treat substance abuse. For the co-dependent addict there is Alanon, a related twelve-step program, as well as private organizations affiliated with those that treat substance abuse.

The loss of a beloved dog, cat or other animal companion can be heartbreaking. For many of us, it is the loss of the only unconditional love we have experienced. It, too, can come suddenly and unexpectedly, despite our knowledge that the animal's lifespan will be shorter than ours. An accident or sudden illness can take away the easy love and companionship that was there always, waiting and available, asking so little in return. A veterinary student once told me that she thought humans had mistakenly imagined angels to look like us. "I think they usually have fur and like to get close to you," she said.

The death of an animal companion can catch at the vulnerable, unguarded part of loving, opening the door to other pockets of grief that had been shut away. "I thought I was getting hardened after so many friends died," one man told me. "But when Elizabeth got sick and I had to put her down, it was a chain reaction. My grief was a flood and I was lost in it."

It shocks me when someone says, "I don't know why she's carrying on so. It was only an animal." I wonder if this lack of sensitivity betrays a rigidity of perception, a lack of understanding that love has many faces—some with whiskers.

Whenever there has been an unanticipated loss, or when one is confronted with imminent loss, there is grief and mourning to come.

It is a good idea to consider seeking counseling and to make use of a support group, if possible. The loss, or prospect of it, may open up a nightmare world of fears that were brushed aside, out of conscious awareness. Humans are marvelously adaptive, but we need help getting through dark places, and more often than not, the help is there if we let it be known that we need it and are not too filled with foolish false pride to take the offered hand.

We cannot dwell on all the uncertainties of the future or anticipate and prepare for losses in our lives. It would cause emotional imbalance. We can, however, accept the fact that it is likely that we will face unanticipated loss and be prepared to ask for help to get through it. We can also do the best loving we can do and stay up-to-date in our important relationships, treasuring rather than wasting the days we have together.

We remind ourselves that change is constant. The world is changing always. Gay people are changing, coming out, demanding equal rights as citizens. These rights are appearing.

Politicians and religious leaders who fall victim to their need for power do prey on people's fear of an unknowable future. Some are able to blind themselves to their true motivation, spouting platitudes and imagining that their god has ordained their actions. But somewhere in such a deluded mind there is awareness that they are harming others. If they truly believe in their god's omniscience they must believe that they are being watched and will be called to answer for their actions. If they cynically use God as a club while not truly believing such an entity exists, there must be a shadowed awareness that they will one day come to their own end and face memories of their deeds and misdeeds. They will wonder about the value of their lifetime. No amount of rationalization can comfort them as they confront the truth.

They may be bold and desperate enough to ask us to forgive them. For our own good, and the good of the world, we must strive to develop our compassion. We may be compassionate enough to offer such forgiveness when their misdeeds are confessed. Maybe.

16

PRIDE

IT WAS A SUNNY SUNDAY morning in June and the annual gay parade on Market Street in San Francisco had been in full swing for hours. I saw a space on the curb next to two women and asked if it was free. The sun reflected brightly on Ruth's bifocals as she squinted up at me, patted the curb, and said, "Free for the right person. You a senior?" I assured her that I qualified and could show identification.

"You live here?" I nodded affirmatively.

"Gay?" Another affirmative nod.

"And you?" I asked.

"I'm Ruth—Ruthie to my friends and this is Brenda." Brenda smiled and extended a hand. "I'll answer the rest in a minute. But first you should tell your mayor of this wonderful city that they should line the whole parade route with little chairs for seniors on this day. The graying of America, you know. Some of us can't stand up all day."

"There's a cable car on wheels for seniors who want to be in the parade and don't want to walk," I offered.

"Yeah, well, that's it. First of all, who wants to be cooped up with a bunch of old people—and second, who knows if we're gay? We were just saying how maybe we should say we're gay lesbians."

"That's redundant," I laughed.

"What, you know something we don't know? We're two widow ladies from Brooklyn. We grew up near each other in the Bronx but then married twin Italian brothers from the neighborhood. We always called them the Brothers Garabaldi. We all bought a big house together, far away in Brooklyn. Brenda's folks were from Puerto Rico and mine were Jews from Russia—don't ask. We had quite a little United Nations. So when the husbands died—a year apart, God rest their souls, the old folks were gone, the kids were grown and scattered, so Brenda and I moved into the biggest apartment together and rented out the rest. Last spring we did Greece and this year California. Food's definitely better here. And Brenda's son is in the Gay Physician's group.

"Gay lesbians?" I smiled.

"Well, you know, we love each other and we live together. What's the matter with that. Do we qualify? How about a float for Gay Celibate Lesbians Who Aren't Very Religious?" I made a face.

"No? Maybe just Gay Chaste Lesbians—not like the ones chasing each other on motorcycles at the front of the parade. You know, the Dykes on Bikes? So why are they so hot and famous to be at the front of the parade with their bras off anyway? What's so special about owning a motorcycle and having those...? And who are all these different people with their designer label signs? It's confusing. We just saw some Transgendered, Bisexual, Something-or-others from some island somewhere go by—all eight of them." She stopped for a breath and looked at me. "Plenty of variety but I guess it wouldn't be fair for us to be Gay Lesbians, huh? 'Redundant,' you said. See? I listen while I talk. Now about you..."

"I meant that if you're a lesbian you are gay so you don't need to say it twice."

"So, that brings up an interesting question," the loquacious Ruthie persisted. "What makes somebody gay?"

"You mean the definition, not the joke?"

"What joke?"

"You know, the old one scribbled on walls: 'My mother made me a fairy' and then under it someone scrawls, 'If I give her the wool, will she make me one too?' "

Ruthie slapped her knee and repeated the joke for Brenda. "That's a good one. But, no, not the joke—the definition. Who qualifies as gay?"

After dropping some names such as Alexander the Great, Plato, Sappho, the Emperor Hadrian, on down through Walt Whitman and Gertrude Stein to Eleanor Roosevelt, Truman Capote, and Rock Hudson, I said, "Okay, definition. I would say most simply that it's women who love women and men who love men—love all the way, including sexually. But homosexual sex isn't enough. Many people do that who aren't gay—especially in prison. If your deepest sexual attractions are for people of the same gender and you act on them, you're homosexual. But it's the willingness to admit your homosexual orientation and the deep affections that go with it—to yourself and others—that takes you over the line from homosexual to gay. Partly it's a political statement, I guess."

Ruthie looked at me. "You talk almost as much as I do." She put her hand on my arm. "No, dear. That's a compliment. So, what about all these others. The transsexuals, transvestites, bisexuals, transgendered and what-not? What are they doing here?"

I laughed. "I guess, when in doubt, we have a tendency to be inclusive rather than exclusive. Difficulty in shutting people out when we're so often shut out. But it is true that most transvestites are heterosexual rather than homosexual in orientation and so the only transvestites who would really be gay would by the homosexually oriented ones."

"Drag queens, like that tall number in the big hair and red sequins over there?" she said, pointing down the parade route.

"And the person standing behind you," I said, as she craned her neck back to look up at the women in a cowboy hat, blue work shirt, overalls and western boots who, at the moment, was kissing a woman companion.

"And behind you, my darling? How about the leather everything with various parts of himself getting a suntan?"

"Very probably gay," I said, "but you'd have to ask to be sure. We come in all shapes, sizes, and costumes and are known to be trendsetters in style."

"Transsexuals?" Ruthie asked. "Gay?"

"Well, if you're a male who feels like a female trapped in the wrong body or, the other way around, a female who feels like you're a male trapped in the wrong body, and you're in the process of getting your life in order and having the necessary medical help to get your body rearranged, you then become the person you have always wanted to be and are seen as such in the eyes of the world and the law, free to marry someone of the other gender, etc. I would guess that means that you are heterosexual and therefore not gay. You're a woman loving men or a man loving women. Unless you are a woman trapped in a man's body, you have the hormone shots and the surgery, and live as a legal woman but one who loves women—then that's a lesbian and you're gay!"

"Oy, enough already. I'm getting a headache," Ruthie said. "So the parade could be called Gay People and Friends."

"That would be good," I said. "You could march. By the way, do you and Brenda know about Parents and Friends of Lesbians and Gays—P-FLAG? They'll be coming along here if they haven't already."

"Stop! We're joining. They went by just before you got here and handed us the sign-up literature. See? We're in the family. Too bad about the bible people on that other block. Such a waste. They could be loving."

She was referring to a group that I had seen on the sidewalk, holding Judeo-Christian bibles and cardboard placards in the air, screaming "We pray for you" along with angry unpleasantries at the paraders, assuring us that we would spend eternity burning in Hell unless we repented. I was amused to see one of the women wearing a red dress and wondered if any of them would be eating shellfish at Fisherman's Wharf, since both are forbidden in that same version of the bible that prohibits a man from spilling his seed or lying down with another man.

Such people are not a novelty to us. They are the heirs to those who tortured and murdered in centuries past in the name of some religious virtue, desperately seeking an assured place for themselves in eternity—at any price.

The gay parades and festivals that have become annual events in cities around the world are often referred to as Gay Pride Day or Gay Pride Week, the latter sometimes including a gay-oriented film festival, theater, dance, readings and exhibitions of gay-oriented art. We have become newsworthy and are being counted as consumers. But such events are also a good opportunity for us to examine our individual and collective identity. Our inclusive community is sometimes called LGBT&Q which recognizes lesbian, gay, bisexual, transgendered, queer and questioning. For me the day of the parade has become a day to remember the dead. I smile, laugh and cry—visited by my spirits as I watch us emerge in greater numbers each year.

The day or the week is also a good opportunity to examine our pride. Gay pride, the same as any other form of pride, is earned rather than given. Stepping out into the light to face whatever prejudice may come your way and asserting the right to be who you are is certainly a reason for pride. But, for me, there is more. I think that each year we must examine what else we have done to earn pride. Have we stood fast against bigotry and prejudice in all its forms? Have we tried to educate those who know us only by prejudicial reputation? Have we helped to make the world safer for the gay children who hide in waiting, hoping to live to join us? Have we done a better job of reaching out and caring for one another? Have we done our best to eliminate the blight of prejudice that we carried from the outer world into our own community?

We have a history of tolerance and acceptance which can slide into careless indifference. There is illegal drug use and misuse in our community as there is in every oppressed group—the ancient temptation of temporary escape. In our community some drugs also are used experimentally to expand consciousness and explore spiritual realms. The illegality, per se, is of some concern—but less. It probably would be better if all drugs were legal, medically controlled, and citizens were educated as to the potential benefits and dangers of each of them, rather than continuing to infantilize the populace and support an industry for the criminals, the catchers and the punishers. That system is so expensive in both human and monetary cost. But we have a responsibility to continue to question drug use in our community and to tell a friend when it looks as if addiction is around the corner or already becoming a habit and to make sure she or he knows where and how to get help.

We also have a responsibility in our community to work against segregation of any sort, including color, age, religion or national origin and prejudice of every kind. We all have been and are victimized by the presence of segregation and prejudice in the larger surrounding community. It is incompatible with pride within our community. There is no acceptance or appreciation until *everyone* is accepted and appreciated on the basis of individual merit rather than pushed aside or excluded because of such classifications.

The patrons, owners, and staff of gay gyms and dance clubs must go out of their way to welcome every possibly gay person into the establishment, onto the exercise machines and onto the dance floor—including elderly and disabled lesbians and gay men. It might sometimes mean showing someone how to use a piece of equipment, having earplugs for sale in the louder dance halls and places for people to sit, as Ruthie would point out. Reaching out with a warm smile and a welcoming touch makes all the difference and is the responsibility of every gay individual who claims pride.

Gay bars continue to be the most easily found community centers around the world. It is the responsibility of their owners and their gay patrons to see to it that every gay person is welcome. Turn down the volume of the music so that people can hear one another. It is the only way that people can start to become acquainted. Have smoke-free areas, if possible, so that people need not risk their health and those with allergies can breathe. Have doors wide enough and ramps where possible so that people in wheelchairs can feel genuinely welcome. And make it very clear that all skin colors and languages are equally welcome.

"So what is all of this about gay lifestyle that the soreheads are always getting so wrought up about and saying they don't approve of?" Ruther asked me later that day.

"I'm not sure," I answered. "I know they seem to disapprove of homosexuality for a wide variety of peculiar reasons. Maybe they have fantasies of all of us living our lives in endless orgiastic debauchery or having secret magic rites that involve eating babies. I honestly don't know."

By this time Brenda was in the conversation. "You'd have to have billion-dollar corporations and their smooth-talking, free-spending lobbyists kissing up to you like the lawmakers do in order to live that kind of life. Face it. You people have style and they don't. And just when they try to copy some fashion you've set, you change it. And you wonder why they hate you? Easy, Honey, they're falling all over each other, having fights, flapping their gums about nothing and they can't keep up. They hate your style because they don't have any."

I told them that I am very appreciative of our detractors when they speak out. They cause discussion. They bring us out into the light. Every time that one of them says that we are not fit to be parents, serve in the military, have a security clearance or have the same civil rights that other citizens have, they cause more of us to get angry, be interviewed, be quoted in newspapers and magazines and be seen on television. People look at us and listen to us and begin to see that the problem is not with us but with our detractors. It takes time. Education always takes time. But the only way they could have kept us as their victims would have been to keep us locked out of sight and remain silent about us.

I told Ruthie and Brenda that my favorite Gay Pride parade had happened in 1977. A one-time beauty pageant contestant and some-time pop singer named Anita Bryant, who sold frozen orange juice on television commercials, had become a self-appointed spokesperson for those people usually referred to as right-wing Christian fundamentalists. She began to attract attention from the media when she proclaimed her ideas about the sinful ways of gay people. Her presumed insight was that since homosexuals could not reproduce they needed to recruit innocent youngsters. Just a few weeks before the parade in San Francisco, her *Save Our Children* organization had managed to overturn a Dade County, Florida, civil rights ordinance that would have made it illegal to discriminate against gay people in housing, employment and public accommodation. This inspired a California legislator named John Briggs (who hoped to run for governor) to launch a witch hunt. He arrived in San Francisco to announce his plan to take away the state teaching credentials of anyone who was discovered to be gay or who spoke out in support of gay people.

"Anita Bryant and John Briggs really rallied us," I told them. In earlier years the parades had been relatively small. But there was a strong plea from local gay activists that year for gay people to come out as gay and to march in the parade. It was also suggested that we lessen the carnival atmosphere that year and let the public see us as we are in everyday life in our jobs and professions. And there was a tragic but catalytic event only days before the parade. A young gay gardener, who worked in San Francisco's Golden Gate Park, was murdered in a senseless hate crime. It was suggested that every participant in the parade bring a flower and leave it on the steps of City Hall as a remembrance.

"The parade was enormous," I told them. "There were men in suits and neckties and women in skirts and heels; placards announcing affiliations or jobs such as telephone and other utility company workers; veterans, reservists, active-duty military and local law-enforcement officers; doctors, lawyers, and many other professional groups, including teachers—all of us marching smartly, deadly serious in a show of our force and solidarity. And at the end of the day there was a hill of flowers that had been left, one by one, on the steps of City Hall. We had come out and our announcement was both strong and clear. It was another turning point, like the Stonewall Rebellion in New York eight years earlier. From that day forward the gay people of this city and in the world would be a force to be reckoned with—we would not turn back—harm one of us and answer to all of us."

"Why the tears?" Ruthie asked, looking at my face.

"Because it was the end of being alone for so many of us," I answered and set down on the curb again for a shameless cry, remembering friends who had been present that day, now gone—my spirits in attendance with me as always on that very special day of celebration and remembrance.

"Your High Holy Day," Ruthie later named it.

So much has changed since then. If you move past the boundaries of state or national lines, there are places in the world where it is legal and respectable for you to be a gay person serving in the military and law enforcement agencies today. There are places where you can be a gay single person or a gay couple and adopt a child to whom you can give your love and a home. There are places where you can be appointed or elected to high office in government. There are places where gay people legally marry. There are places where any gay person is entitled to the same full range of civil rights granted to any other citizen. There are many places where we can be seen in our amazing variety, holding hands and simply loving one another.

The world is seeing us—and our style.

[PART THREE]

Loving
Someone
Gay

17

LEARNING THE TRUTH

WE FIRST IMAGINE that we know all about the person we love. It helps us to feel more secure in an unpredictable world. Imagining becomes believing. We *believe* that we know all about a daughter, son, husband, wife, brother, sister, mother or father.

Accepting the truth can be difficult for all of us. Whether you are a parent, husband, wife, daughter, son, sister, brother or friend you have your own individual quirks, weaknesses, moments of pride, doubts and dreams.

The same is true of gay people. Each one of us is different. Each of us has individual qualities that may endear us to you or cause you to react with distaste or distrust. I cannot tell you about the individual gay person you love but I can offer general thoughts and probabilities that may help you to clarify the unique relationship that the two of you have now and the relationship that you may develop together in time.

Each decade there are more and more stories of parents being supportive of their lesbian daughters and gay sons than there were in previous decades. Witnessing and experiencing inhumanity in the world has helped many people to comprehend the value of acceptance, compassion and love within their own families. Unfortunately, however, there continue to be too many other stories of family love that becomes distorted by irrational pressures to conform to some ideal of *normal* existence. But it is always possible for those who love someone who is gay to see the person more clearly and, therefore, more positively—if they are willing to try.

I presume that you are reading this book because you want to know more about what the subjective experience of being gay is like for the person you love. The earlier sections of this book have given some of that flavor. One common denominator for most gay people throughout the world is that their experience has been difficult. It has been difficult not for any reason that need be true in the infinite scheme of things, but because many contemporary cultures do not yet fully value diversity.

Lack of conformity makes too many people uneasy, and uneasy people too easily strike out to hurt anyone who seems different. In all probability, that phenomenon has made it necessary for the gay person you love to hide his or her true identity at one time or another. And when it is necessary to hide part of your true self it is very easy to begin to feel worthless, no matter how convincing the façade of achievement or apparent self-confidence. You can express your love for someone gay by learning more about what it is like to be gay and offering unconditional caring. Such commitments facilitate the growth of self-respect.

The gay person you love has held tight to an inner truth and identity in the face of formidable opposition. Gay people do not consider this fight for integrity as a mark of bravery. Most do not even consider it a fight. People who grow up in the Arctic expect cold weather. Most gay people are accustomed to the world the way it is. Each of us has found a way to survive day by day. But there is, for me, something touching about it. It brings to mind the childhood story of *The Emperor's New Clothes*. Everyone in the empire agreed to agree that the emperor had purchased a fine new suit of clothes, despite the fact that he had been duped into buying nothing at all. Only a child, who had not yet mastered the art of self-deception, spoke the truth when he saw that the emperor was actually naked. Each gay person grows up like that child, seeing a personal truth, threatened by the general conforming consensus, yet somehow needing to hold on to that truth and share it with others. In a world so full of willing conspirators in deception, I hope that this book helps you to find pride in sharing love with someone gay.

The only thing predictable about the *coming out* or *disclosure* experience itself is its unpredictability. Two of my colleagues had similar experiences. One had prepared himself while in college and came home to break the news to his parents. Both parents sat in the living room and listened quietly until he was finished. He braced himself, took a breath and asked them if they had any questions. His mother rose from the sofa, took his hand, led him into her bedroom and pointed. There, on the bedside table were books. Each had the world *gay* in its title. "We've been getting ready," she said and kissed him as his father entered the room to join them in a warm hug.

The other was in his mid-forties when he became convinced that he must tell his eighty-year-old mother, lest he wrestle with her ghost for the remainder of his life. He planned the event with great care, first going over all possibilities with friends. His greatest fear was that she would die the moment he told her. She had complained about her weak heart for as many years as he could remember. He wanted to let her know that he really did care about her and believed that his actions would speak louder than words.

He planned a special winter vacation in Miami Beach, Florida for just the two of them. They stayed at a hotel she had wanted to visit for years and took two of her friends out to dinner on their first evening. The next day they went out together on a brief shopping jaunt, during which he bought her a colorful silk scarf that he could see had captured her admiration—though she protested that it was foolishness to spend so much money on something that would be a rag one day. She napped after lunch and joined him on the beach for an hour before they went to their rooms to dress for dinner.

That evening he took her to an excellent, quiet restaurant away from the hotel. Near the end of the meal he reached across the table and took her hand. "Mother, I want to tell you something about me that I have never told you. First, I want you to know that I love and respect you. Second, I want you to know that I have held off telling you for years because I was afraid it might hurt you. Now I know that it is good news and that I am cheating both of us by not sharing it."

"So, what is it, already?" she asked. "You've got a secret wife, or maybe two of them?"

"No, Mom, it's that I'm gay. It means that I'm more attracted to men than to women."

His mother's brow wrinkled as she thought it over. "That's how come you been living with Tommy all these years? That's how come you bought the building together?"

"Yes, Mom, Tommy is my lover and it is like we are married." My friend was now perspiring freely.

More wrinkled brow. "So how come all these years I never met his parents?"

"Because, like I said, I was afraid to tell you, and Tommy was afraid to tell his parents."

Her brow arched. "Funny world, different than when I was young. Tommy's nice. You could have done worse."

There was a long silence now. His mother seemed lost in thought. She looked around the restaurant at the other diners. "Is there anything else you want to ask me, Mom?"

"About that? No, Tommy's nice, but I think I should meet his parents."

"But you were so quiet, Mom. You must have been thinking about something."

"I was thinking about how nice Miami is. Just like I expected. And I was wondering what kind of a restaurant we're going to eat in tomorrow night."

Telling someone who is important to you that you are gay is a big event. There are times when the announcement slips out but, more often, the gay person is likely to have spent many hours in thoughtful preparation and shares the information with keen awareness of the possible risk. It is an offering. The most important thing that you can do when presented with this opportunity to improve your relationship with a gay person is to pay appreciative attention when the disclosure is made.

There is no way for the gay person to predict your reaction accurately. You may well have spent all or most of your life in a society that teaches people to despise gay people. Although this particular gay person is someone important in your life, there is no way for her or him to know in advance how able you will feel to throw off a lifetime of negative training and respond spontaneously, positively and with gratitude to such an intimate offering of self.

It is a moment like no other. You will never forget it. There is almost no parallel to the situation in which two people who have known one another very well—perhaps for a lifetime—face each other. One of them risks abandonment by revealing a pervasive fact of identity that may have been invisible to the other. Appreciate how deeply you are valued by this gay person to justify taking such a risk.

Both of you will be changed forever by the moment of disclosure. The gay person gains special freedom and the strength of integrity. There is no longer any need to hide this fact of self in your presence. And you are changed because you are no longer asked to, or permitted to, ignore an essential part of this person you love. The situation demands that each of you relate more completely to one another from this moment forward.

Yet the gay person before you is the same person he or she has always been. It is important to understand this. You may be shocked by the revelation, but this is the same person you have loved and who has loved you. Do not let the shock change your view because a label has been assigned. Do not permit the years of negative conditioning to transform your perception of the gay person you love into a monster who fits the stereotypes. What has been kept from you is a truth about loving and identity. You now know that this person can love someone of the same gender completely. You have no reason to suddenly believe that this person has become emotionally unbalanced, morally deficient or depraved.

When the gay person you love makes the disclosure to you, search your thoughts and feelings for the information you need and then ask. Do not ask questions that would have been considered rude within the relationship you had before the disclosure was made. Your gay friend or loved one continues to have the same sensibilities as before. But you may well need to do some catching up. So push your-self to ask. Some common questions are: How long have you known or suspected you were gay? Will you introduce me to your gay friends? Why do you say *gay* or *queer* instead of homosexual? Is there someone special in your life? Has it been difficult for you to carry this secret? Is there some way I can help you? Have I ever offended you unknowingly?

Be honest and express your feelings. It makes the sharing more complete and makes change come more easily. If you find it difficult to believe that it is true, say so—and tell why, if you know the rea-sons. If you find you are reacting with emotional repugnance, but want to learn more so that you can throw off your prejudice, say so. If your feelings seem to be totally negative, you can say that too. It is a reaction your gay friend has certainly considered. But in fairness to yourself, admit aloud that the negative feelings may change so that the door remains open for you to return if and when you are able to get past your years of conditioning. Gay people are accustomed to pain, but with someone close the rejection may hurt too much and she or he may have to maintain some distance.

Beware of trying to induce shame or guilt. By the time we have developed the strength to make the disclosure, we are usually suffi-ciently in touch with our feelings to respond to such attempts with understandable anger. Even such mild attempts as, "Why did you keep me in the dark for so long?" or "Why didn't you tell me long ago?" can get you in trouble. Use your common sense and realize there are many pressures operating on gay people and be glad that you have been told now. You may have been trained to believe that gay people are bad and might be irrationally tempted to elicit proof in the form of shame or guilt. Resist meeting your irrational needs and give yourself time to get rid of such toxic thinking.

What do you value about this person? Receiving the disclosure of gay identity does not happen in a moment—it can go on for weeks or years. During this period of readjustment, try to remain aware of what it is about this person that you value, and share that information aloud. It may be a sense of humor, intelligence, compassion, fairness or perhaps small things like remembering your birthday each year or a reliable smile in the morning. Sharing your appreciation aloud will be reassuring to this courageous person who has risked it all with you. It will also help you to stay focused on the individual and not get swept away by generalizations about *people like that*.

You may well be tempted to break the bond you have with this gay person. Though she or he has not changed, the information that now confronts you may trigger your own homophobic training. Conflict may be inevitable. Just as some people develop specific phobias (heights, snakes, deep water, etc.), some people develop homophobia. It is a disability like any other phobia and you can get help through psychotherapy, provided that the therapist does not share your phobia. Just as the person who is phobic about deep water may be unaware of anything more than a discomfort with and avoidance of oceans, lakes and rivers, the homophobe may be aware only of discomfort in the presence of gay people and the desire to avoid them.

A friend told me about a social gathering he had attended where a woman whom he had met on other occasions sent a mutual friend across the room as emissary to ask if Mr. X. would welcome a conversation with Miss Z. Amused at the coy courtliness of the request, he returned word that he would, indeed, welcome such a conversation. Seconds later, Miss Z. had crossed the room, stood at his side, smiled, and asked him how he had been. He told her that he had been having a wonderful time because a few months earlier he had acted on a decision to *come out* and let everyone who was of any importance to him know that he was gay. The woman stared at him with an expressionless face, her jaw dropped slightly and, without saying a word, she turned on her heel, walked briskly away and he never saw or heard from her again.

You may not act as peculiarly as Miss Z. if you are prone to homophobia, but your fear may well tempt you to rid yourself of this previously valued relationship by quick rupture or by a slower erosion of the relationship. If you sense these symptoms and want to help yourself, try to find a gay-affirmative psychotherapist. Do not risk working with a counselor who privately shares your homophobia. If you destroy the relationship, chances are that the gay person will be hurt but will survive, having been prepared by life for such a reaction from others who share your disability. But you will have lost.

If your homophobia is of the very mild variety (like the person who can take the elevator up twenty stories but does not want to visit the roof garden of the tallest building in the city), you can get help from reading and from making social contacts with gay people. Prejudice thrives on the lack of contradictory information. Integration destroys stereotypes. The more gay people you meet, the better your chances of ridding yourself of mild homophobia.

The gift of disclosure provides the opportunity and perhaps the incentive for you to begin questioning many of your assumptions about the rights and wrongs within your culture. In most parts of the world, gay people must question conformity and the given morality, building a personally satisfying code of ethics as a matter of survival. Friends and relatives may be influenced to do the same. As a result, you may find the scope and quality of your own life improving.

More than a few recipients of a disclosure also have found it a stimulus to taking on more civic responsibility. We must live in the societies we create. Inequalities and injustice can be changed. The place to start, if you love someone gay, is where you live and work. Get involved in law reform and resist discrimination whenever and wherever you see it. This is not a charitable gift to the gay person you love, but is a result of the gift that she or he has given to you. The disclosure can be an eye-opener, showing you more clearly the sort of world you have been tacitly supporting with your lack of protest.

If you received the disclosure some time in the past and now feel that you handled it badly, it is a waste to blame yourself. Like the rest of us, you can only do as well as you can at any given moment in your life. If the gay person is still living, you might write a note from the vantage point of your current understanding and feelings. The relationship may have been irreparably damaged and you may not get a reply, but surely it will be of some value to each of you if you demonstrate that you know better today. Perhaps your gay friend or loved one feels that he or she did not handle the revelation very well either and has done some learning since then.

If the gay person is no longer living and you feel the pressure of unfinished business, search for a positive experience that can help you to feel closure. A generous contribution to a gay organization, an outspoken and heartfelt letter to an editor, or a chat with a friend or relative of another gay person can leave you feeling more positive about yourself.

If you know or suspect that someone you know is gay but you have not yet been told, appreciate the fear and anxiety that may inhibit the disclosure. Usually, all that you can do is to make it known that you appreciate gay people. Actions speak louder than words, however. Gay friends and gay-oriented reading material that is visible in your home do more than announcements of pro-gray feelings, which can sound affected and inauthentic.

In some relationships the silence goes on too long and is too costly. If you feel oppressed by the secret, you may need to say so and precipitate the disclosure. In weighing your decision, however, bear in mind that your gay friend may be building strength, getting ready for the possibility that you will react badly. He or she may also be battling internal anti-gay feelings. Approach with care. The person who is doing such battle within would sometimes truly rather die than have anyone she or he values guess at the hidden gay identity. In fact, this is a struggle with homosexual desires and gay feelings within someone who has not yet become gay. She or he is not yet ready to disclose an identity that has not yet formed.

Discussions based on your own pro-gay reading can help to sound out the person and, if needed, may help him or her to move along the path toward celebration of gay identity. One sign of readiness for the confrontation is when you notice that the person about whom you are concerned no longer denigrates anyone else for being gay. A better sign is if he or she has one or more gay friends who are admired and respected. From there on it is a matter of using your sensitivity. When the topic comes up, observe how your friend or loved one reacts. If you can sense that he or she feels threatened, back off and wait a while longer. And let it be known, now and then, that you are learning more good things about gay people as time passes.

18

ACCEPTANCE, COMMUNICATION, AND APPRECIATION

W HERE HAVE I FAILED?" she asked in a parody of parental alarm. A lesbian was telling a group of friends about her disclosure experience with her parents. She had prepared carefully and done well. Both parents had listened quietly, looked at one another, and then her mother had said, "It doesn't matter. It does-n't make any difference. We love you just the same as always. You're no different to us now than you were before."

"Doesn't matter? You'd think I could get a little credit for all I've been through!" She was only half joking. She was relieved that her parents had taken the news so well. And it was too soon after the disclosure to know all of their feelings. But she did want some credit.

Most of us have learned that being gay, at best, is wonderful and, at least, respectable. But all of us know that it has made our lives more difficult. Few of us would have had the courage to be gay if the inner truth had not been there pushing us along. We want and deserve some credit for paying the price of being different. We want our friends and loved ones to appreciate that there is more to us than they had thought. This usually comes with time, however, as it becomes more comfortable to share the events of our lives from past and present.

A gay man told me that two months after he disclosed his gay identity to his family, one of his brothers telephoned him with the news that he was being transferred by his employer. "We're going to be living near each other again. Isn't that great? But there's something I need to bring up with you that's worrying me a bit. How can I get your friends to like me and accept me? I'm not gay."

His brother reassured him that it was not likely to be a problem but thanked him for bringing it up. "As long as we're talking to one another we can always get things sorted out. I'm only sorry I didn't let you know about me being gay sooner."

It is usually easy to be accepted and appreciated as a non-gay person in gay social circles. All you have to do is be yourself, be respectful of our gay identity and show that you like us—or at least that you are not prejudiced against us. Most of us are friendly to people who want to be our friends. Our hostility is reserved for people who choose not to know us and/or who believe us to be inferior in some way.

Like non-gay persons, we want to be accepted, appreciated and loved. Those relatives and friends of gay people who have the most difficult time accepting, appreciating and loving us are the ones who never learned to love themselves. If you do not love yourself, it is difficult to offer love to another person. It is the reason why those non-gay people, who have gotten to know themselves through the hard work of soul-searching are more at ease with themselves *and* with people who are different from them. If you accept yourself, you are much more likely to take others as you find them.

Ignorance is a barrier to any sort of relationship. Warring factions generally do not know one another well because they have been fed stereotypes. No matter what the seeming differences—nationality, skin color, age, language or customs—humans are varied but more alike than different.

When family members tell me that they are worried that they will not get along well with a sibling, son, daughter, father, mother or grandparent now that they know the person is gay, I say that they are probably right unless they value the person and the relationship enough to get to know the person better. Getting to know someone when you already care is very enjoyable work. But biological families do not always function perfectly. Just because two people are biologically related does not mean that they have enough in common to enjoy one another.

The same is true for today's chosen families, those developing networks of friends and relatives that become one's real family through the years of a lifetime. If you discover that someone in your chosen family is gay, and you want to keep her or him in your chosen family, it will not work unless you value the fact that the person is gay. And in order to value that fact, you have to learn what it means to be gay.

Books are available and so is the person. Most of us appreciate it when we know that someone loves us enough to put effort into understanding us better. We are more than willing to assist.

"Do I need the homosexual vote? Who are these people, anyway? Lesbians? Gays? Where are all these homosexuals coming from? Why are there so many of them all of a sudden and who says they vote, anyway?" Words worthy of the flustered and bewildered politician who spoke them to one of his advisors. "We have a mandate and are going to continue our march into the future," he said firmly, as if that somehow answered his questions. He was managing an unusual political maneuver of marching resolutely into the future while failing to move forward. He did not know or understand gay people.

The simple truth is that while there might appear to be more lesbians and gay men around with each passing year, it is an illusion due to the fact that we have been making it easier for one another to be truthful, *come out* and be visible. There is every reason to believe that we represent the same percentage of the human population that we have been in all parts of the world and in all times in human history. When the social environment is less punitive, and there are visible role models already *out* and living with self-respect, it becomes easier to be truthful about your identity. It is a relief to stop hiding your true self, even if some people still would like you better or feel more comfortable if you continued to pretend to be just like them.

Another potentially confusing issue that comes up when family members learn that someone in the family is gay is the fear that they may have inherited "it" too. It is very likely that there is a *predisposition* that has a genetic basis, as is also true in preference for left-handedness. In the past, some people were forced to learn to act right-handed even though they were predisposed to be left-handed. We now know that this was a mistake that was harmful as well as unnecessary. We now accept the simple fact that some are left-handed and some favor their right hand.

When asked about it, I like to look the inquisitor in the eye and tell her or him that, if they have a homoerotic preference, they are aware of it already. We all know whether it is males or females that most often make us want to turn our heads and have a second look on the street. It is an automatic and involuntary physical and emotional response. If the preference is there, one may choose to hide it or exercise it. If it is there, it is healthier in the long run to exercise it, if the environment is not too punitive. And if the preference is not there, you know that too.

I hasten to reassure people that you cannot catch a homoerotic preference any more than you can catch a heteroerotic preference. Neither is contagious. If they were, strongly heterosexual societies would not have to bother with the constant punishing suppression of homosexual desire and behavior. But if you are related to someone who is gay, you can catch some acceptance and appreciation. Gay people have worked hard for it and will be glad to help you gain it also.

It is too bad that many families learned of a loved one's gay identity only because he became ill with AIDS. It is very difficult to hear the gay identity as good news when it is combined with bad news. But once the truth is out, more often than not, families become more concerned with helping a loved one who needs them than with passing judgment on which gender he finds most attractive.

It is not always true that to know someone is to love them, but it is true that you cannot love someone unless you know them. Only foolish, unfounded fears stop non-gay persons from wanting to get to know a gay person they care about better so that they can care more.

One of the most serious social diseases of contemporary times is prejudice. As information is more and more easily obtained and attractively presented, there is less and less excuse for the existence of prejudice and for the terrible toll it takes in human suffering.

Prejudice is a matter of prejudging, making a decision about someone or something with insufficient evidence. The damage is done when one acts on the basis of prejudice rather than reality. No one is immune from this disease. In most parts of the world, even the most respected citizens carry it in some form and willingly spread it to others. It may be as innocent as a belief system that concludes in advance that all cooked vegetables are tasteless and have lost all nutritional value. It may be as dangerous as the untested belief that all people with a certain skin color, language or erotic preference are untrustworthy and second rate. It is the latter sort of prejudice that causes people to be beaten and killed in war and for sport.

I once made a similar remark in passing while discussing another subject at a professional meeting. A non-gay colleague turned on me with considerable anger and said, "You're a fine one to talk. When are the homosexuals of the world going to clean up their act. I'm sick and tired of being the recipient of their prejudice."

I answered that there might be something in the behavior of gay people whom he had met that he did not care for but that I doubted very much if it was prejudice. Prejudice breeds and grows on ignorance. In order to keep your prejudice intact you must be sheltered from too much information about the people who are the targets. Almost every gay person in the world grows up in a non-gay family and in a non-gay community. We are regularly exposed to non-gay school mates, merchants, neighbors, teachers and co-workers. "I think it is safe to say that we know a lot more about you than you know about us," I told him. "We have lived very close to a wide variety of people whom we knew were non-gay. Some we have loved and some not. I doubt if you have lived very close to a wide variety of gay people whom you knew were gay. And I doubt if you were aware that you loved some of us."

It is curious but true that many people who are not naturally predisposed to prejudice will follow the prejudiced perceptions of their leaders. A clear example is the religious leader who justified a holy war by promulgating stereotypes about *the enemy* that could not possibly stand the test of personal investigation. A less vivid example is the parent who passes along the stereotypic images of prejudice that he or she received from parents and grandparents.

It is extraordinary to think that only half a century ago many people believed that Jews had horns on their heads. A few sadly sheltered people probably believe it still. But then some people today still believe that gay people are those *dirty queers*, who lurk in darkened alleys waiting to prey on *innocent young heterosexuals*.

In the early days of this wave of gay liberation, we used to suggest half jokingly that prejudiced people should *take a lesbian to lunch*. We were trying to suggest that it is hard to hold onto your prejudice if you get to know a few of us.

I am sorry to say that I continue to hear stories of sons and daughters whose parents have *accepted* the fact that their offspring is gay but absolutely forbid the son or daughter to bring any gay friends into the family home. It is almost as if they sense they would receive evidence that would destroy their prejudice!

But then people cling to old beliefs as they sometimes do to comfortable old shoes that are no longer doing their job well. A mother who had refused to meet her son's partner, or any of his friends for fifteen years, met them all when she visited her son in the hospital in the last weeks of his life. "I am so ashamed," she told me. "They showed him more love than I did and they were more wonderful to me than I deserved." Now her son is dead and his partner and friends finally are welcome in his mother's home.

Prejudice is no one's fault. It is a disease of the mind and spirit. The existence of a disease is no one's fault. But it is the responsibility of every sane human to do what he or she can to resist and counteract any disease that threatens human life. It may be difficult to challenge a prejudiced statement the first time, but it gets easier.

The same mother told me about someone at her place of employment who did not know the circumstances of her son's death, saying casually at the lunch table that one thing good about AIDS was that it was cleaning a lot of the undesirables out of the world population. "I just couldn't speak. I knew I would cry. But another woman at the table said, 'If they make you a judge, be sure to let me know because I want to live in another country where it's safe to have somebody think I'm undesirable.' "

The first woman laughed and said, "Don't be silly; I'm talking about queers and drug addicts. Everybody knows they're undesirable."

The second woman said, "You'll have to introduce me to the ones you know. On second thought, don't. I think I'd still like the ones I know better. The ones you know must be some kind of weird."

Point made.

If you care about one of us, you will have to do what you can to combat the prejudice about all of us. Look in your own heart first. If you believe that lesbians and gay men should not be free to marry one another, think about it long and hard. If you think you know one thing that is true about all of us, you are wrong and you are prejudging.

In a world full of chatter, most of us have difficulty in expressing that which matters most to us. We can talk about the weather or the news, but—though you may want to do it very badly—it can be most difficult, even frightening, to anticipate talking about feelings with the people who matter most in your life. We fear judgment, misunderstanding and loss of appreciation.

There is always more to learn about another person, and there is always more to tell about yourself. It is sometimes tempting to try to shape someone you care about into the person you think he or she should be. Since the other person cannot oblige and be exactly the person you would wish him or her to be, you are apt to do some trimming, adding and altering in your perceptions. Learning more about the person you care for means daring to rid yourself of false perceptions. Telling more about yourself to someone for whom you care means helping that person to see you more truthfully, without their own false perceptions. It feels risky because we do not like to see our privately manufactured perceptions evaporate in the light of truth, and we are apt to fight it one way or another.

When I am consulted by loved ones who want to know how to improve their relationship with a gay man or a lesbian, I state the obvious. I advise that people say what is on their minds and in their hearts, ask the questions that are hidden inside and express emotions aloud. You can do all of that while retaining sensitivity to the other person's feelings. Talking out your feelings is much less hurtful than acting them out in behavior that is a code you expect the other person to understand.

I still am bothered by the story of a man who came from a very large family. It was very difficult for him to come out of hiding and admit to himself, and then to his family, that he was gay. He sent copies of the first edition of *Loving Someone Gay* to his parents and to his widely scattered grownup siblings. He had a variety of reactions from his brothers and sisters but never recovered from having been told by one sister that another sister's husband had burned the book in the living room fireplace without anyone in the household having read it. Whether or not the nonverbal message was correctly decoded, it hurt him deeply. It had taken great courage and caring on his part to try to open the lines of communication. The violent response was an unhealed wound that hurt him to the day he died, a year later. His family mourned deeply, perhaps more deeply because some of them had been unwilling or unable to communicate with him about his true identity and his struggles.

It often seems difficult to know how to begin communicating. If you love someone who is gay, tell her or him that you do. Then back up the words with actions by trying to learn as much as you can about the person, about what it means to be gay and about your own feelings in response. Remember to *talk* it out rather than act it out. Words can be confusing until their meaning is untangled. Behavior meant to take the place of words is even more confusing. Show that you care by being unwilling to give up on the effort to sort things out by talking—even if you have only negative thoughts about homosexuality. Remember that no matter how many seemingly appropriate greeting cards you send, you do not love another person until you are willing to give up your old false perceptions and improve your understanding of that person.

For many people, communicating love is the most difficult. Some have learned to say "I love you" with such superficial regularity that it loses its meaning. Others are stingy with the words. When you mean it, say it. It is very reassuring to hear it when you sense the other person is saying it because they feel it. This can be especially difficult between men. Male training rarely includes one male feeling and saying "I love you" to another male. It can become a monumental problem between a father and a son, between brothers, or even between male lovers. Because of such cultural conditioning, men may have to force the words out until they come more easily. Women who have been exposed to the opposite training may have to check themselves on the all too easy, and therefore relatively meaningless, use of the words.

When I think of communication, I like to remember the lesbian who fell in love with another woman "... when we were both past forty, Honey." She told me, "Those first weeks were wonderful and awful. I didn't know what I was feeling exactly, how to say it, or if I should say it. But she helped me. She used to hold me quietly sometimes and say she wanted to speak from her heart. One day I understood the difference. There was all the usual talk and then there was our heart talk. When she spoke from her heart, all I had to do was listen and love her, and care. Sometimes I would feel hurt or angry or whatever, but if I spoke from my heart, no matter what it was, she was always there listening, caring and loving."

True communication comes before all else in any loving relationship. To neglect it is to invite trouble into the relationship. And telling is only half of it. Listening with care is the other half.

A man who grew up near Barcelona told me that he fell in love with another young man when he was nineteen years old. "My father had died in the war and I am the only child. I decided right away to tell my mother that I am gay and that she would have to accept it." Her response, however, was to say, "Okay, I understand what you are telling me. You are my son. Also you are gay, but I do not accept it."

He had not known what to do. "It made me crazy. It was like she was not accepting a package someone was handing her. Finally, I said, 'Listen, this is not something you can not accept. The sun comes up in the morning. You cannot look at it and say you do not accept it. That's self-indulgent foolishness you get from a child. I *am* gay and the sun *does* come up in the morning.'"

Each of us wants to be appreciated by those we love. Acceptance of the facts of one's life must come before appreciation. Without the acceptance of reality, appreciation is false—wishful thinking, at best.

The problem is that most of us have trouble granting acceptance without conditions. It is difficult for us to accept another person *as is*, though experience should have taught us before the end of childhood that we cannot change other people. Nor can we change most of the events that come along in life and impact us. We must learn to accept that which we cannot change, or we will know no peace in life and will miss the opportunity to give those we love the most precious gift we are capable of giving.

For a non-gay person to give the gift of true acceptance to a gay person, it is necessary to learn as much as possible about what it means to be gay and to unlearn the negative stereotypes that are so plentiful. This can lead to personal conflicts in beliefs and values.

Religion, for instance, can present conflict to someone who would like to be more accepting—just as it often has presented conflict for gay people working their way toward integrating their gay identity with the other facets of their lives. The conflict runs just as deeply whether the religion is fundamentalist or liberal, highly intellectual or salt of the earth. I was reminded of that fact by a man whose large family belongs to a religious group that is self-described as *creationist* and a woman who comes from a highly intellectual and orthodox family.

"*Creationist* sounds good," the man told me, "but I've had trouble fitting into it and my family's having trouble now. I wrote and came out to my sister and she told my brother. She wrote back demanding that I not tell my parents because it would break their hearts and cause them trouble with their faith. My brother moved away but kept the religion. He's got a job cutting down trees that are older than the family religion. How's that for respect for creation? He told me that if he ever sees me again he'll see to it that he and his buddies beat some sense into me. Very loving and accepting, huh?"

The woman has two sisters and a brother who have chosen the family religion as their vocation. "God save us from people who have a religion based on a book," she told me. "I came out to my family before I left our country and they ran to their book right away and said, 'Oh, no, no, no. You cannot be this. Look here in our book. You cannot be that way.' I asked them who wrote the book and they told me, 'God did.' What can you do? I say that they believe in a cookie cutter with sharp edges and I will not submit to the cutting. Their cookie-cutter book is more important to them than I am. They pray all the time for me to change. So I live thousands of miles away and we write letters about the weather."

The religious conflict may not be resolvable. Religions change their dogma or their interpretation of it very slowly and, while some of the faithful may recognize that there are good gay people being shut out and are attempting to recognize them and fit the conflicting realities together, there is a long road to be traveled, one very slow step at a time. Learning that someone you love is gay may seem to put that person on the other side of the door that presumably leads away from the sanctuary. Yet, like the mother in Spain, you must accept that the sun comes up in the morning and you must accept the fact that this beloved person is gay. Until you do that you cannot hope to move toward mutual appreciation and resolution within the relationship.

Sooner or later, sex must be confronted in the process of communication. Unfortunate but true, since it is homosexuality that separates us from people who consider themselves to be exclusively heterosexual in orientation, sexuality is treated as the most important facet of being gay. If someone you love is gay, homosexual desire is a part of her or his nature and homosexual behavior of some sort is usually involved.

You must come to terms with any and all of the reasons you have heard in your lifetime that are supposed to prove that homosexuality is bad. If you are successful in your quest to honestly re-examine your learning, you will come to the inevitable conclusion that sex is sometimes hurtful and it is also often wonderful. The difference has to do with what is happening between the people involved in the sexual act. You will find that it has little or nothing to do with the gender of the people involved.

Because gay people have been exposed to the same societal training in their lifetime as non-gay people, there is a sharper focus on sexuality. We pay attention to it. As a group, we tend to be more frank and honest about its good and bad aspects. To a non-gay person who has been trained to think about sex but to mention it only in certain *acceptable* ways, it can be shocking to listen in on gay talk about sex or to hear the sexual innuendo in general conversation. Sometimes it is exaggerated. Young gay people are particularly likely to emphasize it as they try to find their way through the thicket of fiction and facts about gay sex and learn what it means to their generation.

If you love us, you must try your best to accept us as we are. Like the young man in Spain, each of us is trying to be the best person she or he can be, whether that fits your idea of how a good person should be or not. Most of us spend all of our lives trying to get free of the oppression to which we have been victim since birth. We continue to try to be worthy of our own respect and love. Your acceptance can help a great deal; your conditional acceptance can slow us down.

Gay or non-gay, most of us are so inexperienced in giving the gift of unconditional acceptance that we may think we are doing it when we are not. Being neutral about being gay in an anti-gay environment is not quite enough to qualify as accepting. A neighbor once said to me, "As far as gay is concerned, I'm neither for it nor against it. It's up to you whether you're gay or not." It sounded almost right. I know that my gay identity is my business and not my neighbor's. It would have helped more, though, to hear something like, "I think gay is just as good as not gay. I like you. Being gay is part of you, so it's part of what I like about you."

The message you need to try to get across, once you feel it, is that you accept *and* support the person's gay identity. Often the word *accept* is used with no meaning. Many times relatives will tell a gay person, "I accept the fact that you are gay but I don't like it." There we have the acceptance that the sun comes up in the morning but not acceptance that is dynamic enough to permit you to move on to appreciate it. Either you accept the person or you do not. If I tell you that I accept something about you but I do not like it, I have done no more than admit that I cannot find a way to change you into the person I require you to be.

It is difficult. You must be who you are and hope that your gay friend or relative will accept you too. All of us are changing. We can only hope and try to change in better ways while hoping that the people we care most about accept us and appreciate us as we are at any given point along the way.

I once met a man who told me that at one time in his past he had been gay for a year. That interested me since I know that all the professional and unprofessional claims of *curing* people of gay identity are, at best, false advertising.

It happened that all of his best friends in college were gay and involved in the same attempts to win social change in the world that interested him. He knew that he found several of his male friends attractive and so he reasoned that he, too, must be gay. He had a boyfriend for a short time and then a serious lover relationship for some months. It was one of his gay male friends who helped him to recognize that while he was capable of sharing affection and enjoyable sex with a few males, the people who most strongly sparked his erotic attraction and the individuals to whom his heart was drawn most strongly were women. He had gone overboard in his attempt to be accepting of gay identity. He had correctly located some gay feelings of his own but ignored his stronger non-gay feelings. He laughed when he told me about it but also admitted that it was not at all funny at the time. "I had to go through a long period of coming out to my gay friends as being basically straight."

Whatever our erotic orientation, each of us can be no more and no better than the person we are. If you love someone who is gay, try your best to learn about us and about your gay loved one in particular. Try your best to offer the gift of unconditional appreciative acceptance and you may find yourself the recipient of that same wonderful gift.

19

PARENTS

HERE IS PART OF A LETTER that came to me from a mother in a distant country. "When my youngest child came out to me three years ago I was in the middle of my degree course in social sciences. In theory this should have meant I would have no problem on this subject. On an academic level I didn't, but as a parent I had every emotion you talk about in your book.

"This was one of the most isolating experiences of my life, as my son at the time felt unable to come out to the rest of the family. I felt frightened because of all the negative pictures flying around in my head, confused, sad because of the loss of our expectations, no marriage, no grandchildren from this very special son. But also sad because of the extra difficulties he would endure throughout his life because of our homophobic society. I felt guilty, a greatly loved child to all the family, had we loved him and spoilt him too much? Had I made him this way because he and I were so close? I felt angry too. Angry at him for bringing this sorrow and what I saw as public disgrace to the family, but also very angry at myself for the way I, who thought of herself as such a liberal, could react as I was doing.

"In the end I think this was what helped me to seek answers, to want to understand, the need to overcome this feeling of disgust at myself. I was able to study homosexuality as part of my course... ."

This mother found her way through the forest of feelings that surrounded her and was able to give her son and herself the gift of understanding. It was a hard-earned triumph that is not difficult for any parent to appreciate. Another mother, discussing how she came to terms with the fact that her daughter is a lesbian, said, "What else can a parent do? We learn early that we can't anticipate everything and when something comes along, we deal with it. We do the best we can."

That last phrase reminded me of a kind nurse who, looking at my face as I was about to leave the hospital with the new life of a first child in my arms, said, "Don't worry, babies aren't as fragile as they look. You already know how to hold her. She'll let you know what she needs and you'll do the best you can."

Flying over the vast Pacific, I once found myself in one of those intimate talks with a stranger that sometimes happen in airplanes. He told me that he and his wife had arranged a meeting with their two adult children for a very important talk about the future. "We were very frank, you know, talking about passing on and inheritance and all of that. I said something flippant about it all being about passing on, one way or another, and the two of them picked up on it right away. Funeral arrangements and wills didn't take long at all but we got into several hours of good talk about the really important things that parents pass on to their youngsters—sometimes on purpose and sometimes not. You know the little mannerisms, quirks and habits, as well as important values you don't even think to talk about. Our son said he had learned a love of nature from me and a love of music from his mother. Our daughter said she had learned from her mother how to take what her children bring into her life, make use of it and to not indulge in making something bad of it. That's very important, don't you think?"

I told him that I did, indeed, think that was very important. The world has every imaginable kind of parent in it, some more thoughtful, generous and competent than others. All parents, unavailable and self-centered or available and giving, whether shouldering the task of parenting willingly or not, do pass on something to their children. Parenthood is a responsibility.

If you are reading this book because a son or daughter is gay, you are undoubtedly trying to live up to your responsibility . If you have chosen to read it on your own, it indicates that you are the kind of parent who will go out of your way to understand and help facilitate the growth and well-being of your offspring. If you are reading it because your daughter or son has asked you to, they are trying to tell you that they value you as a parent and want to use the book as a means of strengthening the bond between you. They may hope that the book will speak to you in ways that are difficult for them.

I asked a gay man who was cutting my hair how his parents had reacted when he told them he was gay. "They had already been in this country for ten years or so. They were cool," he said. "They already had some gay friends, though I can't say I liked them very much. My dad just took it in stride. It didn't make any difference between us. My mom, after about fifteen minutes of silence, said, 'Oh, good, a *fruiter*—a funny boy. My sister has one. Out of the six of you, I hoped I'd get at least one!'"

That is not a usual reaction. Parents usually have strong emotional reactions to learning that a daughter or son is gay. You are apt to feel frightened. New information is often frightening, and it is not the first time you have experienced fright during your career as a parent. As always, you take it as it comes, one step at a time, learning more, helping to reassure your youngster and staying alert to ways that make the situation better. It is the same with a skinned knee or a first date. As you learn more you will feel more comfortable and be better able to help.

Although gay people are becoming more visible, some of the fear you feel when suddenly confronted with the gay identity of your son or daughter may be due to feelings that they are part of a world that is unknown to you. This can cause you to worry about his or her well-being. You may also experience guilt because of a false but prevalent belief that it is bad to be gay and that parents are responsible for it. It is the unusual parent who is so familiar with gayness and has such a solid communicative relationship with his or her off-spring that sincere appreciation for the information can be expressed immediately.

A frequent first question is, "What did we do wrong?" Well-educated parents who have read the wrong books or advice columnists may be too prepared to answer their own question. "It was because we: didn't pay enough attention to you; smothered you in love; favored your sister; let you get too close to Uncle Al; lived in the wrong neighborhood; sent you to the wrong school; burdened you with our drinking problem; didn't talk to you enough; frightened you with the example of our bad marriage; were too close to one another and shut you out; let you play with the wrong kids; kept you home too much; didn't make you go to church; let you get too close to the pastor; forced you to be good; etc."

All parents have done some things "wrong" in the rearing of their children. But the fact is that we do not know why some people retain awareness of attraction to people of the same gender and others follow the dictates of a culture and lose that awareness. Nor does it much matter, unless we accept the destructive assumption that gay people are bad and innately unhappy (or unless we want to rear all children to retain gay awareness). Gay people are gay and the non-gays are non-gay as a result of a combination of factors. These include: factors present at birth—usually described as *temperament* (how active or passive one is and whether visual, auditory or tactile stimuli are most likely to cause a reaction, for example); early and later learning experiences—some of which are related to child-rearing practices; all of which, together, build the core of the person—sometimes called *character*. And the millions of experiences inherent in living in an unpredictable world that build on the temperament and character create the unique individual outer layer that we call *personality*. The reason the causative factors are not important is that gays can be every bit as happy, satisfied and productive as non-gays and perhaps live in a wider, richer world than most people. Their *problem* comes to them from a punishing environment, not from their own identity, desires or behavior. Besides, any single factor could as easily contribute to a heterosexual as a homosexual preference or orientation.

Parents are not entitled to the credit or the blame for a gay daughter or son. They can be held responsible for how they behave after learning this information, however. Granted, you have your own years of prejudicial training to overcome, but love has been known to help parents fight greater odds. Experienced mothers and fathers know that children grow best when given daily doses of love, respect, understanding and support. Grown children continue to develop when parents continue to offer these important emotional vitamins. And your gay offspring, denied the full love, respect, understanding and support of the larger community, is especially in need of yours.

Parents often say, "How can I be expected to receive it as good news when I know it means pain and a more difficult life?" The answer is that you are not expected to be joyful in anticipation of pain and difficulties. You're asked to face that pain and those difficulties as an adult and parent, to help your son or daughter to get through tough times and grow from their experiences. You are asked to do what you can to fight the malaise of community ignorance and prejudice that creates the difficulties and inflicts the pain, to voice opposition to politicians and religious leaders who insist on rules that harm your children. You are asked to rejoice in having a son or daughter who is willing to fight to preserve integrity and truth and who cares enough about you to risk your withdrawal of love in order to share his or her truth and come closer.

In ancient times, people selected the most beautiful and talented youths of the community and ceremoniously threw them into the molten lava of boiling volcanoes as offerings to appease the presumed angry gods who might otherwise destroy crops and homes. Some parents are willing still to sacrifice their beautiful gay offspring to appease a god of conformity. Parents are no better and no worse than other people. They have their own pitiable anxieties and weaknesses. I feel anger but I also feel compassion for the mother or father who breaks that most sacred bond and turns away from the outstretched arms of a son or daughter because of having been taught that it is the *right thing to do* if a child is gay. Somewhere within that parent there is a deeper level of truth that is stronger than any social conditioning. This truth has been violated, thereby creating an unbearable burden that must be carried to the grave.

For most parents of gays the disclosure of gay identity rarely comes as a complete surprise. You usually know your offspring well enough that there have been clues along the way. After the initial confrontation, however, your job as a parent is to encourage your offspring to become a self-respecting person who need not hide anything. To do this, you must quickly learn what it means to be gay. Your daughter or son is one expert, but only one, and may be inexperienced or misinformed. You need to turn to all available sources of information, including books and other people.

A word of warning is due, however. I regret to report that there still are some psychiatrists, psychologists and other supposed mental health experts who build professional reputations and livelihoods on the presumption that gay people are *sick*, emotionally disturbed or emotionally underdeveloped. We have had more than enough solid evidence to the contrary since the early 1960s, when it finally became possible to publish studies such as that of the American psychologist Evelyn Hooker, who scientifically compared the psychological test results of gay people with matching groups of non-gay people. The *evidence* of those *anti-gay*, prejudiced mental health workers rests on their own observations, perceptions and experiences with patients seeking help, having already accepted the advertised sickness assumption. The point of view of these presumed experts was the only one permitted in print for many decades and they continue to speak with an air of absolute authority. They are absolutely wrong. Do not let them intimidate you.

These so-called professionals neatly subvert parental support by pointing an accusing finger and saying it is your fault that your child turned out so badly. In my more forgiving moments I try to remember that they began with prejudice as well as misleading information, went on to develop blind spots and eventually realized that their reputations and livelihood depended on proving themselves right. But when confronted with the dead and the wounded who have been subjected to the unnecessary pain caused by these individuals, I am not so forgiving. Cynical or stupid and well-intentioned or not, they have gay blood on their hands and have no intention of acknowledging true evidence and becoming rehabilitated.

Many parents have united in their support of gay sons and daughters. There are organizations of parents, families and friends of lesbians and gays such as PFLAG (found on the web or in telephone directories) that effectively work against community attempts to harm gay people.

Sometimes there is a culture gap as well as a generation gap. It may be difficult to understand the gay subculture of your daughter or son, just as the culture of a different generation often is mystifying. You can ask questions, read and honestly communicate your incomprehension and differences of values. You need not suddenly become *gay* any more than you need become a generation younger or older in order to span the gap. All that is required is good will, support and effort.

It is the trying to understand that communicates your caring and that is a most important parental gift. It is a parent's responsibility to promote the welfare of her or his children. In order to do that job we are called upon to do the best we can. In the process, we pass on to our offspring the best qualities that each of us has—and that, not property, is the true legacy of any parent.

20

WIVES AND HUSBANDS

T HERE WAS A HUGE, ancient tree growing on the slope behind my grandparents' house," she told me. "It was very beautiful but because it was so old and so close to the house, people would sometimes tell my grandparents it should be cut down. My grandfather always told them that since it was ancient, something of nature's beauty, and living, we must respect it and let it live out its years in peace. Then he would tell me quietly that if it ever crashed into the house there would be a problem. Well, one stormy night it did crash down—right into their living room and kitchen. It was a disaster except that they were asleep at the other end of the house and not harmed by it."

An Asian woman, married to an American man whom she had met while he was in the armed forces and stationed near her home, was beginning to tell me about the day that her husband told her that he was gay. When I asked her more directly about her feelings at the time of her husband's disclosure, she said, "It was the end of the world. Nothing would ever be the same. There was no harm to my body or to his or to our two children, but our world had come to an end and nothing would ever be the same."

I know that there are people who believe that gay women and gay men never enter into heterosexual marriages honestly for love. These same people usually do not believe that lesbians or gay men can function sexually in a heterosexual marriage and thereby become mothers and fathers either. They are wrong.

There are many gay men and lesbians who have been, or continue to be, in heterosexual marriages. Most of them have children. Most of them married with love. Most of the marriages were or are better than average. I have seen many such people in my office, along with their wives and husbands. I also have met many socially.

The mythology of prejudice would have us believe that this cannot be true because the gay person carries too much *hatred of the opposite sex* and is, therefore, unable to perform the necessary sexual acts. Any gay person in a heterosexual marriage is using it as a *cover* or has a non-sexual marriage of convenience, or so the story goes. I do know of a few such marriages, not infrequently for the purpose of permitting one person or the other (or both) to live legally in the same country as his or her spouse. It is the only legal solution sometimes to prejudicial immigration laws that exclude the possibility of international love and marriage for gay people because of nationalized bigotry.

A marriage of convenience or cover marriage may be demanded by the managers of a gay film star or athlete if it seems that the fans require a totally heterosexual image for their idol. And, as always, such a cover can be necessary in parts of the world where employers or repressive governments make it dangerous to be found out as a gay person.

Usually, however, the gay person and her or his non-gay spouse have entered into the marriage for all the best reasons, but run into troubles when the tree of discovery and disclosure crashes into the home. The woman at the beginning of this chapter said that one of the reasons that she was attracted to her husband was because she saw that he was capable of open affection with other men rather than being aggressive and oppositional with them. "I suppose that, in a way, I knew about his loving other men before he knew it. He was in the service but I could see that he was not that killer-warrior kind of person. I had seen enough of them and did not want one for a husband. We had the best marriage of anyone I know, but now he has come awake to his desire to be with another man."

The only unusual thing about her story was that he had managed to remain unaware of his gay nature until he was twenty-six years old. For men the awareness is usually much earlier, often reported as "I guess I always knew, sort of, but without knowing what to call it." It would be less unusual to hear about a lesbian awakening to her nature in her adult years, not infrequently after a period of marriage and motherhood.

Most married people experience changes in their spouses, in themselves and consequently in their marriages. Sometimes changes are minor, sometimes major. There are changes that come because of illness, jobs, disability, income, different rates of maturation and sometimes shifting interests and affections or love affairs. As the two adults learn how to work together on solving problems and cooperate within the context of change, their relationship can become deeper, more secure and more satisfying. But if they neglect the relationship and one another, the changes easily can be come divisive and destructive.

Change can come unexpectedly and be frightening. A woman from the southern part of the United States telephoned my office to say that she had read an earlier edition of Loving Someone Gay and had found no help for her in it. She had learned that her husband was gay and had tested positive for HIV. "I have two children and he almost killed all of us," she said. She felt that someone should speak out about the harm done by such gay men.

It is to be hoped that she was able to get more information about the viral infection and how it is spread (almost always by unprotected sexual intercourse or direct blood-to-blood contact) and that the information was enough to allay her anxiety regarding her family's exposure to the disease.

If the couple had been having unprotected sexual intercourse, however, it certainly was the husband's responsibility to know his own HIV status and to inform his wife if he had any reason to believe that he might put her at risk. Whether or not he was HIV-positive, it was also his responsibility to practice safe sex if he was having sexual contact with anyone other than his wife.

Lack of responsible behavior on the part of a spouse or sexual partner does not have to do with whether or not the person is gay. Another woman, coincidentally, from the same geographic area sent an e-mail saying, "My husband and I are in a twenty-five-year mixed orientation marriage. We have three children, a great life and are truly devoted to each other." She was writing to thank me for what they had found in the book. "So much of what is written about our choice is negative; many people from both the gay and straight community think it is unworkable. However, we are happy, and I wanted to let you know..."

A married man and woman came to see me together for the purpose of improving the quality of their marriage. Both were extremely attractive, bright, busy executives who were happy with their careers. Each traveled to distant locations regularly but tried to stay in touch by telephone, spending most weekends and an occasional weeknight together. Both said they were satisfied with the marriage and that they loved one another but felt their communication was not as good as it could be. Both felt that something was missing. And there was the question of how, when and where to start a family.

On their third visit, the handsome husband seemed distracted and the beautiful wife looked tired and strained. "Something's in the air," she said. "Last week I brought up plans for a vacation next summer and no response." She looked at him directly. "What?" she asked.

There was a long moment of absolute silence and then, his handsome face twisted and contorted, he burst into violent tears. Sobbing, he said, "I've been seeing someone else for a year. I didn't think it would amount to anything."

She stared at him—arrested, as if watching someone suddenly becoming grotesque before her eyes. She did not move.

"Oh, God, I don't want to hurt you," he said. "I love you. But I love him too. I want to live with him."

I remember the woman who decided she needed to get out into the world when her four children were all old enough to be in school. She took an entry-level job in a publishing company that did not pay well but gave her flexible hours. Both she and her husband were happy with the new arrangement that also lessened some of their financial pressures. But when the company had a *team building* retreat, she met another woman who worked as a sales representative for the company. The other woman was divorced and had older children. They felt drawn to one another, stayed in touch by telephone and e-mail and began to see one another socially. Within months they realized that they had been drawn into a profound relationship. Unanticipated change had descended.

Some wives and husbands know that their spouse is gay or has homosexual inclinations before marriage. Sometimes it is assumed by both people that the marriage vows of fidelity will be strong enough to keep the marriage secure. This is sometimes, but seldom, true. As years go by, unfulfilled yearnings begin to gnaw at the homosexually inclined partner.

In many areas of the world the institution of marriage is changing. Separation and divorce are common. It has become almost ordinary to think of a first marriage as just that—a *first* marriage in which we learn more about ourselves and much more about the skills of conflict resolution and cooperation required in a satisfying partnership. Many couples are opting for one or more live-together relationships of some duration and depth before choosing to enter into marriage. More and more industrialized societies are making that sort of arrangement socially acceptable again (as it was in centuries past), recognizing it as ordinary or normal, and thereby removing stigma and shame assigned by government in collaboration with the dominant religion.

Coming to the realization that one's mate wants to or *must* share his or her deepest feelings and desires with someone else does not feel good. It is painful no matter how well you comprehend the reasons. Whether or not it has been blessed by a religion and state, with any bond between two people there is the promise of growing security. This expectation is part of our innate nature and experience as social primates. Two of us together are safer than one alone. There may be less freedom but there is certainly more security. From the first day of infancy there has been a potential fear that can easily escalate to terror—it is the fear of abandonment. Listen to the amazing power of the scream of any infant who senses that it has been abandoned. Reason does not easily touch this fear. The discovery that one's mate has been or will be bonding with another person is reason enough to set off alarms that signal the primal fear of abandonment.

Stories of gay disclosure within a heterosexual marriage can have happy endings but they do not have happy beginnings. From the first hours of awareness that this awesome change is impacting the bonded relationship, both partners must exert nearly superhuman efforts to accept any and all emotions as they surface and are expressed. They must try their best to offer genuine words of comfort and reassurance to one another. And most importantly, they must continue to communicate physically and verbally, no matter how much it hurts or how unnatural it seems. You are trying to gain ground, to rise above primitive impulses.

The first impulse may well be to run from each other, go to separate quarters in order to feel some safety. Do that if you must, but try to keep the lines of communication open and active. Apart and alone, all of the worst fears flourish, a private nightmare can take root and the anguish of imagined abandonment may overwhelm you with anxiety. Fury and fantasies of revenge come naturally but they are dangerous, ultimately delivering harm to all concerned unless they are understood and controlled.

It is a time when a gay-affirmative therapist can be of help. If he or she is an experienced and well-trained professional, there will be no sides taken by this referee-witness. The therapist may not have quick answers that will soothe the hurt, but having someone with perspective listen to you with understanding can make is easier to find your own answers. It can also help pave the way for further communication with your spouse or partner.

If you did not know that your wife or husband was gay before you married, there may be very good reasons for that. Most of us who are gay and heterosexually married entered the marriage in good faith, having been led to believe that our heterosexual feelings combined with love for our intended were proof that our gay feelings could and should be discounted as being not very important. Most of us were taught by books, therapists, counselors and cultural mythology that if one has both heterosexual and homosexual feelings and there is real love on the heterosexual side, then the homosexuality is just a phase. It is the experimentation or *fooling around* reported in novels and biographies detailing boarding school days. It is the harmless childhood infatuation with a friend or older idol that helps one learn one's proper sex role through identification. At worst, we are told we were developmentally delayed or a bit confused, but a good heterosexual marriage should take care of all of that.

After the marriage vows, some of us realized that the feelings were not going to go away and some of us began to suspect that they might possibly be a decent, respectable and worthy part of the self. At that point, the married gay man or woman faces a decision of whether or not to share this additional information of gay identity and, if so, how much and how soon. The risks are great. There is the real fear of frightening and hurting the spouse because of his or her own sexual identity training: "Why am I not man/woman enough to satisfy you entirely?" or "You don't really love me. You're abandoning me!" There is a fear of losing the important loving relationship altogether. If there are children there is the possible loss of their love, custody or even contact with them. This is a very difficult decision, and it is small wonder that so many gay husbands and wives choose the lonely path of secrecy rather than risk an open road to catastrophic consequences.

If your wife or husband is gay and has taken the risk of sharing those feelings with you, you probably feel as if your world has turned upside down or ended. None of the usual expectations of marriage could have prepared you for this eventuality. Hopefully, however, your experience within the marriage has taught you to face each problem as it comes and to work together with your spouse on solving it. You face some awesome tasks ahead: You must learn more about what it means to be gay to avoid anti-gay misconceptions and prejudices, while also keeping your head above water and your self-esteem afloat so that you and your marriage do not capsize beneath this gigantic wave of confusion.

In reality there is no reason for your self-esteem to be damaged, but it will feel threatened for all of the wrong reasons. During the initial period of reorientation, try to hold on to the fact that you are not worth less because your husband or wife happens to be gay. You did not make your spouse gay. You will hear echoes of anti-gay mythology telling you that it is because you did not provide enough sex, demanded too much sex, drove your spouse away, held on too tight, and so on. Try your best to let go of the guilt. It is not your fault. You deserve neither blame nor credit. The fact is that your spouse has a greater than average respect for inner truth and integrity and loves you enough to have chosen you for marriage and to receive this intimate revelation. From there you go on, with the additional information that you now have—your spouse is gay.

Try to take your time in deciding together whether or not to stay married. Even though the marriage contract makes it more difficult to dissolve a relationship, it is a decision faced frequently, privately, by most married individuals even when neither of them are gay. Each partner continues to change after the original commitment and the changes may lessen compatibility. The gay spouse's gay needs must now be considered in the ongoing discussion of whether to continue the marriage. The non-gay partner must decide if the revealed gay identity reduces the desirability of the partner, for whatever reasons, or takes too much away from the union.

A spouse's anti-gay training or homophobia may surface immediately along with rage at the prospect of abandonment. Sometimes the suitcase is irrevocably packed soon after the disclosure is made. More often, because it involves two people who love one another, the sorting takes much longer. The gay identity of one partner becomes yet another ingredient in the constant weighing of satisfaction in the relationship. Sometimes the decision is made to stay together because of the children. If this is the *only* factor keeping the marriage going, it is almost always a bad idea. Two tense, unhappy parents can make life far worse for children than a considerate divorce or separation done with care would do.

Remember that there is no particular reason for the marriage to be less sexual or less sharing than it has been all along. The announcement of gay identity does not reveal a totally new person, it simply adds a new dimension. The quality and quantity of sexuality and sharing change throughout the years of marriage anyway. The changes are not likely to be the sole result of the disclosure.

For a few gay people, the disclosure is about as far as it goes. They abide by their vows of monogamy and, in terms of behavior, there is no change in the marriage. More often, however, there is a certain amount of change. The gay spouse is likely to insist on exercising some personal freedom, establishing some social-emotional-sexual involvement with one or more other gay people. The non-gay spouse may need to claim the same freedom at this point or he or she may find the gay spouse's freedom intolerable. In rare cases, hardly a feather seems to be ruffled.

It is most important to continue talking and sharing feelings! There is no knowing where or when the roller coaster ride will end, but you need one another more than ever during the ride. The only certainty ahead is that the status quo will change. The formula for balancing the needs of both parties evolves according to the needs and temperament of the two individuals.

If the two of you decide to preserve your relationship and your marriage, more questions will come up. How much information does the non-gay spouse want? Should details of gay activities be shared or kept separate? Which friends, neighbors or relatives are to be told, and how much are they to be told? When and how much are the children to be told? How are times apart to be arranged? It is possible to make these decisions with sensitivity and respect for one another's feelings. Continue to talk! First decisions are not always the best ones. This is, by definition, a period of change.

The more willingness there is to share feelings (including the non-gay spouse's possible hostility and feelings of betrayal and the gay spouse's possible feelings of oppression, deprivation and anger), the greater the basis for discussion and a more satisfying, altered marital arrangement. It is important to remember to respect one another and to offer mutual support during this sorting period. It is also a good idea to set aside quiet times of appreciation during which you enjoy your relationship rather than examine it. When it all seems too taxing and complex, and it will, think whether you would change places willingly with bored couples who seem to have nothing left to say to one another.

Each of you must try to remember that the other person is an independent, individual entity and does not belong to you like a possession. While you are entirely responsible for communicating your own thoughts and feelings, you do not have the right or responsibility to renovate or rehabilitate your spouse. You can say how you feel when he or she behaves one way or another but demanding exact changes in attitude and behavior is not usually productive. If your spouse cares for you and the relationship, changes will come in time as he or she understands exactly what bothers you and how strongly it bothers you.

Your sense of well-being need not depend upon the other person's being in attendance at all times. Sharing your spouse's love with others gets easier if you remember that the more one loves, the more capable of loving one becomes. There is no need to worry about less love being available for you unless you have some evidence that love for you is being withdrawn.

Primacy of relationship is very important. When the sobbing man in my office told his wife that he had been seeing someone else and wanted to live with him, it was a triple blow. He was making the disclosure of his gay identity and it was coming as a surprise to his wife. In addition, he was telling her that she was no longer the primary love in his life. That is really too much for anyone to hear all at once. All sense of security is shattered.

Do not underestimate the importance that reassurance of primacy in a relationship can have. After much sorting, the couple often decide that the crucial factor is declaring the primacy of their relationship to one another—as often as needed. "There may be other people in my life but there is no person nearly as important to me as you are. You come first. I want to grow old with you."

Marriage is a partnership. Each partner is devoted to the well-being of the other. Both partners are devoted to the well-being of their shared enterprise—the relationship. It requires the loving work of building, repair and maintenance. Sometimes it requires sacrifice and sometimes it is painful. If either partner is distracted to the extent that you are focused on your own benefit more than your partner's benefit, you are neglecting your responsibility as a full partner. Three questions must have equal weight and worth. How can I make my own individual life more satisfying? How can I help my partner to have a more satisfying life an as individual? What can I contribute to the growing strength and stability of this partnership? Skip one question and you are no longer operating as a partner.

Occasionally, the husband or wife of a gay person seems so well prepared by experience or disposition as to make the disclosure of gay identity a mere matter of minor surprise and/or appreciation. I remember two people who illustrated this well. The first was a wife whose gay husband prepared his disclosure for many months. Within an hour she learned that her husband was gay and had been all of his remembered life. She also learned that he had had brief amorous adventures during the marriage and in the past year had settled down with one lover who long ago had been presented to her as his best friend.

Her immediate response was, "I can't say that I care much for the deception, though after some explanation I see how he felt it was necessary. I'm envious of all those secret adventures but I don't feel cheated." She said that he had been an excellent husband and father and the information helped her to understand other characteristics of his that she admired.

She went on to say that her father had a best friend with whom he went on hunting expeditions. They had been extremely close all of her life, up to the time of his death. "For all I know they had sex, though I certainly never thought about it." She came to the conclusion that what was involved in her own relationship was a broader understanding of the *best friend* relationship her husband and his lover had. She was secure in knowing that she came first with her husband, she knew and liked the man who was his best friend and lover, and felt no threat to the marriage and home.

The other example is about a man whose wife traveled as part of her job while his own work kept him at home. Through the years, their shared responsibilities had shifted to the point where he was the one who had primary responsibility for maintaining the house as a home base for his wife and their children who were away at college. When she told him that she was a lesbian but wanted to continue their marriage, he listened carefully and asked many questions. She reassured him that he was the most important person in her life but told him that she wanted to have a sexual relationship with two other women she knew in another city. He took some time to think and feel it through and then said he understood and it would be good for her and he wanted her to be able to have that. He went on to say that he might want to have the same freedom, heterosexually, but he first wanted to make sure that it would be good for him and them and that he was not merely trying to compete in some way.

Sex outside the marriage is usually the big issue. The gender is less important. You may have feelings about the kind of people your gay spouse picks for partners; if they have a lot in common, it may be threatening; if they have too little in common, it can be seen as demeaning, since sex is the sole apparent basis for the relationship. You may be worried about contracting a sexually transmitted disease if your spouse indulges in casual sex with strangers. You may worry about blackmail if your spouse is not open about being gay and becomes sexually involved with strangers. These are the considerations, rather than gender, that cause concern and must be discussed and worked out to mutual satisfaction. It is very difficult to be gay and remain monogamous in a heterosexual marriage.

The disclosure forces you to re-evaluate what you want from your marriage. You may be glad you were stimulated to reconsider this question now, rather than permit your life to be guided by the unquestioned values that were formed in youth, long before you decided to marry. You may find you have a better chance of getting your needs met with this partner than with any other person you have met. You may find that your love for your spouse is such that you want her or him to discover true self, even if that means that your paths may separate you one day. This is truly unselfish love. You may have the kind of love that rejoices in the loved one's pleasures and victories rather than the kind that holds tight and strangles growth. You may discover that you are in love with the *person* rather than in love with the *marriage*.

At best, the disclosure will stimulate growth within your relationship and encourage mutual respect for differences of all kinds in people. At worst it will mean a parting of ways—and if that is necessary it *can* be done with love and respect.

It is not unusual for couples dissolving their marriages to be subjected to terrible pressures from relatives and friends. She (non-gay) is told that he is a despicable person to have passed himself off as an eligible husband when he was nothing but a homosexual, and that she should get every penny she can from him by way of compensation. He (gay) is told that if he had married a truly feminine and caring woman, the homosexuality would never have become an issue and he could be a happily married man with children. It is not difficult to imagine the other variations on these prejudicial themes. It makes it very difficult for a couple who truly care for one another to stay focused on the positive experiences they have shared, the rich pool of memories they will always have and their genuine good wishes for one another's future.

If the partners decide that it is best for the marriage to end, it is possible for both people to be devoted and caring—perhaps more devoted and caring than the couple who does not pay much attention to their relationship. Former partners who end the partnership carefully can be formidable friends. In leaving, they have learned more about strong loving than most people will ever know.

21

SONS AND DAUGHTERS

I N NATURE, IT IS A PARENT'S responsibility to protect and assist the development of their young as they grow in self-reliance. The parent encourages the acquisition of skills that will help the offspring to survive and thrive as independent adults. For humans the task is best accomplished with love. Some parents, of course, are better prepared and more able than others.

It is different than the sort of interdependence chosen by two independent adults. The adults can manage life alone but choose to share it. The love in a good parent-child relationship between an independent adult and a dependent youngster, requires that both grow increasingly free of that dependency. The unbalanced interdependence requires ongoing change. Parents can experience unselfish giving, the ultimate reward being the satisfaction of accomplishment. Parents may also be rewarded with affectionate appreciation and reciprocation as they grow old and less able to function independently.

Infants, young children, preteens and adolescents need guidance in more ways than you can possibly imagine until you are faced with parental responsibilities. Electrical cords can be dangerous as necklaces; the attractive shiny glass of a broken bottle on the beach can wound; becoming a good reader is more valuable than watching television; offensive language makes you *less* rather than *more*; being different for *show* is unattractive while being different because of inner conviction is courageous. Sex is good, not bad, however.... .

During your child's early years, you may be asked repeatedly to define *gay*. Since the word is used with increasing frequency but seldom talked about positively in school, it is an understandable request. If you are a gay parent, it is an important request. "Why are you different, Mommy (or Daddy)?" The same question is asked of parents who speak with an accent and have an ethnic identification that is different from the majority of people in the surrounding community.

The choice of words becomes more sophisticated as the child grows older, but the basic message is simple because it is truthful. We gay people are men who have very strong love feelings for some other men and we are women who have very strong love feelings for some other women. It is the same way men who are not gay feel about certain women and the way women who are not gay feel about certain men.

Try not to give more of an answer than the question demands. The child can always ask additional questions. The story often told as a reminder is of the child who comes home from school and asks the parent, "What is sex?" After a much too lengthy explanation that goes from birds and bees to mammals and parents, the fidgeting child looks askance at the parent and says, "But there's only a tiny space to fill out on the form next to the word sex." Oops. If the child is old enough to be asked to fill out a form, the explanation of choosing *male* or *female* does not take very long.

Generally speaking, the best policy is to be open and honest about your own or your spouse's gay identity as early as possible. If your children are old enough to have a question and articulate it, they are old enough to consider your attempts to answer it truthfully. They are too close to you to be kept in ignorance. If you hide something it takes on an ominous quality of secrecy and seems shameful. The belief that a parent is living with shame does not produce a good feeling in a child.

The longer you wait to tell, the more difficult it is. The inevitable questions, whether spoken aloud or not, are: "Why did you wait so long to tell me? Why did you let other people know but not me? Is it really bad? Didn't you trust me? Is it fair that you expected me to share my thoughts and feelings with you when you were not willing to share with me?"

If you are already *out* when your children are infants, there is no problem. If you talk freely about being gay, have gay friends in the home and gay reading material around, they will take it in as a natural part of life as they are growing up. Making the disclosure when your children are older is more difficult. As they move into preteen and the early adolescent years, anything having to do with sex is overloaded with significance and likely to produce blushes and giggles. But the rule of thumb still holds. If they are already teenagers it is better now than later.

Some gay parents hold off telling for fear of influencing the sexual development of their offspring. That is a symptom of the homophobic, anti-gay prejudice that still pollutes the social environment in too many places in the world. No one minds the overt attempts to influence children to become heterosexual that happen every day of their lives. If you remove the assumption that heterosexual interests are superior, it no longer makes sense to fear such influences on their development. Heterosexual parents have been producing homosexual offspring throughout human history and the reverse is not also true.

If telling is difficult and getting ready to tell is taking a heavy toll on your energy, perhaps it is best to take the plunge as you would into a cold lake. I like to tell a story about a friend of mine who had been getting ready to tell his two preteen sons for six months. Finally, he set aside an entire evening and worked up his courage. Over dinner he set the stage in a manner worthy of the well-trained college lecturer that he was. He went through the history of the world, including war and slavery and the varying customs of different cultures. He covered the struggles for civil rights elsewhere and at home and tactfully led up to his question. "How come you guys never ask anything about the gay struggle for civil rights? You know we have gay friends and you see books and articles about it around the house, but you never mention it. I want to have a serious discussion of it with you." One boy said, "Could we do it tomorrow night, because I have bowling tonight." The other said, "And Joe's Mom promised to take him and me to a movie that's in fifteen minutes." So much for the preparation. He vowed that he would take the plunge the next week, and he did. His wife was much amused by the whole drama. She had been encouraging him to get it all out in the open for months.

Contrary to anti-gay mythology, children everywhere have gay parents. They may be kept in ignorance of a parent's gay identity for fear that they will tell their peers with disastrous repercussions to follow. If you live in a part of the world where the life and liberty of gay people is threatened, this may, unfortunately, be the best policy until the political climate changes.

If you live in a place where the struggle for gay civil rights is ongoing, it is probably better for the children to know where you stand. They are forming their values. Given the vigor with which children can mirror a society's punitive enforcement of conformity codes, there may be genuine cause for concern. Their peers may give them trouble for having a nonconforming parent, but they can learn how to handle it and will grow stronger and more empathetic, as other children of oppressed minorities have done in generations before them.

If you are the son or daughter of a gay parent, it is easier to hear the disclosure directly than for you to discover it on your own. Anti-gay prejudice being as virulent as it is in some areas, too many children are traumatized by making the discovery in a television, radio or newspaper account that describes their father's arrest or their mother's court case. Others have learned by overhearing neighborhood or schoolyard gossip.

If you learn about your parent's gay identity from someone other than your parent, the first thing you must do is to ask your parent about it. It may be true and it may not. It may take your parents weeks or years to find all of the right words to explain the gay feelings, the circumstances, why you were not told sooner and what it all means. You can ask your questions, express your feelings truthfully *and* be supportive. It is now your turn to try to support your parent in the same way your parent would be expected to support you.

If you are learning that your parent is gay, it means that your father or mother is different from most other people, different from the way many say a parent should be. Your parent is different because he or she is able to love another man or woman fully—body and soul. Is that so bad? Do your own thinking. In a world where grownups can be seen competing, cheating, stealing from one another and even killing one another for what they believe are good reasons, is it so bad to have a parent whose "crime" is the ability and need to love?

Having a parent who is different can make it easier for you to be who you truly are. Hopefully, it will help you explore your own gay feelings, but that is only part of it. It can also make it easier for you to dare to be different in other ways. You will not be as tempted to take other people's word for what is right and wrong. You are much more likely to think for yourself at an earlier age, and that means you are much more likely to build a life that is personally satisfying.

If no one helps you get free of the prejudices against gay people, you may think that your gay parent is bad. You may feel resentful that it was kept secret from you, not understanding how self-hatred can take root and grow inside someone as good as your mother or father. You may not have considered the possible fear your parent has had of losing your respect and love. Once you know the truth, you can begin to think these things through for yourself. Consider the possibility that your parent is a better person than most because she or he has retained true self-respect, maintained integrity and displayed courage in a world where people try to force you to be like everyone else at any cost.

Your gay parent may turn out to be a person with whom you can share your most private thoughts and feelings. Some people may tell you that you should feel ashamed or guilty. Why? You have done nothing wrong. You are not bad and your parent is not bad. Your parent is *different* and we need differences in our world. Who wants to live in a world in which everyone is just like everyone else? Not only would it be boring, but how would we know how to deal with the unpredictable events that shape our lives? Anyone who suggests that you should feel wrong, guilty or bad is *not* someone who can help you sort out your feelings. Your gay parent can probably help you the most.

Children and preteens will need guidance and answers to questions about what it means to be gay. One or both parents will have to undertake the job of giving this guidance initially. There also are some gay-affirmative books written for children, but some are difficult to read and require interpretation. For adolescents and adults it may be possible to find or form a discussion group in which thoughts and feelings can be safely shared. Those with more experience can help those with less experience come to terms with feelings and judgments, and those who are interested can coordinate efforts to support gay people in their quest for equal civil rights.

But if you are a child who is teased by other children about having a gay parent, try to remember that it is exactly the same as any other kind of teasing. It is no fun and can make you feel miserable unless you do something about it. The children who tease you are trying to get rid of their own unhappiness and are looking for a distraction. Trying to make you feel bad by pointing out some way that you are different helps them avoid their own pain. They are not mature enough to know that all of the greatest people who ever lived were different in some way. They know they can hurt you most by attacking the mother or father you love. Deal with them as you would with any bully who is stuck in anger and misery. Stay out of their way until they are more calm and have more self-control. Then tell them you are proud of your parent's courage to be exactly who she or he is—*different*.

But if you feel threatened with real physical harm that you cannot avoid, find a responsible adult or hit back if necessary. These unhappy people may seem strong because they do not admit how frightened they feel. If you hit them with your own awareness of how unhappy and unsure they are, it is difficult for them to keep their balance. You have nothing to be ashamed of and no need for fear. It is they who have something to be ashamed and fearful of—if they don't change they are going to be very unhappy adults. You have a parent who is different but not bad. It is the child bully who is behaving badly.

Sometimes, daughters and sons must help their parents. If you learn about your parent being gay when you are no longer a child yourself, and if your parent does not feel self-respect within that identity, you can help. If you believe that you are from a less prejudiced generation, you can introduce your gay parent to the idea that there is richness in diversity and that each of us is free to grow and develop if we are not trying to conform. You might also do some research and help your parent find reading material and contact with other self-respecting gay people and gay organizations.

If you have sad or bad feelings about your gay parent, try to express them out loud. You might talk them out with a close friend, with your other parent or with another trusted adult who is not troubled by the circumstances. But if he or she gives some hint that it is anything less than good news to be gay, beware. It is an indication that this person has been infected with anti-gay prejudice.

When you feel ready and are no longer worried about hurting your gay parent, talk to him or her about your feelings and see what you can work out together. By letting your parent help you with your bad feelings, he or she may clear some things up, too. Parents who hide their gay identity often become bitter and lonely, all because they were afraid of rejection by their daughters and sons.

You may sense some ambivalence in your gay parent when you try talking things out, and this can be confusing. The ambivalence is due to *being* different. The children of immigrants experience it. Their parents want them to integrate into the surrounding dominant culture and become a seamlessly assimilated part of it. But they also want their offspring to value what they have brought with them from a different culture with its customs, language and attitudes. Whatever your age, you can help yourself and your gay parent by sorting through your thoughts and feelings and learning from them. If you are honest, you will come to feel proud of your parent's difference, in time. Sharing and showing that pride will encourage everyone concerned.

Sometimes a parental marriage ends and it seems to be because one parent is gay. In other circumstances, when a marriage ends, the children sometimes feel relief if the parents did not get along well and did not seem to like one another, thereby creating a constant tension in the household. When the marriage ends because one parent is gay, the children may be more mystified and hurt. There may have been no discernible tension and little, if any, indication that the parents did not like one another or were not getting along.

There is more of that kind of divorce now than in generations past. It is not the result of hatred or cruelty. It is the result of two people having lived together as partners for some years and then realizing that each of them has grown in different ways that makes them no longer suitable as partners. Each realizes that she or he must follow a different path in order to continue the process of self-exploration and growth. If they defy this basic rule of nature and stay together there is the possibility of despair and eventual resentment of one another. One contributing factor to the increase in this more constructive sort of divorce today is the growing awareness that one partner may have hidden from the truth that he or she is gay.

The younger the children are when such a marriage dissolves, the more difficult it may be for them to understand. But it also can make simple acceptance of the situation easier. The important thing to find out from parents is that each of them loves you and that the struggle surrounding parting is not in any way because of you. The parents may be so preoccupied with the emotional and practical complexities of disengaging that they forget to let you know this. You may have to ask. Do it. You will feel better if you ask more than once, in several different ways.

If your father is gay and goes to live with another man whom he loves, or your mother is gay and goes to live with a woman she loves, it may be difficult for you to accept this other, almost-parent into your life (but probably not much more difficult than it would have been to accept your mother living with another man or your father living with another woman). Try to be patient—with yourself and with them. The simple passage of time is a great healer and teacher. Try to believe that your parents are doing what they need to do. Try to focus on their love for you while each is trying to get their own life in order. You can learn a great deal about getting through difficult times by watching them. There will be times in your own life when it will be necessary for you to make difficult decisions and you, too, will need to find courage and the self-confidence to make your own changes.

Social foundations are changing slowly but surely all over the world. We continue to question old assumptions, such as those that have kept some adoption agencies from considering gay people and non-gay single people as suitable adoptive parents. There are children who are shifted from one foster home to another and children who have been passed over for adoption because they have behavioral problems or some sort of physical handicap. These children need parents who will love them, help them through difficult times and give them a secure and stable home. You cannot learn compassion if you do not experience it. You cannot relax unless you are secure. These are vital ingredients for growing well. The gender of the grownups sleeping in the parental bed does not matter if they can freely give these gifts.

I once participated on a panel in Reno, Nevada, for a meeting of child welfare agencies in the United States. The panel was made up of four openly gay parents who were also professionals with something to say to this sort of audience. Our discussant was a judge from Arizona who was charming and intelligent and went out of his way to be friendly to the panelists. After our presentations, however, he announced that he was a judge who felt that it was his duty to reflect the mores of the community and that if those mores were to change, we gays would have to shoulder the burden of education and furnish our *visible martyrs*.

He described the cases that came before him for custody or adoption involving one or more gay parents as rarely "*clean*" because the applicants were often unfit for parenting for some reason other than gay identity. I am sure that I was not the only person in the room who was wondering about prejudice at that moment.

He said that he was about to face the problem of the first clean case. He said he had never met the two gay men who were trying to adopt, but that, by all reports to the court, they had everything to offer as parents. They had a stable relationship, good education, money and status in the community—but they were gay.

In response to a question from the audience as to how he might rule in the case, he said he would rule against the adoption because the community was not ready for it. At that point, a handsome, well-dressed, soft-spoken and articulate pediatrician arose from the audience and announced to the judge that he was the clean case and had traveled from Arizona to Nevada that day to see the face of the man who was to judge his fitness to be a parent without ever having met him. It was a scene that I will never forget. For one moment, I think it must have been clear to everyone in that room which man would be a better parent.

There is one last untruth that must be brought to light. I know many gay people who are parents, and I do not know one gay woman who loves a son less because he is male or one gay man who loves a daughter less because she is female. Openly gay people have given up the pretense that they are able to love *only* people of the opposite sex. A gay person may be more *sexually* attracted to people of the same gender, but we have learned through our hard-earned freedom that it is only possible to love a person because of who that person is. Your gay parent loves you because you are you, and not because of your gender. But if you are unsure of this, don't be afraid to ask.

Your gay parent may require some special understanding, but in the end they have the same responsibilities in relation to you that all parents have for their children—to protect and promote growth. If gay parents are to be judged it must be on the basis of how well they care for their offspring. Did they do their best for you? When you are judging your mother's or father's parenting skills, her or his gay identity cannot be set aside. It is an important facet of their identity and, therefore, an important factor in their life and in yours. Do both of you give that special identity full value? Has it been used to help you grow?

Not all gay parents are great parents, but most are. They deserve your love.

22

SISTERS AND BROTHERS

How much does it matter to you that a sister or brother is gay? How does it impact your everyday life? Is it your business? What do you need to do about it?

Two brothers and a sister sat in my office. The two brothers were gay and the sister was not. "I guess I'm the one who fell out of the nest," the older brother said. He had left home at the age of sixteen when his parents discovered that he was involved romantically and sexually with a man ten years his senior. "I was the one who started it. He was afraid to get involved with me but I wouldn't take 'no' for an answer. Our parents were determined to put him in jail one way or another, so I wrote a letter to him and a letter to them saying he was not to blame and then I left town."

"I was only fourteen at the time, but I knew I was gay too," his brother said. "I didn't know who I could talk to about it. I certainly didn't know that my honor-student, good-looking, star-athlete, all-around best-boy-brother was gay. I was really scared when you disappeared, Paul, as well as mad and worried about you—and me. I needed you. I didn't dare tell anybody that the second son was also gay until I left home when I was eighteen."

"I was shocked to find out about both of them," the sister said. "I'm the one who stayed in the nest—probably too long, with what was left of a family that had twisted itself into a pretzel. Every one of us is a little crazy. So here we are ten years later trying to get together again, maybe better this time than before. We've all had trouble forgiving but we found out that forgetting is even harder. We just couldn't forget one another."

That describes what most brothers and sisters feel—unable to forget one another. The feelings, both positive and negative, seem to be stronger in relation to the number of years spent together in the nest. Twins feel it most, together since conception. Sisters and brothers separated at birth who later learn of one another are usually very curious and strongly drawn to meet.

You may or may not have suspected that your sister or brother was gay but the moment of discovery or disclosure usually comes as something of a shock. Whether it confirms your suspicions or takes you by total surprise, there are several predictable emotional states that follow.

The first is worry. We all are aware of the prejudice and potential abuse waiting in the world for people who are *different*. Humans collectively have not yet evolved enough to rid themselves of destructive behaviors. Consequently, when you learn that a brother or sister is gay, you have good reason to worry about his or her safety.

The second is emotional distance. As the sister of the two gay brothers said, "For years, I kept wondering who these two guys were. It was like they were strangers. I thought I knew my brothers and yet it seemed like I didn't. Then I didn't know if I wanted to know them."

Like her, you may feel as if your gay brother or sister has put distance between you. It may feel as if he or she has done it or is doing it on purpose. You may fall victim to common homophobia and feel disgust, or you may want to have some distance or separation for a time. It can become complicated by a psychological defense called *projection* when, in truth, you are the one who wants or needs emotional distance, are unable to admit it and blame your sister or brother for having put it there—and then feel additionally hurt by that.

The third predictable emotional state is anger. Whether or not it is conscious, most brothers and sisters cannot escape feeling that the gay sibling has created a problem for them or brought a problem into the family. Sometimes it is deflected. "It's something that I can handle but it just doesn't seem fair to Mom and Dad. They don't need this kind of problem at this point in their lives." Or "We are adult parents now and can deal with this but it is definitely not fair to the kids. Why should they have this problem to complicate their lives?" It's an attack of common homophobia again. The problem is not the sexual orientation or identity of the gay person. The problem is the destructive prejudice in our world.

The fourth and most pervasive emotional state is a period of disorientation. A brother told me, "It was like the front of our house was still the same and the address was the same, but when I stepped inside the door the rooms were different. You just stand there blinking your eyes, trying to get used to it."

You have received important information and it has to be integrated. It takes time to sort feelings and imagine all the ways in which this fact of life may affect your own life and the lives of others in the family. The value of this period of disorientation resides in the opportunity it allows to reorient or reform family relationships in a constructive way. Relationships can be made closer and more satisfying than they were before. It is likely that you have been exposed to plenty of misinformation that can be corrected by reading, talking to a gay-affirmative counselor or by having talks with your gay brother or sister.

A gay male friend of mine was asked by his younger brother if being gay meant that he liked dressing in women's clothes. He explained that he did not like to do that, but that if he did like it and made it a regular part of his life, it would mean that he was a *transvestite*. He explained that there are both men and women who are transvestites, both gay and non-gay, and that it has little or nothing to do with being gay.

His brother's other question was whether he wanted to have surgery to become a woman. He explained that he did not want to do that and that a person who wanted to change from male to female or from female to male was a *transsexual*—and, again, it had nothing to do with being gay.

The new relationship that develops after you have learned that a sister or brother is gay can be an excellent one. If you too are gay, you can talk to your sibling about your gay feelings and attractions and he or she will understand and appreciate them. If you are not gay, you can still do a lot of sharing with your gay brother or sister. If you grew up in the same home with the same parents, you have a store of shared experiences to look back on together. To that can be added your very different and unique individual experiences and points of view.

It is as if your brother or sister has spent some years in a foreign country. You're sure to have many questions about the differences in language, values and how they can be explained. Your brother or sister may not have all of the answers, but together you can explore possible explanations. Anyone who knows more than one language and is familiar with more than one culture is richer because of it.

You will have to let your gay sister or brother know that you want to reform your relationship and make it closer. It will be necessary to both *say* it and *act on* it. She or he has reason to anticipate possible rejection. You may find unexpected anger in your gay sibling. "Where were you when I needed you?" Ride out the storm. Sort it out together. Honestly expressed feelings from both of you will carry you to resolution and make a closer relationship possible.

After learning that a sister or brother is gay, you may fear that you too are gay. Such fears are based on misconceptions. The first is that there is something wrong with being gay; otherwise the prospect of being gay would not be so alarming.

The second question may be troublesome. Is it inherited? Might I too be gay and not know it? The evidence suggests that the predisposition for sexual orientation is most strongly influenced by factors present before birth—genetic inheritance and/or biochemical influences during pregnancy. But the predisposition is a matter of *more or less* rather than *either/or*.

If we were totally relaxed and unprejudiced about sexual orientation, we would probably see that it is *normally* distributed in the population, which means that a minority of people would have an exclusively heterosexual orientation and a minority would have an exclusively homosexual orientation. Most people would be more or less homosexual and more or less heterosexual in their attractions at various times in their lives, depending on attributes *other than the gender* of individuals available and the strength of desire or need at the time. Some people would be more homosexually inclined more of the time and some would be more heterosexually inclined more of the time. This flexibility is less visible when the surrounding society insists that you must get into a category and be either homosexual or heterosexual in orientation.

If you are afraid that you are gay because you inherited it or that you may have caught it by growing up in close proximity to it, relax. It is not a disease and it is not contagious. You know your most secret desires. You know whether attractive men or attractive women catch your eye more often. You know whether your predisposition is more homosexual or more heterosexual no matter what your history of actual sexual behavior has been. Most people have some homosexual feelings and are capable of homosexual behavior if the circumstances are right. Being gay, however, is an ability to love and you must develop that on your own.

Having a gay brother or sister is likely to stimulate you to search out your own prejudices, not only against gay people but against other disadvantaged groups also. It is likely to make you more sensitive to the injustices in the world and more likely to make you a socially responsible citizen. It can open up enough questions in your mind to make you more appreciative of people's differences and more open to your own personal change. All of this may begin to show you that you are actually indebted to your gay sister or brother for helping you to seek and find a richer life.

Your gay brother or sister needs your open demonstration of love, respect and support. The gay person's path is a lot less lonely if the family is cheering along the sidelines. But do not hold back on your negative feelings. Your hidden prejudices and bad feelings can change only if they are brought out into the open. Once revealed, they will not do as much damage as you get to know your gay sibling and his or her friends.

You also may be able to help your parents leap the gap since you are distanced only by differences in subcultures while they have to contend with generational differences as well. Whatever you do, let it be wholehearted. Your gay sibling needs your appreciation (or clear rejection), not patronizing acceptance.

The two gay brothers and their non-gay sister found that with willingness and effort they were able to build very satisfying relationships with one another. The last time that I saw them, the younger brother said, "I noticed how many times we talked about the nest. It wasn't all that comfortable there back then, though. The nest was too small—too tight, not enough elbow room. We were more crowded than close. Now we're getting to know one another and to be the close family we were supposed to be in the first place. It's bigger than a nest—it's great."

If you are not gay but you have a brother or sister who is, you are in a position to help our damaged world to heal. You can talk about your gay sibling to your non-gay friends. You can display your love and pride. You can talk to bigoted politicians and religious leaders and offer them your superior knowledge.

If you have children, you can talk to them and their friends too. The young always offer hope for a better world but they need to know what needs fixing. Bigotry is an affliction Prejudice is a social disease. Both must go.

23

FRIENDS, RELATIVES
AND NEIGHBORS

M Y UNCLE JOINED THE ARMY when he was fresh out of high
school," she told me. "He thought it was his chance at an
education. He never thought he might face killing or getting killed. He
wasn't allowed to say he was gay. They sent him into a war that
needn't have been. He got killed at half past five in the morning over
there, at nineteen years of age. Two days later my wife and I found
out that our government wouldn't honor our wedding. Yeah, I'm
depressed and I don't think pills will help."

Friends, relatives and neighbors can do a lot to help gay people
stay afloat until such time as they are recognized as deserving equal
rights. Love is love. When it is discovered, it must be honored.

Great differences in age and generation or in geographic and
cultural backgrounds can be a hindrance to understanding—but
sometimes they help. I have heard many tales of grandparents who
were comforting and understanding when parents were disabled by
shock and prejudice. The same is often true for aunts, uncles or
cousins whose personal experiences give them perspective that makes
them more understanding. And, of course, true friends are amazing

in their ability and willingness to leap any barriers that stand in the way of compassion.

A man told me how he had dropped out of school, quit his job and been close to suicide when he received a one-page note from his grandparents that changed everything. He had disclosed his gay identity to his mother and father and their reaction had been to enlist all of their friends to pray for him. They did not want him to be gay, and he did not want to be gay because it was making everyone so miserable.

His grandparents' note invited him to come and help them with their cherry harvest. "It sounds dumb but all I could think about was the taste of my grandmother's cherry pie still warm from the oven. It filled my whole mind. It was my whole focus. So I went. The second day I was there, my grandfather sat me down on the ground next to him in the orchard and asked me what was bothering me, so I told him. He bowled me over. He said he didn't see the use in talking about it with anyone else in the family because they were obviously too easily upset right now. But he wanted me to know that he had had the same feelings when he was my age and he envied me, living at a time when it was possible to do something good with those feelings. He said, 'You go find yourself a good man to love, love him good, and you bring him back here to meet your Grandma and me and we'll help you celebrate.' I think my Grandpop saved my life."

A lesbian from a small town in Canada, who is now quite advanced in years, described visiting her aunt and uncle in New York at a time when she was feeling deeply ashamed of the fact that she had secretly fallen in love with the girl next door. Her aunt and uncle had just returned from a trip across the entire United States and invited their friends to a big party. "I'm sure they both noticed my subdued mood but my uncle caught me looking at a gorgeous woman at the party and said, 'You find her attractive, I see. Good for you. So do I. You know many women prefer the company of women. Sometimes two women settle down together for life. They are usually superior women.' He went on to tell me about how he and my aunt met Gertrude Stein and Alice B. Toklas. I was astonished. I had been sure I was the only one like me on the planet. He was calm, relaxed, sophisticated, and just flat out giving me permission to be who I was. It made an enormous difference for me. I try to pass it along to young people."

"Coming out for me was a very swift way of learning who my friends were and what friendship really can be," another woman told me. "There I was on a class trip in Hawaii—a long way from Utah—with dozens of my friends. We all displayed happy smiles all the time. When I cut through the nonsense one day and told my friend Mary that I loved her, word spread like a dry grass fire on a windy day. You would think people have lives of their own to live. I was the center of attention. Backs were turned. Authority spoke and more backs were turned. But a total of four friends told me they were with me no matter what—whether or not they were punished, sent away or whatever. We're all friends today, many years and many emotional hurdles, tragedies and joys later. One is a lesbian and the other three are straight and married with huge families. We five are *really* friends. I really don't know what all of those other people think friendship means. I guess it's just a comforting word for them."

Two very close and dear friends of mine, a husband and wife, were surprised but took my own disclosure in stride. They were determined in their support and persistent in seeking information anywhere and everywhere to learn more about what it was like to be gay so that they could understand. As the years passed, they were surprised at first to find that an increasing number of their friends in various places around the world were gay. They had sailed through the invisible, divisive shield of prejudice with such force that they had hardly noticed it.

Some friends and relatives of gay people want to relate better but are not sure how to do it. If you truly care about your friend or relative who is gay, take the trouble to talk with him or her about it. Do some reading and thinking and try to educate yourself. Dare to talk about it in public places. Do not treat gay identity as a forbidden topic, because it only protects and preserves the prejudice. It is the responsibility of anyone who cares deeply about someone who is gay to become educated about gay identity and to talk publicly about the injustice of prejudice.

Not all gay people are wonderful. Some have swallowed the stereotypes and act out accordingly. These are badly wounded people, damaged by prejudice. Others have the same limitations and lessons yet to learn that are found among the less desirable members of any population. People who are not decent are not decent—and are, understandably, avoided. But if your reluctance to become more familiar with gay identity and gay people is based on a general distaste for the subject and the people, you are suffering from common homophobia. As suggested earlier, you can seek help for this condition. At the very least, you can be honest enough to admit that you have a problem about associating or being associated with gay people. The response that you get may well be anger, but that is an appropriate response to an honest slap in the face. You can keep a healthy distance until the time for healing comes.

If you are a relative, friend or neighbor who is not close, but learns of someone's gay identity and feels supportive, make your support known in some way. Let your colleague or acquaintance know that there are other gay people in the world whom you value. It may strengthen and enrich your relationship. Even if it does not, voicing your support is sure to make both of you feel better. Remember that a brief note inviting someone to come and help pick cherries once saved someone's life.

If you are a relative or a friend who has hidden your own gay identity or your homosexual inclinations, here is a person with whom it may be safe to open the closet door and share your secret. You may not be ready to disclose yourself to most other people and may need to request that your needs be respected for now. But in the meantime you might share common experiences, concerns and joys and it could help both of you feel less lonely.

If you want to relate better to someone gay and are not sure how to do it, the first step is to tell him or her how you are feeling. The second step is to do some reading. And the third step is to start meeting more gay people. If you want to be closer to someone who comes from a foreign country, you must make some effort to learn the language and customs of that country. If you know that the people of that country are disadvantaged and discriminated against, you would naturally make it your business to fight that discrimination and protest the disadvantages in any way that you are able to do so. You must show by your behavior that you want to be closer and are willing to do the work involved.

If your gay friend or relative does not seem to appreciate your efforts at first, there are reasons. When gay people begin to reclaim their feelings, they are often in touch with anger that has been stored for years. Much of it is anger at the unthinking cruelty of the average person—and of non-gay family and friends in particular. As you begin to become more sensitive to gay people, you may become aware of their anger toward you and other non-gay people. The anger is real and legitimate, no matter how unfair it may seem to you at first. It is only by being aware of this anger and expressing it that the gay person has any real hope of reclaiming all feelings and surviving.

When the overflow in the reservoir of anger has drained off, the gay person will calm down to the extent that anger will be expressed in your direction only when you do something or say something provocative that deserves a negative response. Then the anger is efficiently expressed and quickly over.

It is a phenomenon that has puzzled many people in dealing with members of other oppressed minority groups. The initial rush of anger is unexpected and frightening. It is inexplicable unless you have some sense of how it is to live with such anger dammed up inside of you and how liberating it is to release it.

It is neither necessary nor appropriate to prostrate yourself in the path of the anger nor to invite punishment for the sins of all thoughtless non-gays in human history. But it is necessary and appropriate to understand where the anger is coming from and try to avoid inciting it. You must be honest with your own feelings also and sometimes those include anger in response. Sort it out. Stay honest. Talk. Seek resolution.

That is what is asked of you as a loving relative, friend or neighbor of a gay person. If you're reading this book, it is unlikely that anti-gay bias has closed your mind and heart. You're trying to understand. You are asked to listen to the gay person with the intention of understanding, to be honest in presenting your own feelings and to show that you care when you do. It is the gay person's responsibility to do his or her half of the communication.

You will find that most gay people make good friends, good relatives and good neighbors. We know how to appreciate differences, make the world more livable and fund fun even during periods of painful growth. Above all, we know how to love and appreciate the love of others.

And lest we undervalue caring neighbors, I must relate a story about the family that was in an uproar because their one son and one daughter had both come out to them at the same time. Though their daughter and her partner were intending to have a child with the aid of a gay male couple who were friends and would act as donors and fathers, the parents mourned the loss of all that might have been if their offspring had been normal and entered *normal* marriages. They were able to confide and share their feelings with their broad-minded next-door neighbors who were from Denmark, and who always listened with concern.

The neighbor wife said, "My brother and his family are coming in two weeks for a visit and you will love them. They all speak English too. They will be good to talk to also. The children are adorable." What she did not mention was that it was her brother, his *husband* and their son and daughter. But she was right. They were good to talk with and be with and it provided more reassurance than many thousands of words could have done.

Have you ever noticed how an individual's exercise of compassion makes him or her stronger and more loveable? We all look up to those who perform everyday acts of heroism by offering a hand or speaking out.

[PART FOUR]

Professional
Services

24

HELPING

IT IS REASONABLE TO EXPECT professional service providers to be familiar with the values, customs and ceremonies of the people to whom they presume to offer service. You offer limited service, at best, if you do not understand the world in which your client lives.

"I know I've got a big mouth and I'm taking it to another dentist. There I am with my jaw open while my dentist's assistant is cleaning my teeth and she starts talking about the parade and says she doesn't understand why so many good-looking men turn out to be gay when it only means asking for trouble. When she got her hand out of my mouth, I told her that I'm gay and that I didn't ask for it, but I thank God I had the courage to claim the name when I saw the truth of my sexual orientation. I've done my lonely time. I've lost friends. I've been sent away by some of my family. But yes, thank you, I do have gay pride. I damn well earned it. I'm doing my share to make this world a better place and I'm not alone anymore. If anybody doesn't approve of me they can take a hike or dig a hole and crawl into it." So spoke a man in an ongoing psychotherapy group. It was days before the annual San Francisco Gay Pride Week parade. "I just might put on a dress this year. It would be a first time for me and it probably would do me good. Maybe I'll scare a few homophobes."

The final section of this book speaks to and about the genuinely professional person who is dedicated to helping, offering service to other people when asked to do so. If you are a helping professional you realize that each person with whom you work is an individual, not quite like any other person. No set of generalizations applies entirely to that person, but generalizations can help when they are used to focus more quickly on the individual by enabling you to scan and compare which factors are and which are not relevant to the individual.

If you work with people who are gay, or with the relatives and friends of gay people, keep in mind a few generalizations that may or may not apply to the individual. They can help you remember to pay attention to what may be happening or might have happened to this particular individual.

1. The gay person has probably learned to feel *different*, to hide behind outward appearances and real evidence of success and accomplishment.

2. The gay person may have learned to distrust her or his feelings. This process often begins with the first, dim awareness of attraction to people of the same gender when the message communicated by the surrounding environment is that such feelings of attraction are wrong or bad.

3. The gay person may have a higher degree of self-consciousness. Having been exposed to both subtle and overt anti-gay mythology, one learns to be on guard.

4. The gay person may have decreased awareness of the anger generated in response to a punitive environment as well as the anger at the self for being different. Though out of conscious awareness, such anger can continue to accumulate.

5. The gay person, often invisible as such to others, is assaulted frequently with attacks on character and ability. These attacks are in the form of anti-gay jokes, prejudiced statements or omission when heterosexuality is praised. Awareness of the hurt associated with such assaults is usually kept to a minimum so as to keep anger under control.

6. A gay person is more likely to fall victim to depression. Much of this stems from hidden anger and insufficient emotional support in his or her environment.

7. The gay person can be tempted to dull the pain that surfaces by making use and misuse of alcohol and other drugs. The misuse of alcohol is reinforced in loud gay bars that make conversation difficult, especially if such bars are the only community-sanctioned meeting place for lesbians and gay men.

8. The gay person who is respected and loved, but who is hiding his or her true gay identity and facing what he or she believes would be a ruined life if the truth were to be discovered, is at high risk for a fatal accident or a seemingly inexplicable suicide. This is particularly true for adolescents.

9. A gay person usually has lived in two worlds simultaneously. The less public world has important reference points that are not visible. If you would know the person's history, you must learn about the person's experience in both worlds.

A professional who offers service to a gay person and who is not aware of the generalizations sketched in this list is likely to miss the reality of the gay client. I was reminded of that recently.

"I think the counselor just didn't get it." It was the tired voice of a friend, tearful and depressed, less than a week after his dog, Es, had suddenly become gravely ill on a Saturday morning. "She was just seven years old—halfway through her life." He was talking with difficulty, through tears. "We were going to help one another start toward old age soon—after I retired. She had waited patiently for me to have more time. There was going to be time enough at last for those long walks and playing ball and her snoozing in my lap or beside me while I read." Stopping to breathe, his quiet sobbing continued.

"The older and more lined my face got, the more she wanted to kiss it. Her affection and acceptance was so sweet. At the vet's on Sunday, we held her and talked to her while they gave her a shot that took her away in seconds. It was all over so fast. And today, the sky is blue here and the sun is shining and it doesn't matter one bit to me because she's not here to touch and hold."

I was hearing grief and more. I knew that there had been three dogs in his life, the first a stray mongrel who followed a lonely boy home when he was eight years old only to die two years later after giving birth, and then one of her puppies—hit by a speeding car and left to die slowly as the eleven-year-old boy sat by its side through the night—petting, talking and trying to comfort.

He told me that he had thought maybe he should see a counselor for a few sessions to try to head off the depression he feared that he was falling into. "I didn't think it would matter in this situation that the counselor wasn't gay. She seemed nice enough. I told her what was going on and what had happened and I cried a lot while she listened. I was really raw. But she startled me. She said, 'You can get another dog, you know.' I guess she meant well. But I was trying to tell her how much love I'd gotten and been able to give with Es and what it all meant to me." More tears.

"Then she shook her head and said, 'And to think that in some parts of the world they eat dogs.' That was it. I had to leave. I guess it was her way of trying to be sympathetic, but she didn't get it. I was trying to explain how Es and my other two dogs taught me about unconditional love. They were my best friends and family—souls I could confide in who would hear my confessions and accept or forgive without judging. But also they were like my children because they depended on me as totally as I depended on them. This person was on some abstract plane, miles from gay me. What if I had said, 'Well, lady, if your kid or your best friend ever dies you can get another one—and to think that in some places, you know, they once ate human flesh—including kids!' Imagine that as a way of helping her with the loss of love with her child or her friend? We're in different worlds. Es was just a dog to her. Maybe she's never had a pet and doesn't understand that animals don't give a damn whether she is gay, straight or getting old."

The professional who intends to help gay people can work toward reversing the psychodynamics in the preceding generalizations. But it is wise to give careful thought first as to how and when help is truly helpful.

"So in comes Lieutenant P., both guns smoking, so to speak. It's the annual dinner to honor the fallen, commiserate with those not promoted and congratulate the ones who were making it to retirement. She had a reputation for being mean and tough but not a lesbian. She was on her third husband and had seven kids and liked being a cop. Anyway, she had heard there was some *lesbo* name-calling going on in the department and makes this big show of sitting at our table, putting her arm over my shoulder and talking loudly, saying she personally is not going to put up with any kind of prejudice from any officer at any time for any reason. I was not quite ready to come out yet but she might as well have painted a pink triangle on my forehead."

Help can be offered but not forced. Gay people have had too much damage done by would-be helpers who forced us to move in ways we sensed were wrong or foreign to our nature. We will be rightly suspicious of help offered until we can determine its usefulness—that it is the right help coming from the right person at the right time. You would do well to describe in advance what sort of help you intend to offer and say why you want to help. We are not likely to ask for or accept help until a bond of trust has developed and been tested.

Your primary objective should be to help people to become more truly themselves by helping them become more truly gay. That means the development of conscious self-appreciation and integrity that includes the full integration of gay thoughts and feelings. You never encourage self-destructive behavior and attitudes. You do not encourage conformity. You encourage integrity by encouraging behavior and attitudes that match internal feelings.

Find whatever anti-gay or homophobic feelings you have. Try talking them out with friends or seek whatever professional help you may need to rid yourself of them. If you keep them hidden they will act as blind spots and sabotage the service you offer to a gay person. Anyone who has grown up in a society that has anti-gay prejudice is not entirely free of these feelings.

Be willing to admit your own homosexual feelings and other feelings of attraction to people of the same gender as you. If you do not recognize and honor such feelings within yourself, a gay person is likely to feel that there is no basis for trust. You may choose to act on those feelings seldom or never, but your reasons for that choice must be clear to you.

Do not inform on or "out" gay people. Be aware of how this information can be used against us. We must choose for ourselves who and when to tell. Divulging information about gay identity is an absolute violation of trust as well as a probable violation of ethical confidentiality.

These ground rules can easily become a natural part of your style when working with gay people. You may find it helpful to add other ground rules because they suit your personality or the particular job that you do. Neglect of ground rules, however, is likely to slow down, disrupt or terminate the professional relationship.

Taking one profession, teaching, as an illustrative focal point, here are some examples of how a professional can be of conscious help to gay people in the context of everyday situations. The teacher's style would vary, of course, with the teacher's personality and the grade level taught as well as with socioeconomic and cultural backgrounds, intellectual abilities and the personalities of the students.

1. CONFORMITY. When a teacher gives an assignment to be written on lined paper, someone is sure to write on unlined paper. Someone else is sure to add some absentminded drawings or decorations. It is an opportunity for the teacher to explain why the original request (to do the assignment on lined paper) was made and to appreciate, nevertheless, the originality that may have prompted a few students to execute the assignment differently. While the papers are being returned, the teacher might smile and say, "I really liked the trees that Jean drew on the side of the paper because it's something of Jean's. I never would have thought to ask each of you to add a drawing of trees because it would have been more difficult for some of you. Anyway, your trees were an unexpected treat for me while I was reading these papers, Jean."

Or, "Mr. Smith did his composition on unlined paper. My reason for asking that it be done on lined paper was to make it easier for me to read. But your handwriting is so clear and attractive, Mr. Smith, that I had no trouble reading it at all and it stood out from all of that lined paper. I hope it doesn't embarrass you if I use this as an example to point out to people how you can make yourself noticed and valued by other people if you dare to stand out from the crowd by doing something your own way while not making it a disadvantage to anyone else."

2. DISTRUST OF FEELINGS. In a secondary school class discussion, a student says, "Well, Narcissus fell in love with himself and that's wrong." The teacher enters the discussion. "That's an interesting statement and I wish everyone would think about it. I know that I used to think some of my feelings were wrong. Then I began to see that all of my feelings were right because they are *my* feelings and they are there—and that includes feelings that some other people might not think are right or good. It's my *behavior* that I have to be careful with so that I don't behave in ways that cause unwanted trouble. I've learned that if I accept all of my feelings, it's actually easier to control my behavior. Now what about Narcissus? Can you separate his feelings from his behavior?"

In an early elementary school classroom there is a heated discussion about where the group will go on its class trip. The question is decided in favor of a suggestion made by Tim and Alex. Amid the mild uproar of jubilation at having the decision settled, Tim and Alex spontaneously hug one another. Sara, who is sitting near them, giggles and points, saying, "Look, Tim and Alex are in love." Everyone laughs. The boys look embarrassed. The teacher says, "It takes more than a hug to show someone you're in love. But I'm glad Tim and Alex know how to show it when they feel good about one another. I know some people who are too scared of what other people think to dare to let anyone know what they're feeling even when they're feeling good. It's too bad to be robbed of your own feelings that way, don't you think? You can always control yourself but it's nice to be able to show some part of every feeling you have."

3. DECREASED AWARENESS OF FEELINGS. Anthony swoops across the playground and takes the handle of the wagon just as Alice is about to reach for it. Alice looks glum and retreats from the group. The teacher has noticed the incident and goes to her. "I can understand that you feel bad, Alice. If that had happened to me, I would be really angry."

A teacher in a middle school class is taking a brief look at English history and has come across a king who is considering the execution of his best friend and trusted advisor. One boy volunteers, "He don't care about nothing, man. That's how kings are." The teacher says, "I think that when someone says 'I don't care,' that person is trying to tell you that he wants you to believe that he has no feeling. I never believe that, though. I know people always have many feelings. I know when I say that I don't care, I'm usually hiding feeling hurt or angry. That's what happens, for example, when you get caught loving someone and have the silly idea that you shouldn't. Do you see how the king might have been feeling that way here?"

4. ATTACKS ON CHARACTER AND ABILITY. A girl in the first grade during show-and-tell says, "When my friend Suzette and I grow up, we're going to live together and not get married and go all over the world together, and maybe we'll be astronauts but we're not sure yet." Another girl laughs, and says, "That's 'cause you and Suzette gonna be too ugly to get husbands." The class laughs. The teacher says, "Some of the most important and beautiful people in the world don't marry and choose to spend their lives with a friend. When you get older you may read about two women named Gertrude Stein and Alice B. Toklas, who were famous and very important people in the world not too many years ago. People are still writing books about them. And you will learn about the Emperor Hadrian and Antinous. Antinous was the most handsome man anyone knew and Hadrian was the most powerful king and they were friends who knew that they needed to be together. So even though I know that Denelle

may change her mind when she grows up, I don't think it's silly that she wants to spend her life with Suzette.

A high school teacher overhears the end of a joke just before the bell rings to signal the beginning of class. "So, get this. The private says, 'Listen, honey, I ain't carrying no heavy equipment no more, it ain't comfortable and I'm the one who made the General's equipment comfortable last night.'" Much laughter and knee slapping. The teacher says, "That joke was funny but it was also sad. You know, once upon a time people used to tell jokes like that about anyone who had come from a different country, spoke a different language or had a different skin color. The problem with those jokes is that they get you believing that the stereotypes are true—like believing that all gay men are puny and weak. I've met gay men with a lot of muscle and I'll bet no one here would want to find himself in a fight with one of them." "No, 'cause they might lick you," another boy says and there is another uproar of laughter. The teacher laughs and says, "Are you beginning to get the idea? That one made us laugh because it was a clever play on words but maybe also because it reinforces an idea that gay men are so desperate that they would be delighted to have even the slightest contact with each and every one of you gorgeous men in this room. Could you see how that might not be true?"

5. ALONE AND UNSUPPORTED. On the third day of kindergarten, five-year-old George burst into tears. "I don't care," he says. "I don't want to be a brave boy. I want to go home." The other children do not know it but the teacher knows that he is the only child in the class from a home in which both parents are recent arrivals from another country and are having a difficult time with the new language. George has a trace of an accent himself. The teacher picks him up and puts him in her lap for comfort and says, "You know, George, everyone in this class has felt the way you feel now. It even happens to me sometimes and I'm a grown-up. It's especially hard if you think you're all alone and the only person who feels the way you do. I don't think you have to be brave,

but I hope you'll let me hold you a little while because it makes *me* feel better."

The day following a test, a secondary school girl says, "I don't think the test was fair. It wasn't a fair test of what we learned and I think you should not have given it to us." There is a long silence as the other students watch and wait to see what will happen. The teacher says, "Thank you, Patricia. Naturally, I don't like being told that I'm a poor test-maker or an unfair person, but I'm certainly glad you spoke up and said what's on your mind. I'll bet some other people here feel the same way but were afraid to own up to the feelings because they were afraid it might get them into trouble."

6. DEPRESSION AND IMMOBILITY. An elementary school teacher is worried about a young girl named Grace. The child is in no trouble, but she sits by herself most of the time and rarely interacts with the other children. Nor does she seem busy with her own ideas or tasks. But Grace is always willing to do what she is told. The teacher announces that he wants everyone in the class to help him think of something they can all do each day that will be a new way of doing something they are accustomed to doing. "Let's have fun," he says. "For example, we might try changing the hand we write with today and see how if feels, and tomorrow we could spend the whole morning making sure that each person is holding hands with another person at all times. But I'd like to have your ideas."

In a high school senior literature class, a teacher notes several students who seem quiet, inactive and unhappy. "Where do you suppose writers get their ideas for literature?" she asks. "They have to use imagination and very often they start by remaking the world the way they would like it to be. For this week's assignment, I would like each of you to invent three situations that you have never been in, but that are plausible. In each situation I would like you to invent two people whom you are genuinely surprised to discover you have loving feelings for and a third person whom you are surprised to find makes you angry."

7. ESCAPE USING ALCOHOL, OTHER DRUGS AND SUICIDE. An eight-year-old boy comes to his teacher and says, "I have a funny feeling and I want permission to go to the office and get an aspirin." The concerned teacher asks, "What kind of funny feeling?" The boy responds by saying, "It's not really a headache, but I've had this funny feeling ever since this morning when I said good-bye to my mom and dad when they left on their trip." "That funny feeling may be sadness, or loneliness or missing them—or even anger," says the teacher. "I'd really like you to get to know your feelings even when they seem uncomfortable. Would you do me a favor and see if you can think about exactly how you feel so that I can write it down for you in a little while during recess? If you think you need an aspirin after that, I'll send you to the nurse. Okay?"

25
BEING PROFESSIONAL

SERVICE PROVIDERS ARE considered professional if they are dedicated to making full use of both their learned skills and their earned skills along with their natural talents in helping others. Some take the school courses, pass the examinations and obtain a professional license but lack dedication, natural talent or both. Others who would not be recognized as professionals by state boards because they did not follow an orthodox path or ventured beyond current rules act in ways they believe to be in the best interest of their client or patient, are receptive to evaluative comments of colleagues, clients or patients, and are dedicated in making full use of natural talents and learned skills. These individuals would have to be considered truly *professional* in any genuine meaning of the word.

Our perception and expectations of professionals have changed, are changing and will continue to change. We have an increasing variety of trained service providers called by a variety of names such as *professionals*, *paraprofessionals*, *assistants*, *interns*, *staff volunteers*, etc. We have come to expect less magic, but are entitled to expect dedication and responsibility from all professionals. There are minimal guidelines that we may expect them to follow.

A hospital, for instance, may have a rule that friends are not permitted to visit a very sick person or that they may not stay beyond limited visiting hours—a *family only* rule. If that is the case, everyone on the staff who may be expected to enforce the rule must know who is *family* for a gay person. Lesbians and gay men, where denied the right to have licensed, legally recognized husbands and wives, may be domestic partners legally registered with the state or not. Even that may not be permitted. It would be inhumane to expect the gay patient's spouse, sometimes called *lover*, *friend* or *partner*, to wait in the hospital lobby while a distant cousin or uncle is permitted to visit. Such behavior on the part of the staff would be unprofessional and inexcusable.

We are much more aware of the subtle and not so subtle ways in which some people have used and continue to use positions of presumed authority to intimidate and misuse other people. We are increasingly sensitive, for instance, to sexual misconduct by supervisors in the workplace in professional settings.

A helper must be very careful of sexuality when working with gay people. Sexuality has been made into a major issue for us. It is important for lesbians and gay men to have self-esteem enhanced and homoerotic orientation supported whenever possible. It is important that professionals make appropriate appreciative remarks.

It also must be clear that the professional person is not inviting or threatening sexual seduction. This is most clear in psychotherapy. The psychotherapist must make it clear that she or he is responsible in upholding the agreed upon contract, including prohibition of sexual contact with the patient, so that the patient is free to verbalize erotic and sexual feelings, including those feelings that have to do with, or may seem to have to do with, the therapist. There must be no shame or inhibition and no worry that the therapist will use the revelation of feelings to initiate sexual contact. Sometimes, after the therapy, patients and therapists do become friends. Some have sexual affairs, and some marry. But this happens *after* the therapy is finished— after there has been a cooling off period during which the therapist shrinks down to life-size and is no more than herself or himself. It must be clear that neither person is taking advantage of the other.

Yet appropriate support and appreciation must be there. A gay man I met socially told me, "My therapist is a great guy and I think I'm sexually attracted to him. I was telling him one day how ugly I feel when I walk into a party, and he told me he thinks I'm really good-looking. Do you think it would be really bad or wrong if we had sex with one another?"

I suggested that his therapist probably would make it clear that sex was not part of the psychotherapy contract. I told him it might be a good idea to check his contract with his therapist and that I thought it would be wonderful to speak about his sexual attraction to his therapist. I also said that I hoped he could enjoy his therapist's admiration of his attractiveness and feel safe while doing so. Psychotherapy should be an appropriate place to explore all attractions and attractiveness and learn how they operate as part of your life.

There are tales of lesbians or gay men who believe they are receiving counseling or psychotherapy from a professional only to find that they have stepped into a traumatic, homophobic trap. There is the unethical and unprofessional behavior of the counselor or therapist who suggests, either directly or by innuendo, that the client ought to make sure that she or he has exhausted all heterosexual possibilities before announcing gay identity or the therapist or counselor who overreacts when homoerotically admired. This is illustrated by a story told to me by a lesbian who dared to admit that she was sexually attracted to her social worker and sometimes had sexual fantasies about her. The social worker became flustered and then angry, shouting, "That's not what I'm here for. We'll have to assign you to a male case worker." Her reaction was inappropriate, damaging and thoroughly unprofessional. She need have done no more than smile, say 'Thank you,' and go on with her work.

There is no excuse for responsible service providers daring to dishonor homoerotic feelings in a situation in which they would honor heteroerotic feelings. One of my all-time favorite stories is about a police cadet handling a squabble in a restaurant with admirable professional aplomb. The cadet was with his girlfriend. He was in uniform but not yet on duty. A patron in the restaurant was threatening to assault another patron who had winked at him. The cadet intervened quickly. In response to the man's saying, "I heard him tell his friend that I'm cute and I'm gonna rearrange his face." The cadet said, "So he's wrong. You're not cute. And you're wrong. You're not going to hit him. You're not the first person who's been admired in this restaurant and you won't be the last. It happens. Rearranging someone's face doesn't. Relax. It's no big deal. I get winked at by guys sometimes."

For almost all of us who are in the helping professions, a large part of the motivation for going through all the training is a real desire to help people. Each of us had to learn that even with good training and good intentions it is impossible to help everyone. Each of us has our own limitations.

Many have spent their entire lives keeping their distance from their own homosexual feelings and impulses. For some the strain has been compounded by the homophobic preaching of heterosexual superiority in the guise of objective studies of human behavior from some of Freud's supposedly devout followers. I know psychotherapists whose lives have been tortured by attempts to maintain heterosexual adjustment while their inner nature yearns for gay companionship. Several have experienced grave physical illness. Some, because of their conflict, have put themselves in harm's way and as a result are no longer living.

My heart goes out to these people and to their loved ones. Those who are living still cannot be helped until they are willing to risk giving up the dogma that has instructed them to follow a lonely heterosexual path at any cost. The risk can be taken with the help of gay fellow-professionals and with the support of pro-gay friends.

Any professional who knows that she or he is struggling with this sort of conflict would do well to engage in psychotherapy with a gay-affirmative psychotherapist. As long as the internal struggle continues, it is only fair for such a professional to be very careful when working with gay clients. Anyone conflicted about homosexuality is going to have blind spots. It is a moral and ethical responsibility to admit this disability.

We rely on professionals who have worked to rid themselves of homophobia to use their education, compassion and judgment and take risks when they believe those risks are justified. We admire professionals who take personal risks that they have reason to believe are in the best interest of the persons they are trying to help. If they are good at their work, the risks they take are much more often right than wrong, more often a risk to themselves than to the person they are helping.

It was not considered extraordinary during the time when interest was highest in the human potential movement for a professional helper to use various forms of touch and physical contact, including full body massage, when doing psychotherapeutic work. During periods when society is more constricted, however, a competent practitioner may be more cautious in deciding to touch a client, fearing that the touch will be misinterpreted as an intrusion or molestation. In less constricted times, a physician may depend upon examination of the entire naked body for full clinical information. In other times the physician must make do with what he can learn from the examination of a fully clothed or covered body—or one with only small patches of naked skin exposed.

We make do with these changing tides of social norms and expectations, using our judgment as to what is permissible, how it will be interpreted and what is in the best interest of the client. The *primary* professional consideration, however, is less a matter of what is currently deemed acceptable in the society and more a matter of judging whether the procedure is honestly designed to help, or whether its purpose is to meet the needs of the practitioner. Next, of course, must be the informed willingness of the client to cooperate in the procedure. Without that consent, any procedure is intrusive and less than professional.

I like to tell the true story reported to me by a person with whom I did a psychotherapy session in a hospital during the last days of his life. He was quite lucid but gravely ill as a result of AIDS. He had been denying the gravity of his condition. He told me that in the middle of the preceding night awareness of impending death had come to him. He was in pain. He was terrified. He could not sleep. Neither the pain-reducing medication nor the sleeping pill he had been given seemed to help. He felt chilled and continued to shiver. The gay male nurse on duty understood what was happening. He stayed with the patient, holding his hand, but the patient could not stop shivering. He cried, telling the nurse that he felt himself to be more alone and lonely than ever in his life. He said that he knew he was near death and would never be held in another man's arms again.

The nurse took off his wristwatch and told him he had to go and make some arrangements with the other night nurse. He told him to watch the minute hand until it reached a particular spot, fifteen minutes away. Within that fifteen minutes the nurse had returned, removed all of his own clothing and got into the bed with the patient, holding him close and warm until the patient fell asleep. "It was the most wonderful thing anyone ever did for me in my whole life," the patient told me.

Unprofessional or professional? Judge that as you may, the nurse went beyond fear, took a personal risk and did what no medication or conventional nursing could do. He helped. When you reach the end of a professional career, the question you must face is not whether you did all that you were told you *should* do but whether you did all that you believed you *could* do to help.

From my own personal and professional experience, and the experience of the professionals with whom I have worked and whom I have helped to train, it seems to me that any orientation, style or variety of techniques can be adapted to use in work with gay people. Never has there been any finding in the genuinely scientific studies of techniques or theories that would dictate homophobic practice. The problem is with the preferred societal dictates of the moment and the related prejudice of practitioners.

My own style in individual psychotherapy has tended to be an eclectic conglomerate with telltale traces of professional heroes past and present, including Freud, Reich, Jung, Sullivan, Rogers, Perls and Maslow. Like most therapists who have been in the field for some years, I have had to learn what works uniquely well for me as a therapist and what techniques apply in particular situations with particular clients. I have added or adapted certain techniques because they seem to work well with many gay people. These would include the use of journal writing to explore past history, unquestioned assumptions and value systems; breathing exercises and self-massage to reduce tension and make friends with the body-self; examination of dreams for messages from the inner self about past, present and future; and the search for quiet, nonviolent expressions of anger.

I believe that gay persons derive special benefit from group work because so many of us have endured years of being invisible and alone, building a negative self-image. Throughout my career I have conducted many ongoing weekly groups and supervised others. In addition, I have regularly facilitated weekend and week-long groups. Typically, I find that a gay person profits most when he or she starts with individual psychotherapy, then enters group psychotherapy, with the two overlapping for some period of time, and finally finishes with a comfortable period of membership in an ongoing group, during which he or she is able to reinforce the new learning and help others who have, as yet, had less extensive therapy experience.

The weekend and week-long experiences are not usually as useful for the beginner who has had little or no psychotherapy experience. These groups can be intense and very rich in revelations because there is more time for deeper exploration and greater safety due to the strong bonds that develop among participants. The weekend group is designed in such a way that a community is created, emotions stirred, and the person is better able to see how much more he or she could be getting from life. I have sometimes referred to the ongoing weekly group as a *struggle group*. Participants are continually frustrated because it is not as pleasing as a weekend or retreat-group experience. It is structured to be halfway between the more ideal community of the weekend or week-long group and the pale everyday world. Participants in the weekly group must struggle to change themselves and the group to bring it closer to a satisfying reality in which more needs can be met. It is the *how to* group. The hard won insights acquired in the struggle are directly applicable to the world outside and can be transferred to other relationships the next day.

While psychotherapy groups for gay people usually are facilitated by trained professionals, *community gatherings* that focus on personal and group growth usually are not. Such groups develop their own ground rules and participants guide one another in adhering to them. Almost always, a part of each meeting is devoted to a full opportunity for each person to let others know what he or she is feeling and thinking, speaking truth from the heart.

My own professional opinion is that the most important task for gay people who are focused on personal and community growth is to become ever more able to speak one's gay truth, the truth about one's gay feelings and thoughts. We have been inhibited and controlled by the manipulative use of shame and guilt. We must speak *any* truth that feels connected to shame and guilt while in the safety of community.

Many formed gay communities are explicitly devoted to spiritual discovery and growth, free of religious doctrine. Some are explicitly devoted to erotic or sexual discovery and growth, questioning societal restrictions and customs, inspired perhaps by learning about the bonobo secret of success in peace-keeping. These two missions, spiritual and erotic exploration, frequently fuse in an intentional gay community, speeding the self understanding of gay men and lesbians. These communities can be located by using key words such as *gay*, *spiritual* and *erotic* in searching the Internet.

While these communities and growth groups are seldom led by professionals, more and more professionals are participating in them. They offer ways to learn about one's self, shed homophobia, question assumptions, and find your own way to better offer real professional services.

26

CONTINUING EDUCATION

G AY MEN AND LESBIANS are increasingly visible in the world and those who design training or certification programs have become aware of the need to include issues concerning gay clients and patients in their curricula. Such training is slowed in its development by politicians who promote divisiveness and prejudice in order to keep their jobs. But the training will evolve. The gay professionals and students in such programs will see to it.

There is a need for gay-affirmative retraining as part of continuing education experiences for all professions. But continuing education institutions are often not flexible enough to do the job well. Anyone who is sincere in wanting to become more professionally responsive to lesbians and gay men will need more than an academic course. Time spent *in the field* among gay people, in social as well as social service settings, is essential. It is the only way to learn the customs and the language of the culture.

In order to deliver professional service appropriately, it is necessary to have supervised experience. This permits both the retrainee and the supervisor to contrast and compare their thoughts and feelings about how best to meet needs in a particular situation or a particular moment.

If the counselor who saw my friend a few days after his dog's sudden death had the benefit of supervised gay-affirmative retraining, then that initial session might have been a disaster anyway. But if she had reviewed it with a gay-affirmative supervisor, she might have learned how she had insensitively missed the point. Her client, on the brink of depression, was describing his experience of love in his lifetime, his friendship needs, his loneliness, his parenting experiences, the chilling fear of becoming unwanted in old age and how the sudden unexpected loss had caught him off guard—reopening wounds left by friends dying in the AIDS epidemic. Instead, she saw only a man who was troubled because he had lost a pet and might be helped by replacing it.

Hidden attitudes, prejudices, blind spots and ignorance are notorious for causing problems, not only for psychotherapists or counselors but for all professionals. The presenting problem may be a painful tooth, a budget that won't balance or a will to be executed, but the person bringing the problem must be given full attention and consideration. The following are suggested guidelines for gay-affirmative retraining of psychotherapists and are offered with the hope that *any* professional may find in them the ingredients that will help her or him become a more gay-affirmative dentist, accountant, attorney or other professional service provider.

Appreciation of homosexual feelings. Know thyself. Socrates, who is believed by many to have been one of our gay forefathers, was certainly insightful in offering this famous advice. Getting to know yourself deserves first place on any list that speaks to your interaction with others in the world. While getting to know yourself, it is extremely important that you identify and explore your own homosexual feelings, whether or not you consider yourself to be gay. Since most people are trained to keep those feelings out of awareness, identification of the feelings is much more difficult if you are not gay.

Once located, merely accepting the fact that such feelings exist is not enough. It is important to become comfortable with having those feelings, to appreciate them, to learn that they not only do no harm but, once welcomed, open the door to greater same-gender affectional feelings in general. If you do not own your own homosexual feelings, but cling instead to the belief that heterosexual feelings are better, this will be communicated to a gay client in some way sooner or later and you will leak persuasive, unconscious conflicting messages about his or her worth.

If you have located your own homosexual feelings and believe that you not only accept them but appreciate them, yet find that any fantasy of expressing them in behavior makes you quite uncomfortable, chances are good that you are dealing with some unrecognized homophobia. It is vital that such issues be resolved or relieved or you again risk transmitting subtle, conflicting messages to gay clients.

Of course you may choose to restrict your sexual behavior to heterosexuality because you are monogamous and in a satisfying heterosexual relationship. Or you may choose to restrict yourself to heterosexuality because you believe you are incapable of being loving, respectful *and* sexual in any relationship with someone of the same gender. But if you avoid homosexual behavior because you feel that it is bad or distasteful, no amount of rationalization will prevent you from communicating that secret, if silent, message to gay clients.

Anyone who claims that she or he has no homosexual feelings is either one of a very tiny minority of the population or is about as well off as the psychotherapist who says that he or she never dreams. It suggests that you are out of touch with your inner emotions and would do better work in some other non-service field.

Conversion of sexual orientation. Think about why you might consider entering into a presumably therapeutic contract to eliminate homosexual feelings and behavior. Willingness to consider entering into such a contract implies that homosexuality is pathological and undesirable. Though homosexuality and its related sexual orientation have been eliminated from pathologies listed in the *Diagnostic and Statistical Manual* of the American Psychiatric Association, with the hearty endorsement of the American Psychological Association and the subsequent endorsement of the American Psychoanalytic

Association and most related professional associations in other parts of the world, prejudice persists.

There are counselors and therapists who are willing to consider accepting a client with the agreement that they will work together to eliminate *undesired* homosexual thoughts, feelings and behavior. They take the seemingly broad-minded stance that they would not think of trying to eliminate gay identity but are willing to work with clients who feel the need to free themselves from homosexuality, if that is their freely made decision. I hope that any true professional would see the foolishness of such reasoning if the word *homosexual* were changed to *heterosexual*. What counselor or psychotherapist would agree to a contract to help rid a person of heterosexual thoughts, feelings and behavior.

Rationalization provides a very thin disguise for prejudice. *If there is something pathological about a particular individual's homosexuality, it is the pathological facet that needs examination and elimination, not the homosexuality itself.* Every decade brings a new brand of psychotherapy with its own language and its own rationalization for eliminating homosexual thoughts, feelings, behavior and orientation. It attracts unhappy people who hope to escape persecution but who are destined to discover that they have offered their money, time and effort in exchange for more suffering in the offices of their "helpers."

Experiencing oppression. All gay people have experienced some form of oppression related to their being gay. The subjective reality of that experience must be brought into consciousness so that it can be examined. This is an area where a therapist or counselor is at a serious disadvantage if he or she is not gay, is not involved in a gay social network, and has not worked with a large number of gay people. The evidence of experienced oppression is often quite subtle. A client may laughingly tell a story of sitting at a wedding rehearsal dinner when his sister's husband-to-be tells a feeble anti-gay joke that fails to get any laughter. He says that he is amused to think how surprised his future brother-in-law will be to discover that he now has a gay brother. Behind that amusement there is hurt and anger—

possibly rage. Probably there were also feelings at the time of being alone in the family of origin once again.

Very early in life, many of us are exposed to a cultural mythology that mocks gay identity. It suggests that gay people are defective and unable to perform well in areas valued by the society. Most gay people have had times in their lives when, like their non-gay peers, they felt unsure of their ability in a particular area. Consciously or not, it would have been natural to associate that presumed inability with the presumed inferiority of gay people. Rather than be found out, the person may have changed course and tried for success elsewhere.

That is a type of oppression and when awareness of it begins to arrive in consciousness changes can be expected. But it takes a sensitized therapist to recognize the cues. More blatant oppression, such as being fired from a job or disowned by a parent, is not to be passed over lightly either. It is very likely that the gay client pushed aside many of the feelings associated with such experiences because the feelings were overwhelming and there was too little support available. He or she needs to be able to review such experiences with full awareness in order to achieve the liberation of increased self-worth and self-esteem.

Stereotypes. It is very likely that your client has unthinkingly accepted some stereotypes of gay people while growing up. It is important to identify them so that you can help her or him undo the undermining damage to self-esteem that is the consequence of negative conditioning associated with those stereotypes.

Such stereotypes are many and varied: Gay people are sexually promiscuous; unreliable, capable of only shallow affection; weak; passive, gay men are limp-wristed caricatures of females; lesbians are castrating women who are too full of anger to love anyone. The list could go on and on. You may be able to detect your client making a veiled reference to some such trait in himself or herself. More often you will catch a hint of it when your client is talking about another gay person or voicing some negative feelings about you, if you are gay.

Flush out these stereotypes whenever possible. Do not push them away with quick intellectual denial of their validity. They feed on emotional fears of the past and present, not on intellectual facts. Better to let the poison out. Better to incite your client to rant and rave and spit out all of the bad things she or he has ever heard about gay people. Better to help keep the client aware of how much these old stereotypes are alive within, waiting to sabotage growth and success.

After doing this a number of times (most effectively in group therapy), you can begin to laugh together about the bitter foolishness of it all. But do not laugh too soon. Those stereotypes have been killing people for centuries. Each time the toxin seeps to the surface, you must do something to weaken its strength. Ask for examples of known gay people who do not fit the stereotype. Ask for examples of gay people, including the client, who display behavior and abilities that are the opposite of the stereotype. And then laugh again, because it is just as sadly funny that some gay people have gone to opposite extremes to elude identification. The ultimate goal of the exercise is to reach the awareness that it is good to be whoever you truly are, regardless of gender, sexual orientation or stereotypes.

Anger and erotic affection. While working toward expanding the range and depth of awareness of feelings, try to be particularly alert to facilitating constructively channeled anger and openly given affection. Gay people too often learn early in life to hide these and other feelings from themselves and others.

It is similarly true of any oppressed minority group member. Someone from an ethnic minority often becomes adept at hiding feelings from others, but usually has the support of family and friends who share the same minority identification and are relatively safe recipients of the expressed feelings, so that it is not necessary to hide feelings from the self. But the gay person often grows up alone with no one in view who shares his or her feelings or who might be a suitable recipient of mutual respect and confidence.

If you are gay, your early learning probably branded your erotic and affectionate feelings as wrong and bad. This, in turn, generated a natural anger (unconscious or conscious) because you were being told that it was wrong to be you. But the very young are too defenseless and do not feel safely entitled to such anger, and so it is buried along with most of the awareness of erotically affectionate feelings for people of the same gender. This violation of your nature, along with the myriad of insults that accumulate during the years of growing up invisibly gay, create an enormous reservoir of anger which can feel unjustified. Then there is fear that if the anger begins to leak through the dam, there will be no holding back a destructive flood.

Through commentaries on daily events shared in individual psychotherapy sessions and through psychotherapy groups, you can relearn how to express feelings of erotic affection and the feelings of anger in any given opportunity. You can learn that these feelings are perfectly acceptable and that the anger need not be destructive, but can be voiced softly. The erotic affection need not be orgiastic or overwhelming and can be expressed in a few moments of touch and/or talk. Reassurance is gained with each experience of expression.

These two hidden areas of feelings and the need to hide them usually seem so powerful that, over time, they can invalidate a wide range of feelings and cheat the gay person of much of her or his emotional life. Reclamation depends, in large part, on the therapist's alert, prompt and relentless assistance in identifying and expressing all such feelings—with special attention to anger and the feelings of erotic affection.

Body appreciation and sex. The therapist does well when he or she actively supports appreciation of the body-self and body impulses. Though it may run contrary to conservative training and repressive norms, try to learn to lose your fear of touching your client as a means of demonstrating that you value and trust physical contact. The key word is *appreciation*. You must help your client to question what, if any, harm there is in any body impulse or what, if anything is unattractive about any part of the client's body-self—remembering and emphasizing that the body is something you *are* rather than something you own or carry around with you. This understanding inevitably leads to acceptance and acceptance precedes appreciation.

It requires willing and active effort on the part of the therapist to counteract years of training that have taught us gay people to hate our bodies and distrust our body impulses. Direct references by the therapist to the attractiveness of the client's body-self can help. This should be done especially when you sense that your client is discounting the value or beauty of her or his body in some way. That is the moment to reflect on what you are hearing, query the client as to other negative body feelings and make your own positive body observations about the client.

You can also inquire about or suggest techniques that the client can use to reclaim more positive body feelings. Learning self-massage and self-loving masturbation can be very helpful. Anything that helps a person learn to better accept and then appreciate his or her body is a gain.

There is also the matter of touching your client. Some therapists say all the right words of appreciation and never touch a client more than to shake hands, if that. Some go to the trouble to sit as far away from the client as the dimensions of the room permit. No matter how sophisticated your client or how profound the theoretical explanation of this stance, there is a simple and primitive person inside each of us, including your client, and at such a time it is recording a negative message. If it could speak it would say, "If you really thought I was attractive, instead of just giving me some words to make me feel better you would *want* to touch me and you would find a way to touch me no matter what your ethics or training." And it is true. A compassionate hug, a friendly pat on the shoulder or appreciative touch on the arm now and then give the powerful message of body appreciation that goes far beyond words. And in so doing you give the additional message that one need not fear one's body impulses.

This is an area where the therapist may need to see his or her own personal feelings and fears more clearly. Therapists, like other people, may have grown up in a society that is distrustful of physical and sexual impulses. Under no circumstances would I recommend explicit sexual activity between psychotherapist and client. This is not because I believe that sex is bad, that psychotherapists are so overwhelmingly powerful, or that sex between a therapist and client must absolutely be wrong. It is because I do believe that sex is complicated, both for the therapist and for the client, and that if the two engage in sexual intercourse the chances of the therapist maintaining sufficient perspective to do the job for which she or he is being paid is unlikely. When I have been asked this question by a client, my truthful answer has been something like: "My reason for not wanting or intending to act on any (sexual) attraction to you is that I believe it would rob me of the perspective I need to do the work that we are doing together. I have not been trained or learned to handle that level of complexity. I believe that under those circumstances I easily might see you in terms of my needs rather than yours. It is something that psychotherapists may learn to manage productively someday but we're there yet." This is said with genuine sincerity.

It is very important that the appreciative touches of the client's body be welcomed rather than intrusive. A therapist's sensitivity and communication skills must be used in making that determination. It is also important that such touches be sincere. Teasing is not helpful. It confuses both the therapist and the client. I am willing to touch or hold a client, if appropriate, in an individual session, sometimes ending an individual session with a hug. I might be willing to exchange a back rub or a massage with a client in a group setting where there are adequate social controls that give a sense of safety. But I would not do so in an individual session because socially conditioned notions of seduction would suggest a lack of safety.

To the extent that you can communicate ease of body contact that is appreciative of your client's body, you demonstrate beyond words that there is nothing to fear—that just because you enjoy body impulses to touch, there need not be any automatic or compulsive next step toward sexual activity. This is also the opportunity to demonstrate your respect for the client's right to accept or reject behavioral expression of another person's body impulses.

In my experience, therapists who have had gay-affirmative training are much more clear in this area of physical contact and sexuality because it is covered so directly as part of the training. We must be clear about it, because we are dealing with the anti-gay mythology that suggests that gay people are so enslaved by their sexual desires that they cannot be trusted not to translate sexual desire into instant behavior. Ironically, it is the traditionally trained heterosexual-oriented therapist, whose training is inadequate in this area, who is most likely to *slip* into sexual activity with a client.

Support and respect. Like everyone else, we gay people need support from people with whom we can identify, people whom we trust. Most of us grew up feeling alone and lonely, different from others. And perhaps we are. Certainly, for most of us, our reality is a shade different than the presumed reality of our surrounding society. It helps if the therapist encourages clients to establish a gay support system. It is an opportunity to create a chosen gay *family* by selecting people who are gay and whom the client likes and trusts. Of course, the client must check with these people to see if the affection and trust are mutual.

Respect is important. We have been taught lack of respect for ourselves as gay people. It is very important to have mutual respect, therefore, in our personal gay support system. We may not need to see these people very often, but we need to be able to contact them regularly, to keep current on what is happening in one another's lives, to hear the gladness in their voices, to sense the warmth with which they value the relationship and to feel the mutuality of respect.

When you lose a member of your gay family because one of you has moved on in some way—any way, including death—allow yourself whatever grief and mourning is due. In all likelihood, that person cannot be replaced because he or she has become so uniquely dear to you. But as your grief and mourning lose intensity, begin to consider adding another person to your gay family. You may be surprised to find mutual value in age difference. To begin with, you may select people of approximately your own age, with perhaps one or two older people who seem wiser. But people who are younger also may contribute a valuable fresh perspective to the mix of your family.

Your chosen gay family are the people to turn to when the world is telling you that you are crazy, wrong and bad because of your gay identity. After a lifetime of being told that you are wrong, there must be a small circle of trusted, supportive people to whom you can turn to check your reality. If they tell you that you ought to think it over again, you do so. If they tell you that you are being persecuted by a homophobe, you can believe it. They provide the security that a family is supposed to provide so that you can grow. Each of them offers a hand to hold, warm arms to enfold you until you feel safe and a strong shoulder to cry on when the need is there. Together they stand ready to celebrate with you anytime. They represent a beginning to the end of loneliness.

Awareness in community. Like other people who, because of prejudice, find that they are members of a disadvantaged minority group, it is imperative that gay people become aware of themselves, the world and their current place in it. Meeting with other gay people in a discussion or support group is one very helpful way of identifying facets of oppression, but it does more than that. Just to sit in a room full of gay people is a meaningful experience. Remember that each of us felt pretty much alone at one time. Seeing all the different kinds of people who are gay reminds you that you are no longer alone and that you need not fit any stereotype. There is space for each and every one of us.

As people in such a setting open their hearts and lower their defenses, we begin to see the universality of many of our feelings—some, we were certain, were ours alone. Instead, we discover that they are shared by many gay people. It gives an immediate dose of what psychologists call *consensual validation*—the majority agrees with your reality and supports you. As you hear your peers talking about a particular feeling related to some common aspect of gay oppression, you begin to realize that you too have that feeling within but have kept it so buried that you never really admitted it to yourself.

Pro-gay reading and work in the gay community have much the same influence on opening and validating feelings. Ultimately, each gay person must learn to validate his or her own feelings, but this sort of community support gives an enormous boost. In addition, pro-gay reading gives the authoritative weight of the printed word to tell you that you are okay being the person you are. That is difficult for non-gay people to understand, but most of us have done too much reading about ourselves as defective or second-class citizens, and in most societies the printed word has an almost sacred authority.

To see the words of gay people in print gives quick perspective. You are suddenly in a position to evaluate rather than defend yourself against the onslaught of negative judgments.

In most areas of the world, gay communities continue to build themselves. The work depends almost entirely on volunteer efforts. There is every imaginable kind of work to do. Political repression requires our willingness to counter it. The AIDS epidemic brought many of us out running, eager to help one another. It led to stunning achievements in community participation that were and are imitated in non-gay settings. It put us into contact with one another in ways that not only helped those in need but led to new friendships, love relationships and recreational activity groups of all sorts. Working in the gay community does one more important thing: It assures you of your own strength and ability to help other gay people. It assures you that other gay people (and, therefore, you also) are worth the help. It is the ultimate statement of self-worth as a gay person.

Therapeutic equality. It is wise to work toward a peer relationship with your client. The message: You're not a second-class or inferior person. There is an inherent problem of assumed inferiority that probably stems from the *doctor-god, keeper of life and death* medical model prevalent throughout the last century. This notion subsequently infected the mental health professions. Please notice that it also left us with the word and concept of *mental health*. It is troublesome to see so many psychotherapists and counselors lead one another to believe that they are very powerful—caught up in the secret delusion of near omnipotence. This can be unfortunately reinforced by the client's natural need for role models and advice.

In the usual psychotherapy process there is a dependency that develops between client and therapist. Eventually, this is worked through, just as we worked through our earlier dependency on our parents. (This can be done more thoroughly and constructively with the paid help of the therapist.) The client may terminate with gratitude, believing that this wonderful therapist is a superior being, if not actually superhuman. Since life's path usually carries the client away from the therapist anyway, there is no great harm done by this lingering mystique and it makes the therapist feel grand.

But with gay clients, this phenomenon is counter-therapeutic, and the therapist *must* have the courage to prove beyond any reasonable doubt that he or she is no better, smarter or wiser than the client. The reason is that gay people have usually had a dominant society telling us that we are inferior throughout our lives. If this one person who helps us most is superior, we are once again, after all is said and done, inferior.

It is easier for a therapist to show us his or her vulnerability, as well as the unfinished and unpleasant facets of self, in a group setting rather than in individual therapy. But whatever the setting, it is important to demonstrate that you, the therapist, have defects and that you share with your client the same human dilemma of always being on the road and never reaching the destination, while being neither bad nor incompetent. You may even point to an area in which the client is clearly a better person. If you care about the gay client with whom you are working, that should give you a real thrill.

Constructive personal values. The gay-affirmative psychotherapist or counselor encourages his or her client to question all basic assumptions about being gay and to develop a personally relevant value system as a basis for self-assessment. The very real dangers of relying on society's value system for self-validation must be pointed out.

It may be a long, tedious, terrible job but the gay client must be guided back through her or his life (an autobiographical journal is a good stimulus) for the purpose of rooting out nearly every assumption he or she has learned about the goods, bads, rights and wrongs of human feelings, attitudes and behavior. Having identified these learned assumptions, the client must be helped to re-examine them in the light of current information and adult judgment, then decide which assumptions should be kept, which discarded, and which altered. This provides the foundation for a personally relevant value system that can be used as a rudder for steering through the unpredictable and turbulent waters of life.

To survive, gay people must see that we cannot afford to accept unchallenged any prepackaged set of assumptions, even if they were given by such exalted authorities as parents, religion, government, or the newest revolutionary group. Most of us have grown up in a world that uses an interlocking set of assumptions surrounding the basic assumption that gay is bad. Accepting a part of that interlocking package with no questions asked is going to give us a feeling of vague discomfort. This is because of logical inconsistencies that develop when new assumptions are squeezed in to replace the few that were deleted. So the new individually tailored set of values must have its own internal logic and must feel right to the individual. For a gay person to trust any culture's given set of values is suicide—sometimes literally.

Decreasing shame and guilt. A therapist or counselor can help to lessen the shame and guilt surrounding homosexual thoughts, feelings and behavior by pleasantly encouraging graphic descriptions of gay experiences and, when appropriate, sharing something about his or her own.

Our access to *camp* humor has helped us to survive. It pokes fun at the ultimate foolishness of everything and provides a broad foundation of acceptance for that which is human. Humor is by far the easiest way to get at the guilt and shame surrounding homosexual thoughts, feelings and behavior. "Had any good fantasies lately?" with a raised eyebrow and an encouraging smile can go far in helping to move things along. The therapist or counselor may sometimes ask directly that the client be sure to report any thoughts, feelings or behavior that had been homosexual and/or embarrassing in some way. The therapist need only hear it out and calmly state the truth that he or she does not see anything wrong with the homosexual parts of the report, per se. Depending on the therapist's relationship of the moment with the client, one might go so far as to add that she or he found it interesting and/or stimulating.

You are working to decrease guilt and shame. Sometimes there is a wrongness or badness involved; sometimes the client has violated his or her own standards and values and, understandably, feels guilty or ashamed. But guilt or shame need never be the product of the homosexuality itself. The surest way of communicating this, if it is permitted within your style of psychotherapy or counseling, is to mention your own homosexual thoughts, feelings and behavior now and then. You can use group therapy situations to show that you are experiencing such thoughts or feelings on the spot and that you feel relaxed and self-appreciative about it, or embarrassed, but know that such embarrassment is only a habit-echo from your past.

Endorsing homosexuality. It is extremely helpful to use the weight of your authority as a therapist to approve homosexual thoughts, behavior and feelings when reported by your client. This is important in counteracting a lifetime of experience with the disapproval of authority figures. Like it or not, no matter how diligently you work toward a peer relationship, to some extent you will be viewed as an authority during most of the course of the psychotherapy.

In the preceding guideline, it was suggested that you induce the client to reveal more and more homosexual thoughts and feelings so that he or she could be desensitized by the lack of negative reinforcement. In this final guideline, you are asked to use your authority to flatly counteract the authority of a lifetime that has said homosexuality is bad. It can be done with a smile, a handshake, a hug or the use of a simple, sincere word like *good* or a statement like "Gee, that must have been fun and felt wonderful." In a group session, if you see one client touching another in a manner that has sexual overtones and it looks as if both are enjoying the contact, you need only smile and nod to undo some of the damage of past years.

This is the guideline that is most likely to make many counselors and psychotherapists uneasy. It is worth considering that discomfort carefully. It betrays how deeply ingrained is the societal instruction that homosexuality is bad and wrong.

Personal discomfort is a probable requirement in the re-education of professionals dealing with gay identity and the facts of life surrounding gay people. Homophobia does exist in both overt and latent internalized form. Prejudice and blind spots do exist. Hidden hurts and desires exist also. I recommend the use of educational aids that reach the professional's most defended emotions.

The 1997 film *Bent*, based on Martin Sherman's award-winning 1979 stage play, is a good example of such an educational aid. It is set in Hitler's Berlin and the Dachau concentration camp. Any professional who cannot find contemporary parallels is, at present, too well-defended to offer service to gay men and lesbians. It is a film that digs out hidden homophobia and prejudice as well as compassion in the viewer. Focused discussion if its relevance to work with one's gay clients is both instructive and therapeutic.

Re-education must be a part of any continuing education program. When the focus is on gay clients, the education must reach the emotional as well as the intellectual reserves of the professional and that can be uncomfortable.

27
TEACHERS
AND LIBRARIANS

Twenty-first century librarians are far different than librarians in the first half of the previous century. Rather than hiding needed information on high shelves or in locked rooms, they are dedicated to making all information available even when a nation's repressive government threatens punishment. Librarians and teachers are the guardians of the intellectual freedom that advances civilization.

An Irish writer who grew up in a small village told me that he was confused about his orientation while he was growing up. "There was a lot of physical contact between us boys and I liked it quite a bit. Somehow I knew there was more to it for me than for the other boys." He said that he also knew somehow that he dared not ask any teacher or be caught trying to find out about it in the library at school.

"You know we Irish people love words. We love to talk and we love written words. So when I went to school in the big town, right off I headed for the library and found nothing I wanted to learn from the books in the card catalogue. It looked pretty grim. I thought about asking a kind teacher or two but I was suspicious that there would be hell to pay for me if word about me got out and about. It wasn't until I was old enough to discover the gay bar that I met a librarian there and he showed me a few books of his own that started it all making some sense to me."

From nursery school through college, the teacher and the librarian are the two professionals who are certain to have contact with each developing gay person. Much of our early understanding about society and our place in it happens in school. And as a consequence, that is where most of the prejudicial early negative learning about gay identity occurs.

There *are* gay children. They realize that their true feelings depart from the supposed norms of attraction between males and females. Their feelings run deep and are usually kept secret. Gay children are entitled to the same education as other children. They are entitled to learn about themselves and the entire world in which they live and to feel positive about themselves.

Teachers and librarians have thousands of opportunities to teach youngsters to appreciate their unique selves and to appreciate differences among people in general. It is important to help youngsters learn to be suspicious of conformity and to value the differences inherent in a society that values integrity, since it is diversity that offers riches while conformity serves only mediocrity. This is demonstrated again and again, in every area of human endeavor, from the sciences to politics to the arts. Creativity makes the unusual possible. And it is the unusual that offers the potential to advance civilization.

We need to help children learn how to evaluate both the unusual and the usual, to develop both pragmatic and moral judgment, so that they do not fall victim to simplistic worship of the average or norm. We have a responsibility to help children to free themselves from our wasteful habit of labeling behaviors as *masculine* or *feminine*, so that each child can be and become the person she or he is. All of us, adults and children alike, need the intellectual tools that will help us to balance our responsibilities and abide by the social contract of our society while daring to push its limits as we develop an individual self with personal integrity.

Casual remarks can reinforce the notion that being gay, like other natural human differences, is honorable and worthy of respect. There is no shortage of past heroes who were gay. Walt Whitman, Sappho, the Emperor Hadrian, Gertrude Stein, Julius Caesar and Alexander the Great are not presented as whole people if there is no mention of their gay identity. Well-known gay women and men of more recent times are legion in number. It is not possible for their names and claims to fame to *not* come up in the work of librarians or teachers. Their gay identity must not be hidden or ignored. Such omissions are dishonest and defeat the understanding that feeds education.

There also are many opportunities to increase awareness among colleagues, not only with information, but by challenging bigoted jokes aimed at gay people or questioning the supposition that a heterosexual orientation is better, for instance. If it is done with tact and good humor, most people will come to see that their habits of prejudice are not fair. To everyone's surprise, perhaps, some colleagues will surface as gay themselves once the social climate of the workplace is no longer hostile or punitive. They are to be congratulated because gay people are much needed as models in the everyday world of our youngsters.

If you are a teacher or librarian, you may not know, as you look over your learners, which individuals are now gay or who will someday come to realize that they are gay as they mature and unfold. But your pro-gay stance will bolster the self-esteem of these developing but invisible people. You must protect them from indignities the same way that you would protect any other youngster from a disadvantaged minority group. The fact that you do not know which students or clients belong to this minority group makes it more pressing rather than less so. Their invisibility may make it necessary for you to remind yourself more often, rather than reacting to simple visual or auditory cues.

And keep this in mind. If you do not help gay children, who will? There is a touching scene in the French film *Wild Reeds* in which a gay student hears that the man who owns the shoe shop in town is gay and has lived quietly with his male companion for years. His search for integrity as a gay person brings the confused youngster to the shoe shop, where he reveals his sexual orientation and his problems to the man and dares to ask for advice.

Few youngsters know how or where to find validation or even simple information. They rarely turn to family because they fear rejection. Their gay peers are invisible. They can get bad ideas about themselves in libraries that hide the truth. They do not know how to find gay adults or gay organizations that might help. There are serious legal risks for the gay adult who does not have an obvious professional helping role such as librarian or teacher, and who is not in an institutional setting, but who reaches out to help a gay child. Caring can easily be interpreted as *impairing the morals or contributing to the delinquency* of a minor. It may even be seen as outright *child molestation*. Some of these invisible developing gay children are, quite literally, depending on you in your professional role as an educator to help them and possibly to save their lives.

At the college level and in more progressive secondary schools around the world there are gay student unions. Some schools have discovered the obvious fact that many of their alumni are gay and are reaching out with gay alumni chapters. Offers of support from teachers and librarians to gay students and alumni are extremely good for morale and can help the less visible potential members to feel genuinely welcome.

28

PHYSICIANS AND
OTHER HEALTHCARE
WORKERS

D o not assume. That's something every good hairdresser knows. Listen and don't assume. It's not just the people like me, in lavender ribbon occupations, who carry the responsibility of being visible now." So said the young man cutting my hair. We had been talking about a performance of the *Barber of Seville* and its reminder of how the village barber once upon a time carried many responsibilities, including those we now think of as medical. "I guess there were *some* gay doctors and nurses out of their closets before AIDS, but it really is nice that there are so many *out* now. I didn't know one doctor who was gay when I was a kid and nobody was going to mention he was gay to a straight doctor. You could only tell your hairdresser, florist or decorator then!"

Indeed, there are many gay physicians and other healthcare workers now visible and many gay people choose to go to them because there is an ease of communication with those familiar with the language and customs of your people. Rapport between patient and doctor or patient and nurse is extremely important but sharing the same sexual orientation does not guarantee it. If you work in the healing professions, **developing a gay-affirmative orientation is more important than your sexual orientation**. It is essential in establishing rapport with gay patients.

Medical professionals are the group likely to be sought out by the developing gay person who is searching for answers about sexual orientation and identity. There are plenty of data to support you in giving reassurance that, while not statistically average, gay is quite *normal*. It is not a sickness. There is no need to seek medical treatment for it. There can be external social problems associated with being gay, but those are problems that can be solved and there are people available who are glad to offer help with the solving. There also are books and periodicals that discuss gay identity with the respect it deserves.

You can also be of great service by not assuming that a patient is exclusively heterosexual in orientation, regardless of appearance or social history. It can be embarrassing for a patient to have to announce to a doctor or a nurse that she or he is gay. A friend told me about emerging from the sleep of anesthesia in a recovery room when a nurse warmly welcomed her back to life and asked if her husband was waiting for her. She shook her head *no* and the nurse said, "Hard to believe a good-looking woman like you isn't married." She said it just was not the right time to explain that she was married but had a wife rather than a husband. She did not have the energy available.

A well-known twenty-eight-year-old athlete visited a doctor's office while on a tropical island vacation because he was concerned about a rash that had developed and seemed to be spreading. The doctor, trying to be jovial, said, "A rash, huh? Been out with any strange ladies? I'm sure there are plenty of ladies who make themselves available to you." He wondered if he should tell the doctor that he had, indeed, had sexual intercourse with a stranger but that the stranger was a man. Knowing that the doctor would be shocked and fearing that it might fuel a rumor about him, he smiled and kept quiet about his tryst until he located a gay physician.

When examining a patient, taking a history or prescribing treatment, keep in mind that this person, regardless of appearance, may be gay unless he or she voluntarily has offered the information that he or she is exclusively heterosexual. Your tactful and tacit assumption that any patient may be gay will cause you to be more professional and trustworthy by both your gay and non-gay patients. To the gay patient it offers solid support and may save a life.

29

CLERGY

I F YOU ARE TRUSTED, you may be the first person to whom the gay person in distress will turn for understanding and advice. In the past, gay people have quite often been told that they are sinful and immoral, that they must repent and mend their ways. This does not help anyone. Fortunately, increasing numbers of clergy are realizing it and are choosing to become better educated about what it means to be gay.

If you have not already done so, perhaps you could examine your religious beliefs and the teachings of your particular religion. Is there only one interpretation? Would your God, Jesus, Moses, Buddha, Muhammad or other deity have found a gay person distasteful or inferior and demanded change? Really? Are you sure? Are you so sure that gayness is bad? Who says so?

Even if you are unable to see the beauty and dignity of gay people, even if you continue to believe that being gay is sinful and immoral, be good enough to tell the trusting gay person who consults you that it is *your* opinion, *your* belief and *your* interpretation of *your* religion as *you* understand it. Say even that others agree with you, but, in fairness, say that many other respected religious experts in the world do not agree with you and tell your parishioner where he or she can find an authority who has gay-affirmative opinions and beliefs.

Gay people seeking your advice might be interested to know that the Reverend Troy Perry founded a church in Los Angeles, California, that particularly welcomes gay people. Called the Metropolitan Community Church, it has grown quickly across the United States and in other countries. There are also gay-affirmative synagogues in many cities, as well as Protestant churches, that reach out to gay congregants in a positive manner. You could also tell them about a highly respected group called the Council on Religion and the Homosexual, that there is a Roman Catholic gay-affirmative group called *Dignity*, a Jewish group called *Achvah*, and similar gay-affirmative groups that are appended to most major religious institutions.

If you are unable to find it in your heart to serve the gay person with respect, be gracious enough to give him or her a chance to find that appreciation elsewhere. The person may live to thank you. You may save the body as well as the soul and you consequently may feel that you have been truly blessed in your good deed.

If you do not feel positively about gay people, it is important to let the person know that you understand it to be a viable lifestyle. Do not paint a bleak picture because of prejudice. Let the person know that oppression can and should be fought. Every religion has had to fight its own oppressors. You can use religion to show that lack of popularity does not equal lack of worth. As a trusted religious advisor you can show that it is the spiritual quality of your life, the way in which you honor your religious beliefs and serve your fellow humans, that counts, not the gender of the persons to whom you feel most drawn and involve yourself with intimately. Be worthy of the trust placed in you.

If you are gay yourself and keeping your identity a secret, allow yourself to learn about the organizations that exist to support gay clergy. Such a secret can and will eat away at your physical, emotional and spiritual well-being. You can be anonymous on the telephone and meet other people who have had experiences similar to your won. A gay priest returning from a retreat for gay priests and religious workers told me, "It was a good reminder that I am not alone and that it's *our* church too, no matter what the current official political word about lesbians and gay men may be. I got some historical and spiritual perspective and I thank God for these people and the support of this group. Not all superiors are superior, if you know what I mean."

The person or persons selling the social agenda and making the rules for your religion this year will be gone someday. One way or another the agenda and rules will change—in the direction of helping all people or only the favored few. You can help to influence the direction of that change. Your spiritual belief demands more of you than conformity.

30

PSYCHOTHERAPISTS
AND COUNSELORS

I N SOME WAYS, psychotherapists and counselors have become the priests of this new age. People look to us to tell them what is good or *normal* and what is bad or *sick*. Because of the mistakes of past colleagues who masked prejudice and ignorance with supposed professional expertise, those of us with professional training who offer services to the public find that we must prove ourselves to prospective gay clients. They would be more than foolish to believe that we can help them simply because we are licensed as a psychiatrist, psychologist, social worker and counselor. As such, we are part of a small army of professionals who once were very destructive to gay people struggling to understand themselves in a homophobic society.

If only all of that were behind us. While it is true that it was much worse in years past, there are still licensed therapists and counselors who knowingly or blindly work against the best interests of their gay clients. If you know yourself to be less than gay-affirmative and you continue to work with gay clients or patients, **you are an unethical practitioner**. No amount of rationalization drawn from some theory can excuse such malpractice.

It is the responsibility of all ethical practitioners to warn the public away from professionals who consider homosexual orientation and gay identity as less desirable than heterosexual orientation and identity. Such a person is working from a basis of personal fear and prejudice rather than scientific evidence and uses the power of persuasion to do great harm.

Unless you have put time and effort into thoughtful study of gay affirmation, it may be inadvisable to assume that you are competent to work with gay people. There are gay-affirmative courses and continuing education programs available. Even a therapist who is gay would do well to experience such a program and check for blind spots that may have crept in during years of living in a prejudiced society. Certainly no non-gay therapist or counselor should assume competence in serving gay clients without exposure to such courses and programs. Any therapist can profit from supervised sessions with one or more gay clients, if the aim is to root out unseen prejudice and the sessions are overseen by a sensitive, gay-affirmative supervisor.

The world's gay community is growing up very quickly. Therapists who work with gay clients would do well to become familiar with this fast-changing culture. Its rapid development makes it vulnerable to the pathological features of surrounding societies. It could move toward a pattern of exclusion rather than inclusion, for instance. This can be detrimental to the growth and well-being of the gay individual. No one benefits when they are socially stratified or segregated because of gender, age, race, national origin or for any other reason. It is important to be alert to such dangers and point them out to your patient or client. This is especially true during periods of governmental repression.

If you would know and understand this dynamic subculture, you must not exclude yourself from its developing rituals and meeting places. If you believe that it would be inappropriate for you to appear at a gay event or gathering place, there is a *we* and *they* concept operating within your consciousness. This suggests that you do not know this world, are unwilling to know it, or do not approve of it. If that is the case, you have some explaining to do to your client and to yourself.

Near the end of my first meeting with a new client, he spoke about a club where he and his partner had met. "It's a great place really, though I don't imagine you would ever be found in such a place."

"Why not?" I asked, wondering whether he thought it was a bad place (and if so, what had he been doing there and what might that mean about his opinion of himself and his partner?) or if he thought I might consider it beneath my dignity.

"It's a younger crowd mostly and … well, I don't suppose you would be shocked by some of the more obvious behavior there," he answered. "I suppose you've seen worse. But the music's very up—quite loud."

"Earplugs can solve that problem and some of my best friends are young," I answered as I wrote his next appointment in the book. I reminded myself to further explore what this might mean about his feelings regarding the place, himself, his partner and me at the earliest opportunity. But my immediate response had told him that I knew something about the territory and the people who inhabited it. I was not from another world and did not cooperate in segregation.

New priests or not—and far less powerful than we sometimes like to imagine ourselves—we are in a position to help or harm according to how well we understand the world of our clients. Perhaps we are more like lifeguards than priests. We sit in our chairs, listening and watching. But it is important for the patient or client to know that we not only have been certified as competent in rescue and first-aid, but are real swimmers who actually get into the water when we are not on duty. We are affirmative. We like swimming and we like the world of gay swimmers.

31

MASSAGE THERAPISTS AND PROFESSIONAL COMPANIONS

BEING IN THE RIGHT PLACES at the right times, taking charge, pay-ing attention, lots of luck, and more than a little help from my friends, I suppose." It was a party in Danny's honor. He was return-ing to work after five years of disability and returning to England after ten years in the United States. Someone had asked him how he had managed to survive his struggle with HIV infection. "I've learned that struggle in one form or another is never finished and that there's almost always another road to be traveled if you have the where-with-all to get on it," he said. "But, you know, I might have gone down for the count if I hadn't discovered erotic healing and companionship."

Danny was an investigative reporter for a medical news journal in England when he met Ron, an American graduate student. They became lovers. It was early in the epidemic and both tested positive for HIV antibodies. "The rush to Paris for a cure had subsided by then, however. I sat Ron down one evening and told him I thought we'd have our best shot with you Yanks. I could help us find good docs and stay on top of breaking medical news. A kind boss transferred me stateside, Ron transferred his studies and the race was on. But when Ron died three years later, all that I truly wanted was to join him. I was depressed, empty and not looking my best. A woman friend in Cornwall wrote me that when her husband died after thirty years of an excellent marriage, she had absolutely hated the idea that she'd have to find another husband if she hoped to have a sex life again.

"You know, that sparked something in me. I found this massage school in California that had been started by Joseph Kramer, then to be carried forward by Collin Brown, gutsy New Age-type gentlemen. They were enamored with what they called Taoist erotic massage, erotic healing, training people they called *sacred intimates* who would act as *midwives to the dying,* and other fascinating exotica. I thought I might get a couple of articles out of it. But that was before it went international and it was still a bit too 'California' for my rather less imaginative editor back home. I did find out rather quickly how badly I needed to be touched, how much I needed companionship, and that it was not required that I look my best or wait for Prince Charming. I'd have kicked the poor Prince out of my apartment anyway since I missed Ron so badly."

Fee-for-service massage, fee-for-service companionship and fee-for-service sex are far from new. The HIV epidemic caused both to be viewed anew, however. Soon after the epidemic began there were volunteers in major cities who were available to clean house, shop for groceries, cook meals, drive people to doctors' appointments and for companionship. Professional massage therapists volunteered to give massages in the hospital or at home. There was a rush to enroll in massage schools. Soon, in addition to the volunteer services, there were expanding sections of fee-for-service advertisements—first in gay publications and then in mainstream newspapers and magazines around the world—advertising escorts, companions, models and massage.

The advertisements were worded in a local code that usually indicated whether the service offered was nonsexual, *erotic* or sexual. A sleeping giant had been awakened. We remembered how important it was to have sensual contact, sex and simple companionship and discovered again the complex benefits of erotic healing. These needs were real no matter what the medical status, age or attractiveness rating of the person. It was not necessary to exclude people with HIV infection since we were all aware of the requirements of safe sex and the need to practice it. Nor was the elderly citizen, the widowed or the maimed forced to sit on the sidelines watching from a distance. Anyone who considered himself too plain, too heavy, too bald, too thin, too inexperienced, too foreign, too handicapped or of the wrong skin color could hire someone to help him gain confidence and rejoin the active human family again.

The individual advertising his services might be someone who had discovered that he had something to offer his community. Or it might be a sexually talented individual who no longer had to stand on a street corner or in a bar looking for a client for the evening. More advertisements appeared offering qualified massage school-trained practitioners, complete with license or certificate, as well as other background experience. Unregulated Internet advertising helped. Agencies appeared, offering the additional advantage and safety of screening service providers and their talents and then matching them with the requirements of the consumer.

Prostitution? Perhaps. That would depend upon the definition. Dentists, physicians and psychotherapists are also fee-for-service providers. The best of us offer our talent, experience, time, training, caring and professional dedication in exchange for a fee. The worst of us are simply available with one eye on the clock, ready for the next paying customer. As always, the client must find his or her way to the most dedicated and able professional.

"Ill winds blowing good and all that sort of thing," Danny said at his farewell party. "This epidemic has cost more than it ought in human suffering. But perhaps it might pay back a bit if it boots up awareness. Maybe a new generation will legitimize erotically gifted people who soothe with healing touch and ease the plight of folks dying from socially acceptable isolation. Let's see now—if one could choose between the comforting blue light of the television and the great rush of a bingo win, or instead have the loving of warm arms and hands and sweet lips, what'll it be?"

What *will* it be? Around the world, governments and religions change, sometimes becoming more generous or liberal, sometimes more repressive, demanding that citizens conform to dogma. The bonobo keep peace with erotic soothing that is generous and non-discriminatory, chimpanzees require loud aggression and wars.

32

POLICE, JUDGES
AND LAWMAKERS

T HE WORLD IS A COMPLICATED PLACE. People fight. Humans have not learned how to live and let live. We need protection but we must be wary of warlords eager to create laws that they say are necessary in order to protect us if those laws give them greater advantage and make us more dependent because we have fewer liberties. A just society has the least restrictive laws. Its laws guarantee equal rights for all.

Miri grew up on a tropical island, but when she was ten years old, both parents died within a year of one another. Months later, she and a younger sister were sent to live with relatives in a large city. "It was an awful change," she said. "On the island we had only two peace-keeping officers and they didn't have a lot of work to do. It was very peaceful."

She and her sister took very different paths. A teacher took an interest in Miri and helped her find her way through school, including a full scholarship for college that permitted her to become a kindergarten teacher. By the time she had finished her second year of teaching, however, her younger sister had been pregnant twice and was in jail for the third time.

"It was when my sister went to jail the third time that I applied to the police academy. While I was working as a law enforcement officer, I began studying law. Then, while I worked as a paralegal, I finished law school and, after only three years of practice in immigration and civil rights law, I landed here as a judge. I understand that my appointment was an expedient political gesture."

Three years after becoming a judge she met her partner, Riza. "She's worked behind the scenes of politics in various jobs for ten years. She's helped me to see that my next step must be into the peculiar world of the politicians who make the laws. They are the rulers, you know. I need to become one of them to understand them. She believes that I have an excellent chance of winning a seat in the next local election. As a police person and judge, I see that people are victims of the ignorance of others."

In many places on the planet, gay people are extremely reluctant to seek out the police. Law enforcement officers are viewed as the enforcers of discriminatory laws, both written and unwritten, that are born of prejudice. Nonetheless, in such places, the police are often in contact with gay people—often without knowing it.

If an officer considers himself or herself to be a peacekeeper, reinforcing the social contract of a decent society means more than simply enforcing the rules. He or she cannot depend upon stereotypes and must assume that anyone may be gay. An unprejudiced officer learns about many varieties of people from all sorts of backgrounds—their wants, needs and habits. Such police understand that most gay people are law-abiding citizens except when prejudicial statutes force them to break the law in order to seek equality in civil rights or to have contact with other gay people.

Gay people have been threatened in enough ways to have a healthy respect for the rights and property of others and for fair laws. Police need the support of responsible citizens and gay people are quite willing to support the police if officers demonstrate their respect and support for gay citizens.

An officer of the law can help us by showing nonphobic, tactful, courteous understanding and approval of gay people, even when he or she is uncertain that a gay person is present. In those places where it is illegal to be gay, the discriminatory laws will fade one day and disappear as more civilized areas of the world cast a questioning gaze in their direction. When human rights violations come to light, international outrage makes commerce suffer. Social improvement comes less often because rulers have had a crisis of conscience and more often because their economic well-being is threatened.

Some supposedly advanced nations maintain antiquated laws and ordinances that are repressive or unfavorable to us. Such laws may be unconstitutional and are rarely enforced except as part of a discriminatory campaign, vendetta or political attempt to divert public attention when there is scandal in government or during an election. The weight of authority from a law officer in support of a gay individual or group can be extremely helpful as we lobby to right the legal landscape.

In places where outmoded thinking continues to be rewarded with restrictive laws, gay people can be blackmailed, beaten and harassed with impunity. These conditions are intolerable. Such places are sure to have invisible, closeted, gay officers who must endure enormous stress in order to do their work. Non-gay officers with integrity are aware that our tormentors, not we, are the criminals. They must stand ready to use their authority to help us or lose the respect and support of gay citizens and others who care.

Police can also help by educating one another. Some have been guilty of outrageous atrocities toward gay people. Others have witnessed or heard about such incidents. The more professional officer refuses to condone such behavior among his or her colleagues.

I was appalled when shown an episode of a television drama with a reputation for having a social conscience and for its accurate portrayal of dedicated police officers in New York City. One ongoing story line revealed the complex makeup of one of the more conscience-driven officers. The episode portrayed his distress because a female officer to whom he was attracted was not responding positively. It was presented as understandable, therefore, that he used the most offensive imaginable language with two other characters in the episode who had been involved homosexually with one another. If Jewish or Italian identity had been the target rather than homosexual identity, there would have been a cry of outrage in every New York City newspaper the next day. Instead, this strong and persuasive reinforcement of homophobia was quietly excused as mere plot development in a story.

Refuse to subscribe to a code of machismo that damages people and persuades officers to fear association with us. It is always responsible and helpful to raise awareness among colleagues to support us in small, everyday ways such as not laughing at anti-gay jokes or excusing homophobic behavior.

In enlightened parts of the world it is possible to be both *openly* gay and an officer of the law. Indeed, in some places there are outreach programs actively engaged in recruiting gay police officers in order to better match the demographics of the citizens of the community. Not surprisingly, in those communities gay people are very supportive of the police, seeing them as friends and keepers of the peace rather than enemies who enforce rules of prejudice.

Judges are expected to be impartial and even-handed in seeing to it that the law of the land is applied fairly and equally to all citizens. They are also the final human factor in the application of those laws to the community. It is expected that they will use unbiased judgment. When a disadvantaged citizen, such as a lesbian or gay man, appears before them, they must weigh the fact of that disadvantage along with all other evidence in making certain that the law is applied fairly.

Were a judge to apply the law exactly and in the most meticulous detail, without any regard for such an important fact as minority identity, she or he would be unnecessary and could be replaced by a computer. On the other hand, judges who, instead, use their own prejudice in weighing evidence and applying the law compound the error in the discharge of their duty, and do more harm than good. Politicians and lawmakers are responsible for making laws that permit people to live, develop and thrive in society without unnecessary fear or impediment. Too many of them continue to fail to serve gay people well, however, because of their own prejudice.

"They get where they're going by indirection rather than directly. It is very difficult for me to understand them," Miri said. "When I join them, I imagine that I shall be a problem for many of them just as they will present great challenges to me. I imagine there will be many times when I have to smile my big smile at someone who believes he hates me and say, 'Oh, hello. Yes, I heard your speech yesterday. You have a very strong voice and did you know that I am a lesbian? How about we have lunch and have a good talk?'"

She told me about a problem that had come up a year earlier when a powerful legislator learned that she was a lesbian and tried to whip up a storm of public opinion so that she might be removed from the bench. "When the newspapers came to me hungry for good copy, I gave them my biggest, brightest smile and told them that I don't know anything about what he does or where he does it and so I cannot comment on *his* professional life, but I could tell them very truthfully that I do all of my work in the office and not in the bedroom. They picked up on it and started scurrying around for his bedroom secrets—and found a few. So he hasn't bothered me since. Riza said she thought I would handle myself very well when I become one of the rule makers."

Soon thereafter, she and Riza were visiting Miri's sister in Los Angeles. "She ended up working in one of those movie studios, of all things. I'm very proud of her. A single mother with four children and her head held high. I met a big producer there who was begging to meet me like I was some celebrity and he said he was interested in 'developing a property' that was to be a life story about me with some sweet scenes of me as a kindergarten teacher and some big brave scenes from when I was on the police force! I gave him my big smile and said I could hardly wait to see who the actress was who would play me. You know—short, a bit overweight, a little graying in the hair, and the color of this face, lesbian—and, of course, with my big smile. I told him I hadn't seen anyone like that on the big screen yet. So we all had a good laugh."

33

RESEARCHERS

MOST RESEARCHERS ARE dedicated people who have done much to alleviate suffering and have added greatly to our understanding of our world and ourselves. They seldom get the thanks they deserve. Most, that is, but not all. Science is at the service of any master and some masters have better intentions than others.

Genuine scientific research is without bias or prejudice. But the questions that prompt the research are not. There is very little science for the sake of science or basic research that aims only to add to our storehouse of information. Usually there is a desire to use the information in some way and that causes the question that prompts the hypothesis.

A colleague once said, "It would be interesting to know if there are a disproportionate number of gay people who are vegetarians. I bet there are." It was not the idle or random musing of a scientific researcher. She had a hunch that gay people generally are more concerned with the well-being of all creatures than are people in the general non-gay population. Though certainly biased, it is a very interesting idea and might be one place to start to assemble data that could begin to answer the question.

Science never answers a question beyond any shadow of doubt. It merely tells us that the hypothesis has been supported or not supported by the resulting data at a specified level of statistical probability. If enough evidence stacks in one direction, and comes from repeated studies that check the results of previous studies with various hypotheses, we can begin to say with some degree of certainty that our planet does orbit the sun rather than being the center of the universe.

Unfortunately, when we look back at so-called historical research, we find scores of unscientific attempts to identity, classify and scrutinize gay people (incorrectly labeled *homosexuals*). Most of the effort went into looking for the causes of homosexuality. It has been mostly a foolish exercise. The most obvious cause is a combination of opportunity and desire, which is also the cause of heterosexuality. Now, of course, comes the question of what causes homosexual desire? Well, what causes heterosexual desire?

This is a tough question to answer. There are too many causative or antecedent factors and there is no need (other than basic academic research) to identify them anyway. The scientific interest in the causes of *homosexuality*, however, reveal a devaluation of gay identity or sexual orientation and a wish to exterminate it. More often than not, we look for causative factors and antecedents when we want to eliminate something or create more of it. Rarely is it done in pure scientific pursuit of information that will add to our general knowledge.

In more recent times, there have been investigations of various genetic, physiological anatomical, and biochemical factors that might predispose a person to being more homosexual than heterosexual or gay in sexual orientation. The motivation for this research has been primarily political, sometimes pro-gay. The assumption is that if it can be more clearly demonstrated that it is most likely that there is a genetic basis for a gay sexual orientation, we will not be blamed, degraded or asked to change. It is a dubious assumption. I believe it is more likely that a few genetic engineers will set to work to find ways to remedy this *defect* in genetic inheritance. Prejudice does not bow down before the work of scientists. Quite the contrary is true. There are scientists who bow down before the work of prejudice.

One need only look to Hitler's Germany to worry about some of today's scientists and well-funded think tanks.

Openly gay people can be studied to better our understanding of how gay individuals maintain self-esteem and find the strength to survive in a hostile environment, managing to build sturdy and satisfying lives. The information should prove helpful to people working with individuals in other disadvantaged minority groups also.

Studies aimed at identifying gay people as children are dangerous. The children are not able to control or direct their own lives. They are at the mercy of the adults who surround and direct them and the likelihood is high that some of those adults could be prejudiced. Researchers must have a conscience. Learning about atomic energy helped humans. Learning to make atomic weapons did not.

Studies that compare chimpanzees, bonobo and humans can yield helpful information. Perhaps we can learn why humans persist in war and are shy about sexual generosity. It might shed light on queer desires and behavior in humans.

The place where the greatest help is needed from researchers is in identifying the symptoms, causes and antecedents of homophobia and other forms of destructive prejudice. We need that information in order to search for the most effective treatment for this social disease. If homophobia can be eradicated, gay people can live with no more difficulty than any other citizen. Homophobia costs valuable lives. It is a social disease or emotional disturbance that needs very serious attention from researchers.

Epilogue

ME AND THE
FOURTH EDITION

I AM CURIOUS ABOUT THE PEOPLE who write the books I read. I wonder why this person felt the need to write this book. I wonder what it has to do with his or her personal life. The curiosity is there whether the book is one of information or fiction. Particularly, however, if I am reading the book for information, I want to know both what motivated the author and what are his or her life-credentials.

In this case the relevant information about me begins when I was four years old. I have two clear memories of awakening consciousness and identity from that year. The first was the moment when I felt erotic attraction toward a man who went into an outdoor shower stall in Miami Beach, Florida, and held my awed attention as he soaped, rinsed, smiled and sang. The second was a moment of digging in a sandy yard under the hot sun when I suddenly felt *alone* and *different*.

I continued to feel alone and vaguely unhappy while growing up in small town poverty on the northeast coast of the United States throughout elementary and secondary school. Fortunately, I developed a slowly increasing interest in school subjects and found that life was better if I focused on how today was better than yesterday, and how this year might be better than the year before. A combination of luck (in finding the school) and determination (in funding my stay there) saw me through five life-altering years at Antioch College in Yellow Springs, Ohio, with it's work-study program that sent me to distant job sites and helped me to begin to see the world. Two years as a draftee in the army followed, giving me time to read many of the great books that I had not had time for in college and also the reassurance that I was as capable as anyone of performing male-warrior physical feats.

Having finished graduate school at the end of the 1950s, I devoted a year and a half to a clinical research program at the enormous Philadelphia State Hospital. Here I learned that it was possible to help people leave a mental hospital and return to the larger community after ten or twenty years of detention. I also learned that most people were being moved from a warm, secure frying pan where people knew them to a fire of liberty and loneliness.

The next ten years of my professional lifetime was at Hunter College and Herbert H. Lehman College of the City University of New York, involved in the psychological education of teachers who taught the poor. My motivation seemed clear to me. School had been an unhappy place for me as a child and much of it had had to do with poverty.

In the academic year 1968-69, I took an overdue sabbatical and some offered funds from the Carnegie Corporation of New York and conducted a year-long study of the human potential movement and its encounter groups, looking for innovations that might have applications in education and psychotherapy. It was quite a year. I had been enamored of group work since my undergraduate days and had purposely done my clinical internship in California so that I could be in an area where group therapy was flourishing at the time. Instinctively, I had steered clear of organizations of group therapists because they seemed too eager to get it all wrapped up in a neat package rather than exploring new horizons. Over the years I had experimented with my own seemingly daring innovations: first the white coat came off; then people called me by my first name; then I dared speak honestly of my own feelings in groups; and sometimes I even dared suggest that one person could try touching another person.

So when I learned of other people facilitating encounter groups, sensitivity training, sensory awareness, massage with meditation and other explorations, my thirst for the new surfaced again. I spent the year jetting around the country, interviewing the stars of the human potential movement and, most importantly, enrolling myself as an anonymous participant in every sort of group that might hold some promise of being a little different than what I had already experienced.

By the end of that year, I knew that I was changing but I did not know how exactly. I spent the summer writing my report and taking time to read the African-American authors I had not had enough time to read while teaching and directing a clinic. I did not know why I had to do that reading—but I knew that I had to do it.

Toward the end of that summer, it started to happen. I would read *Black* and think *gay*. I would read *Negro* and think *homosexual*. The entire year had made me much more aware of my emotions and by the end of that summer I was shocked at how much hurt, anger and fear I had been holding inside myself all my life. I grew up knowing that I was gay, though the conceptualization and language for it were quite different during those years. Then education and psychotherapy convinced me that I was *normal* with a slight disability in the form of *leanings* in the homosexual direction that I must try my best to keep under control—rather like diabetes. I was married to a woman I loved and had two children I adored. I also had a large empty place inside of me and a terrible ache that was related to the life-long hurt, fear and anger that had begun to surface.

At the end of that summer, the Association for Humanistic Psychology had its yearly meeting in Silver Spring, Maryland. I found myself in a leaderless encounter group with ten hidden leaders. Our second time together, a young man said he needed help from the group. A smartly dressed woman looked at him sagely and said, "I know what your trouble is—boys." He said, "You mean I prefer to have sex with men? That's right, but that's not what I want help about. I want help about a job interview I'm going to tomorrow."

Then, to my astonishment, all of the white-liberal trashing I had been reading about all summer came up. The color was lavender rather than black but the techniques were the same. People actually said things like, "Some of my best friends are homosexuals," and "As long as you stay in your part of town, I don't care what you do." I am not certain how open or verbal my reaction was but I know that it was intense. It seems to me that I sat there for an eternity with my mouth and eyes very wide. I do remember that I announced in a voice trembling with fear and rage that I had had plenty of homosexual feelings in my lifetime and I couldn't believe what I was hearing in that room.

The young man and I made arrangements to get together to talk. He wanted experience in leading groups. I had plenty of experience to share. We both lived in New York City. He knew the gay scene there and I did not. We hatched the idea of trying to do a gay weekend group workshop together. It was a semi-disaster but we both learned from it and no one was emotionally or physically injured as a result of our first clumsy attempt.

I liked the experience of being with gay people in a group. It felt good. I began to understand those years of trying to help African-American and Hispanic people in the ghetto, and why they continued to patiently tell me that I was white or Anglo and that they needed to help one another. I realized that I had found my own people at last and that we needed one another. Slowly I resolved to use whatever talent and energy I had in helping gay people, myself included— though in the beginning I was not sure that I was entitled to full inclusion in the community.

During my years of clinic directing, teaching and research, there had been no time for a real private clinical practice. But now I found gay people coming to me and asking if I would take them on for psychotherapy. I took on a few and found my taste for the academic world rapidly diminishing. With some trepidation I decided to let go of my academic security blanket, the hard-earned tenure and rank, and even the carrot of financially comfortable retirement just twelve to fifteen years down the road. I first resigned as clinic director, and six months later decided to resign from the university.

Ever since my internship days in California I had wanted to return there. It occurred to me that if I was going to shift into a private clinical practice and work with gay people, I could find them in California just as easily as in New York. I was frightened by what all this change might do to my happy, loving family but momentum was carrying me forward. There were many long talks with my wife, who was willing to risk our marriage and be my companion in exploration and growth.

The day after Christmas, 1970, we climbed aboard an airplane bound for San Francisco—all four of us. In addition to the luggage, I carried plenty of anxiety, not much money, and an excited inner voice that told me this was right. Indeed, I was entering the best years of my life—the years of real learning and growing. Reading related to my work had always been a chore but it now became a joy. Every day, my face-to-face contact taught me more about gay people and, consequently, more about myself.

As we had feared might happen, though we valiantly tried every sort of creative arrangement, the natural progression of events led my wife and I to separation and divorce five years later. I lived with a man for the next six years, during which time his two children and my two children lived with us half-time and with their mothers half-time. The loss of the marriage and the excellent home that the four of us had constructed together was a painful loss, though we handled it as well as we were able.

Shortly after the separation, the first edition of *Loving Someone Gay* was published. I had written it in 1975, only to have it refused by a dozen or more *reputable* publishers. More than once the rejection was accompanied by words of distaste—once it was accompanied by a now-treasured letter from a prominent editor in New York who, it became clear, had a psychoanalytic orientation. She and her anonymous consultant took me to task for being shockingly irresponsible and unprofessional by writing about these poor, emotionally sick homosexuals. Celestial Arts, then a small publisher in Millbrae, California, was willing to take a chance on it, however, and both they and I were relieved to find the first printing of 5,000 copies sold out in December, before the official January 1977 publication date.

It was the right time. Anita Bryant, sometimes known in gay circles as "the frozen orange juice queen," was using what remained of her popularity as a former beauty contestant, pop singer and purveyor of frozen orange juice in television commercials to do what she imagined to be her religious duty by telling the world that homosexuals were perverted sinners, some of whom might be saved. Other homophobes were out for the kill in the same hunting party at the same time. Though I am basically an introverted person whose idea of a good time is an evening at home with a good book or, at most, dinner with one or two friends, I suddenly found myself being interviewed on television, radio and in the newspapers and around the United States and in Canada. Since then the book has continued to find its audience around the world.

In 1986 the publisher and others asked me to update the book since the world in which gay people lived had changed so much in the preceding ten years and because we were reeling with the AIDS epidemic. The second edition, *The New Loving Someone Gay*, was published in 1987. The third edition in 1997 was more of a reconstruction than the second edition had been. I tried to be loyal to the words that many people had told me had been helpful to them while also giving due recognition to the enormous changes that had come to gay communities around the world in two decades.

It has been thirty years since I began to write *Loving Someone Gay*. The changes that impact gay people around the world have been amazing. Some good, some bad, but always forward movement. We are visible now. As the marching chant has it: *We're here, we're queer, get used to it.*

I live with my *husband/domestic partner* and our dog in San Francisco. Though he and I are individuals and there have been other chapters in our lives, it sometimes seems that we have been together forever. Symptomatic of the social change, we became domestic partners registered with the city when that was made available to us. We proudly walked down the grand staircase in our beautiful city hall. Then, when the state of California offered domestic partnership years later, we registered with the state.

In February of 2004 the mayor of San Francisco, Gavin Newsom, directed the city to recognize the state and national constitutional guarantee of equal rights to all citizens and issue marriage licenses to any gay couple who wanted to marry. We arrived on line in the early morning darkness and were married at City Hall in the rotunda at 1:30 in the afternoon. Never have I been more moved or more proud. Six months later the state's Supreme Court held San Francisco's gay marriages to be invalid. I may take the hurt of that with me to the grave. I do believe that we will again have the right to marry because the prejudice will be seen for what it is, but I was wounded. During the national presidential election in 2004 the president and his political advisers added insult to our injury by using gay people as bait for prejudiced voters, pandering to fear-based bigotry in a shameful display of political greed. I understand how vital it is to develop compassion and I do it as best I can, but people who practice divisiveness are a problem for us.

Many of the positive changes in the lives of gay people that I did not expect to see within my lifetime have come to pass. We are an enormous, strong, vibrant worldwide community, rapidly growing stronger and larger every day. We have our internal troubles. Having grown so fast, we show occasional dangerous signs of borrowing and incorporating some of the most dysfunctional aspects of the older societies that surround us. I hope that we will be ever more alert to the individual and collective dangers of unprotected sex, the careless use of drugs, prejudice and segregation. We must tend to our youngsters and elders as well as others in need.

I hope that we will learn to honor and harness our anger and use it in a constructive nonviolent manner to teach the world how to change. We are the natural leaders of change that the world needs. We are men who love men and women who love women. We can be the beginning of the end of the tragic waste of tribal warfare. There are too many opportunistic politicians in the world. We must demonstrate a more humane orientation. We can reject prejudice clearly. We can show the world how to have a community that includes everyone *at all times*, regardless of race, religion, skin color, age, language, national origin, looks, disability or any other factor that kings use to build their grand and petty empires by promoting rivalries.

We can honor our bodies, our sexuality and our right to be erotic. In the most politically repressive times and places, human bodies and their potentially subversive biological and erotic needs are made naughty or unlawful. Queen Victoria would have had babies birthed fully clothed if it had been possible.

There are people like her in powerful positions today. Every body needs touch. We have a responsibility to receive it and to give it with respect. We need not imitate a society that designates the young and the pretty as attractive and is disrespectfully intrusive in exercising desire to touch them, while raising the level of skin hunger for ordinary people who are less young and less pretty. It sells products but it destroys people and we need not incorporate such a starvation mentality into our affection-rich community.

My strongest wish is that we be outspoken in our rejection of segregation in *every* form and demonstrate how to be *inclusive* rather than *exclusive* with one another. No one of us is *in* and no one of us is *out*. Such concepts offer only a recipe for community self-destruction that would delight our oppressors. Indeed, gay people must *hang together* or we will throw away our opportunity to demonstrate equality and can expect to be hung out alone in the wind for punishment, one by one.

Since that airplane ride to San Francisco in 1970, I have continued to work as a clinical psychologist offering service to gay men, lesbians and their friends and families, including psychotherapy. I have completed a first draft of a book of memoirs. I also facilitate group retreats, and I write. I am learning to grow old and that involves fewer hours in my psychotherapy office and longer walks on the beach. I also make time for writing fiction and poetry.

I continue to be drawn to the social and psychological explorations that hold some promise of new gains for us—the emergence of fee-for-service companions, for instance. I wonder how the most talented of such service providers might best be trained to offer their talents and skills in ways that would help many and harm few. Erotic healing and various forms of massage, including Taoist massage? How might these therapies be combined with what we know to be helpful in traditional *talk therapy*? There is much more for us to learn.

I am intrigued by the gay spiritual/erotic communities that have appeared. There is hope that we can grow erotic *and* spiritual awareness together in such communities and leave the divisive, rule-obsessed religions to deal with one another.

I do not have the words to adequately describe the joy and richness contained in the learning that has come from my work with gay people in groups and individually. Like all of us, I have accumulated my own scars. But I now know that they can be a source of strength. I am fully aware of how blessed I have been in this work. Each tale that has been told to me represents a gift. Given in trust, each has enabled me to *see* us.

I conclude this final note with the same words that I used in the conclusion of the first edition, thirty years ago. They remain true.

There is a simple Christian hymn titled 'Amazing Grace.' I am not much attracted to institutional religion but its words could apply to my own evolving gay identity. It expresses my experience as a gay person so well.

I am grateful for the special people in my life who have helped me to see my need to change. I am grateful for my work. And I am grateful that I rediscovered my gay identity in time. It has been like coming home, except that there never was any home before.

And all of that is why I wrote this book—again, one more time.

Index

Culture gap, 195
Curing homosexuality, methods of, 7

D
Death, 149–151
Deception, 16–17
Defense of Marriage Act, 88–89, 145
Dependency, on therapist, 263–264
Depression, 23, 85–86, 235, 242
Detention centers, 24
Diagnostic and Statistical Manual, 254
Diaries, 81
Dignity, 147, 276
Disclosure. See Coming out
Discussion groups, 45
Disorientation, 221
Dissociation, 90
Distrust of feelings, 234
Divorce, 215–217
Domestic partnerships, 145
"Don't Ask, Don't Tell," 30–31
Dreams, examination of, 250
Drug abuse, 59, 235, 243
Drug use, 159–160
Dual identity, 39
Dyke (derogatory name), 5

E
Eating disorders, 108
Educational aids, for professionals, 266–267
Emotional distance, 220
Emotional disturbance, 90
Emotions
    complexity of, 84, 240
    expressing, 85
    labeling, 83–84
The Emperor's New Clothes, 168
Equality, 55–56, 145
Erotic, defined, 124
Erotic affection, results of hiding, 257–258
Erotic appreciation, 127, 128
Erotic contact, 120
Erotic healing, 282

Erotic masseurs, 129
Erotic orientation, acceptance of, 188
Erotically gifted people, 282–283
Escape mechanisms, 243
Ethics, personal code of, 54–55

F
Faggot (derogatory name), 5–6
Families
    biological and chosen, 177–178
    creating, 133–134
    designation of, 245
    disapproval by, 7–8, 10
Family relationships, reorienting, 221–222
Fantasy, intensity of, 56–57
Fear, levels of, 43–44
Fee-for-service, 282–283
Feeling different, 234
Feeling identification game, 82–83
Feelings
    awareness of, 78–79
    control of, 35–36
    distrust of, 234, 239
    expression of in children, 240
    identifying, 83
    reclamation of, 79–80, 82
    universality of, 262
    validation of, 262
    see also specific emotions
Feelings journal, 81
FFLAG, 66
Flesh and Spirit Community, 147
4-N Approach, 85–86
Freud, Sigmund, 249
Friends, sex with, 130
Friendship, importance of, 227

G
Gag reflex, 126–127
Gay
    advantages of being, 56
    causative factors, 16
    joy of, 55
    label of, 6–7

Human community, value of, 11
Human potential movement, 47–49
Human programming. *See*
Socialization
Humiliation, 143

I
Identity, 6–7, 66–67
Identity validation, 32
Immobility, response to, 242
Inferiority, feelings of, 22
Intermittent reinforcement, 123
Intimacy, and communication, 120,
132
Invisibility, 31–33
Isolation, 51

J
Jealousy, 138–140
Jokes, 241, 270
Journal writing, 249–250
Journals, 81, 264
Judges, 288–289, 289
Jung, Carl, 249

K
Kinsey studies, 89
Kramer, Joseph, 282

L
Labeling, 88, 93, 269
Language usage, change in, 45–46
Lavender ribbon occupations, 272
Lawmakers, and laws against gay
people, 287
Lesbian witches, 147
Lesbians and gay men, visibility of,
178–179
Letters. *See* Unsent letters
LGBT&Q, 159
Librarians, 269
Library resources, 67
Life, reclaiming, 264
Loneliness, loss of, 45
Love, 140, 183–184
Love-search, characteristics of, 76

Lust, 115
see also Rape

M
Malpractice, by psychotherapists
and counselors, 278
Mariposa (derogatory name), 6
Marriage, 136, 200–201
Marriage of convenience. *See* Cover
marriages
Maslow, Abraham, 249
Massage, 109, 130, 248
Massage therapists, and AIDS
epidemic, 282–283
Masturbation, 35, 109–110, 125
McCarthy, Joseph, 43
Medical professionals, as
information source, 273
Mental hospitals, 24
Mental problems, as source of
homosexuality, 35
Metropolitan Community Church,
147, 276
Metrosexuals, 91
Midwives to the dying, 282
Mind/body/spirit, division of,
107–108
Ministers, 147
Models, need for, 118–119
Monogamy, 139
Moscone, George, 50
Mourning, 149–151
Mutual support, development of,
46–47

N
Names, derogatory, 5–6, 67, 93
Naming phenomenon, 87–88
Narcotics Anonymous, 153
Nature, solace of, 85
Newsom, Gavin, 12
1984 (Orwell), 72
"No," importance of saying, 85
Non-gay-oriented counselors, 66–67
Nonconformity, accepting in
students, 238–239

Nonviolent protest, 50–51
Novel experiences, helpfulness of, 85

O
Obsession, 115
Open relationships, 140–141
Oppression
  community awareness and, 262
  experiencing, 255–256
  in the military, 30
  by religions, 29–30
  systemic experience of, 23–24
  by Zimbabwe government, 31
Oral sex, 126
Ostracism, 7
Outing, forced, 237, 238

P
Paranoia, loss of, 45
Parents
  coming out to, 98–101
  nonacceptance by, 101
  supportiveness of, 167
  understanding by, 189–190
Parents, Family and Friends of
    Lesbians and Gays. See
    PFLAG
Patients, assumptions about,
    273–274
Peer pressure, as source of
  homosexuality, 35
Perls, Frederick (Fritz), 249
Perry, Troy (Reverend), 276
Personal displays of affection, 25–26
Pets, loss of, 153
PFLAG, 66, 100, 195
Physical attractiveness, and
    awareness, 57
Police
  gay attitudes towards, 286
  interacting with gay citizens, 287
  as portrayed in the media,
    287–288
Predator (derogatory name), 67
Prejudice, 180–182, 223, 254–255, 270

Pressures, emotional, 59
Priests, 147
Primacy of relationship, importance
    of, 205–206
Prisons, 24, 36
Pro-gay reading, 262
Pro-gay stance, 270
Professional escorts, 129
Professional service providers, 247
  see also specific types of providers
Professionals, gay-affirmative
    retraining of, 252–253
Protestant churches, and gay
    people, 276
Pseudo-paranoia, 57–58
Psychoanalysts, 28, 75–76
Psychotherapists, history of
    homophobia of, 278
Psychotherapy, 86, 246, 249–250
Public disclosure, 29

Q
Queer (derogatory name), 6, 93

R
Rabbis, 147
Radical Fairies, 147
Rape, 36
Rationalization, prejudice and, 255
Reconditioning, 72–74
Reference points, 235
Regression, 90
Reich, Wilhelm, 249
Rejection, 113–114, 116–117
Relating erotically, 126–127
Relationships
  creating, 136–137
  end of, 151–152
  steps in, 115–116
Religious advisors, prejudice of, 276
Religious organizations
  compassionate oppression by,
    29–30
  gay friendly, 276
  perception of sin and, 35
  treatment of gays, 146–147